WOMEN OF IDEAS

WOMEN OF IDEAS

INTERVIEWS FROM PHILOSOPHY BITES

EDITED BY SUKI FINN

OXFORD
UNIVERSITY PRESS

OXFORD

UNIVERSITY PRESS

Great Clarendon Street, Oxford, OX2 6DP,
United Kingdom

Oxford University Press is a department of the University of Oxford.
It furthers the University's objective of excellence in research, scholarship,
and education by publishing worldwide. Oxford is a registered trade mark of
Oxford University Press in the UK and in certain other countries

First Edition published in 2021

Impression: 1

Published in the United States of America by Oxford University Press
198 Madison Avenue, New York, NY 10016, United States of America

British Library Cataloguing in Publication Data
Data available

Library of Congress Control Number: 2021931338

ISBN 978–0–19–885992–5

Printed and bound in Great Britain by
Clays Ltd, Elcograf S.p.A.

PREFACE

*M*en of Ideas was a 1978 BBC television series in which presenter Bryan Magee interviewed noted philosophers of the time. Of course, it was not just men who had ideas. Yet only one contributor on the series was a woman (albeit a very noble choice): Iris Murdoch.

Forty years later, some things have changed for the better and there is much to celebrate. But still, a 2018 survey conducted by the Higher Education Statistics Agency showed that only 29.7 per cent of philosophers employed in UK universities are women. This is the lowest representation of women in any discipline outside of science, technology, and engineering. And in the US, the latest data assessed in 2011 from the Digest of Education Statistics (a publication of the National Center for Education Statistics) found only 21 per cent of professional philosophers to be women. The numbers are even lower when considering additional factors such as race and ethnicity. As such, there is still a considerable way to go.

Women of Ideas collates interviews from the podcast Philosophy Bites, founded and co-hosted by Nigel Warburton and David Edmonds. Philosophy Bites has been a major success, with over 40 million downloads, and three previous edited book collections published with Oxford University Press: *Philosophy Bites* (2010), *Philosophy Bites Back* (2012), and *Philosophy Bites Again* (2014). It has been an honour to work with Nigel, David, and all the interviewees in compiling the latest collection. I thank Nigel, David, and Peter

Momtchiloff at OUP for this opportunity, and I thank all the interviewees for their cooperation and excellent contributions.

There were around one hundred episodes of Philosophy Bites interviews in the archive covering interesting topics by inspiring women. For this book, I had the difficult task of choosing under thirty from this pre-existing archive. Regretfully, given the underrepresentation and marginalisation of various racial and ethnic groups, people from working-class backgrounds, the LGBTQIA+ community, and those with disabilities in philosophy, for example, there are demographics that are not adequately represented here. This book cannot then be considered as providing comprehensive coverage of women's voices in philosophy, or of women's ideas! Much like the Philosophy Bites books that have come before this, it should be treated more akin to a 'tasting menu'. Yet it is my hope—and plan—that future edited collections, line-ups, syllabi, and what we treat as the 'canon' in philosophy will be more inclusive and representational of the diversity of people and positions within philosophy.

For the first section of this book, I asked the interviewees what it is like being a woman in philosophy (the same question is posed on Jennifer Saul's blog, which is referenced in her answer). The answers are diverse. That is not surprising, not least since the category of 'woman' is diverse (see, for example, the opening chapter of this book from Amia Srinivasan on 'What is a Woman?' which includes a discussion of intersectionality and rethinking gender in light of trans experience). Overall, as this book demonstrates, those who have ideas are diverse, the ideas that they have are diverse, and the experiences that they have are diverse. Also, the diversity of responses to the 'What is it like?' question posed invites a myriad of reactions: from feeling disturbed, to tickled, to encouraged and inspired. It is my ambition that readers take something stimulating from the book's many and diverse contributions.

The interviews themselves have been lightly edited so that they can work well in written, as opposed to the original audio, form. The interviewees and I have made some suggestions for further reading and resources related to their interview, which are included at the end of each interview. The interview with Ashwini Vasanthakumar was for the Philosophy 247 podcast. The interviews with Martha C. Nussbaum and with Anne Phillips were originally recorded for the Open University's podcast series *Multiculturalism Bites*. And the interview with Miranda Fricker was originally recorded for the Open University's podcast series *Ethics Bites*. We are grateful for the permission to reproduce these interviews here. Several of the interviews were recorded at the London University's Institute of Philosophy, and at Oxford University's Uehiro Centre for Practical Ethics, to whom we are also grateful.

Finally, it is traditional to dedicate one's books to one's parents. As a spin on that tradition, I dedicate this book to my academic mother—M—an advisor, a friend, and a truly inspiring philosopher and woman. I have also had the privilege of working with and receiving support from the Society for Women in Philosophy UK, especially from my mentor—J—thank you so much, for everything (which is a lot!). Throughout my time as a philosopher I have been blessed with excellent women supervisors, colleagues, and fellow students, who I have looked upon as role models, yet who have helped me find the courage to pave my own way philosophically and personally—the profound impact they have all had on my life is something I will always be grateful for (you know who you are!). I also give a shout out to my actual mother, Susan Finn (hi mum!), and my father, Laurence Finn (hi dad!)—oh, and for good measure I'd better add my sister Rachel Finn (hi sis!). I love you all loads.

To all the past, present, and future women of ideas—thank you!

Suki Finn, June 2020

CONTENTS

CONTENTS

WHAT IS IT LIKE BEING A WOMAN IN PHILOSOPHY?

Helen Beebee: Sometimes exasperating. (No, I'm not the new departmental administrator.) Sometimes funny. (Seriously, mate, I'm over fifty and we just had a long discussion about UK university bureaucracy, and you just took a punt on 'postdoc'? Still, now I'm going to enjoy watching you get really embarrassed, tell me I don't look old enough to be a professor, and then get even more embarrassed when you wonder whether you've just dug yourself in even deeper. For the record: yeah, you have.) To be fair, though, a lot of the time—for me anyway—it's pretty much like being a man in philosophy. (Or so I imagine. Hard to know, I guess.)

Teresa M. Bejan: Well, I'm philosophy-adjacent. But as a woman in political theory, it's exhilarating, frustrating, discouraging, wonderful, exhausting, and utterly ordinary by turns. A little (a lot?) like being a woman in general.

Emma Borg: It's well known that being a woman in philosophy has traditionally been difficult—the archetype for the profession is resolutely male and there is no doubt that good female philosophers have left the profession, or not had the careers they should, because of gender-based discrimination. I do think things are changing (albeit slowly) and, on the flip side, I have to say that being *this particular* woman in philosophy has been good. I've had a couple of bad experiences in my working life that probably wouldn't have occurred if I was a man, but I feel privileged to have got to spend so much time thinking about things that I find totally fascinating, and to have worked with some wonderful colleagues. So I'd like to send a positive message to the next generation: being a woman in philosophy can be great.

Kimberley Brownlee: I was moved to study philosophy by two desires, both of which have turned out to be impossible to satisfy. The first is a desire to be good. The second is a desire to experience—again and again—that deep, intellectual shock that comes in grasping a great idea. Unlike many women, I have led a charmed life as a woman in philosophy with fully supportive colleagues, respectful students, and deeply satisfying work. That said, I have often had the experience of being the only woman in the room. When I am the invited speaker, this poses no difficulty. When I am an audience member, however, even now I can sometimes turn into a self-censoring shadow. I have found that the best way to overcome this is to tap into a sense of duty: if I have something to contribute, then I have a duty to the presenter to help them to develop their ideas.

Katalin Farkas: For fourteen years, I was the only woman in my department; these things are now noticeably changing. But my own experience of being a woman in philosophy has always been dominated by the 'philosophy' bit, rather than the 'woman' bit. Being an academic philosopher is an interesting, challenging, and incredibly rewarding experience. I have been very fortunate not only in having a job in philosophy, but also in being surrounded by colleagues who have never made me conscious of being a woman in a difficult way.

Sarah Fine: I find it hard, but I draw inspiration and comfort from the many brilliant women doing ground-breaking philosophical work, supporting one another, and changing the face of the discipline.

Furthermore, judging by the wonderful students around me, the future of philosophy is looking bright.

Katrin Flikschuh: The Ghanaian philosopher Kwasi Wiredu once said that, given their views on Africans, it takes considerable discipline for a Black person to find anything of value in the philosophical writings of Hume or Kant (these are just random examples from the discipline). Wiredu conscientiously exercised that discipline, which is one reason among many why he is himself a true philosopher. I think something similar might hold for women: 'given the history of philosophy, it takes considerable discipline . . .'. It is hard not to think that systematic discrimination of both an institutional and an intellectual sort persists in the discipline, and is likely to persist for considerable time to come. It is not clear to me what an individual female philosopher/political theorist can do about it other than plough on. It can be a lonely enterprise, especially if you're not of the sort who finds it easy, temperamentally, to make common political cause with fellow women academics—not least because the political issue is separate from the intellectual/philosophical one (I can't personally do coffee mornings discussing 'women issues'—I'd rather go for a run). But sometimes there can be advantages to *not* gaining easy access to the circle of the naturally elected. Being forced to go on regardless can make one more self-reliant; it can lead one to develop one's own position for its own sake, rather than for the sake of gaining passing acclaim—and it can encourage one to explore areas of the disciplines that are less mainstream. In that sense, there may be advantages to being more marginal, which is not to deny, of course, that there are also countless disadvantages.

Miranda Fricker: What it's like to be a woman in philosophy is a question that will receive almost as many answers as there are philosophy departments. Many of them still pretty negative, I regret to say. For my own part, I'm keenly aware of how lucky I've been.

Tamar Szabó Gendler: It gets better every year!

Alison Gopnik: In general, the fact that human beings have children—a particularly salient fact for women—has largely been invisible to the men, and often at least notionally celibate men, who have dominated philosophy. The 1967 Encyclopedia of Philosophy has four references to children. When I was doing my DPhil at Oxford, I made the argument that paying attention to children could illuminate a wide range of philosophical problems, from epistemology to ethics. The senior philosopher I was talking to looked puzzled: 'Of course,' he said, 'one has seen children about, but you would never actually talk to one'.

Katherine Hawley: It's been made much easier for me by the few but fabulous women of a generation who are now mostly retired. My own generation is a bit more numerous, which often meant that we were mistaken for one another (especially if we had similar hair-styles). I hope that in future there will be as many ways of being a woman in philosophy as there are women philosophers.

Angie Hobbs: There is still much more that could be done to encourage girls to take up philosophy, and—as with all academic subjects—to make it easier to combine an academic career with family life. The latter point applies to fathers too, of course, but it is still women who get pregnant, give birth, and breast-feed. However, the situation has improved from the start of my career: I gave a paper on the ethics of flourishing at a UK university in the early 1990s and was told beforehand, 'Don't worry if we don't pay much attention to your paper: in this department we regard ethics as a bit pink and fluffy and female'.

Susan James: Harder than being a man. Looking back, what stands out are moments of solidarity and support from established women philosophers, who helped to boost confidence. Unfortunately, that remains important.

Kate Kirkpatrick: Since 'woman' and 'philosophy' are both contested concepts, I have no concise answer to this question and I'm sceptical about the aptness of general 'what it's like' claims. But being asked the question gives rise to the suspicion that men are less frequently asked 'what it's like' to be a man in philosophy, which may leave them more time to think, and to be asked about what they think, about philosophy.

Christine M. Korsgaard: There is nothing it is like being a woman in philosophy. There is something it is like being a woman academic, a woman teacher, a woman department member, because institutions and the people in them sometimes treat women differently, often in bad ways with which we are all familiar. But the subject is the same for all of us: both endlessly fascinating and forbiddingly difficult. Like a scientist trying to spot some exotic bird in the rainforest, you move into ever-deeper thickets of confusion and complexity, unable to stop, in pursuit of an insight that always seems to be just out of reach.

Katherine J. Morris: In a world where most of the 'canon' are male, where young women (still!) have little confidence in their own abilities, and where philosophical 'discussion' is so often point-scoring (if not 'willy-waving'?), my women students need women role models. My mother (a philosopher, the noted Sartre scholar Phyllis

Sutton Morris) was a wonderful role model for me, and I try not to forget how lucky I was to have her.

Jennifer Nagel: I don't know enough about gender, or about the sociology of our discipline, to give a good general answer to the question of what it is like to be a woman in philosophy. The question is still difficult if I read it as fishing for anecdotal evidence about my experience as one particular woman. It is hard for me to know the extent to which my experience of my discipline has been shaped by my gender, or—reading the question another way—the extent to which my experience of being a woman has been shaped by being in philosophy. But although I find it hard to be exact, I do think there have been some interactions between these categories in my life, and I welcome a chance to share what I can. Meanwhile, I encourage anyone interested in the larger question to research it more deeply: on questions of gender, I especially recommend reading the work of trans scholars like Robin Dembroff and Talia Mae Bettcher, who are doing exceptionally sharp and creative work on what it is to be a woman, and indeed what it is to have any gender at all.

As an undergraduate, I never had a woman professor or instructor in philosophy, and I took a number of advanced logic classes in which I was the only woman. I remember feeling self-conscious when raising my hand to speak in class, as though I were speaking on behalf of all of womankind, even in asking a tiny question about a proof. People would turn and look at me. I also felt somewhat alone, and wondered whether being outnumbered like this was a bad sign, an indication that I should shift my interests to the kinds of things that were more popular among women; this feeling was then heightened by some dabbling in feminist literature in the Carol Gilligan vein, literature encouraging the notion that women's thinking is naturally concrete and care-oriented, as opposed to abstract. It was a relief to stumble upon Jean Grimshaw's 1986 book *Philosophy and Feminist Thinking*, which gave voice to some of the worries I had felt about the thesis that women have some naturally different way of thinking, while still deeply engaged with the issues of justice that drove me towards feminism in the first place. Graduate school was a much better experience, not least because I had the joy of learning from Annette Baier and Tamara Horowitz, two fantastic women philosophers whose memories I struggle to keep alive in my own teaching.

I have experienced some sexual harassment, especially early in my career, and there are several philosophers I will cross the street to avoid, but I'm not convinced that philosophy is worse than other fields in this regard (I say this as someone who has also waited tables for a living). If there is something gender-relevant and distinctive about our field, it may be that live, face-to-face conversation is unusually important in the development of philosophical skill: it is very helpful to be with peers who will question and challenge you as an equal, and those peers can be harder to find if you are in a group that others are not accustomed to conversing with in this way. It took me a long time to gain confidence in philosophical conversation, to the point where I could forcefully assert my equality with anyone who might take a step towards doubting it. I have some vividly happy memories of discovering this confidence. For example, not long after being tenured, I was challenged by some guy in Vienna who overtly classified me as a 'Lady Philosopher'; while earlier I might have been thrown off-balance by this, I was glad to discover that the encounter just struck me as comical, and a learning opportunity for the students within earshot. I am grateful to everyone—women, men, and the nonbinary—who contributed to my development by being constructive conversational partners along the way. I'm even, in an odd way, grateful to that guy in Vienna: an initial lack of confidence can be paralysing, but once confidence is gained, it can be strengthened by certain kinds of adversity.

On a number of occasions, it has been made clear to me that I was invited to speak or contribute because the organizers 'needed a woman'. I have never been sure what to say in response, especially because I am quite keenly aware of the value of invitations to speak and write. Unsurprisingly, I'm most likely to be told this in situations where I'm outnumbered ten-to-one by men, and although it seems ungracious, I have wondered whether I should take a moment to encourage some reflection on the role of gender in getting those ten men on the stage or into the volume. If they just came naturally to mind as thought leaders, where women had to be dredged up under that special category, subject to a deliberate mandate of inclusion, then that's a real sign of weakness on the part of the organizer, given the current state of the discipline. I feel sorry for philosophers who do not naturally think of women's work when they set out to make a contribution in my subfields now: as a journal editor, I do still see submissions with long all-male bibliographies, and I must say that these submissions are typically under-informed as a result, missing valuable and relevant moves in the literature. Partly because it now confers such a competitive disadvantage, I think the old bias towards just taking men seriously is weaker than it used to be, but it has been a battle to get where we are now. Of course it is not just our fight, and the fight isn't over: concerns about fair participation in philosophical conversations are all the more pressing when it comes to other demographic groups that have historically been excluded from mainstream philosophy, and when it comes to new demographic groups forming out of resistance to old norms, such as the norms that have governed traditional thinking about gender.

Rebecca Newberger Goldstein: As a graduate student and then an assistant professor, in the 1970s, I was often the only woman in the room. My specialty then was philosophy of science, which was intensely male-dominated. I was often made to feel uncomfortable. Then again, if I hadn't felt like such an outsider, I probably wouldn't have ventured outside of the straight and narrow academic path by writing novels. The fiction-writing clinched my outsider status, but it's also led to an interesting life.

Onora O'Neill: I was first taught Philosophy in Oxford in the early 1960s by Elizabeth Anscombe and Philippa Foot. Their generation of women philosophers had faced real obstacles in becoming established in the field, and it was often said that those who succeeded had managed to do so because so many of their male contemporaries had their academic careers disrupted by the war. And there were still disadvantages in being a woman in my generation. But now there are successful women philosophers in every professional generation. It is a great pleasure to see how things have changed. Of course, it is still not easy to find good jobs, but fair treatment is pretty normal.

Anne Phillips: Like Hannah Arendt, I prefer to describe myself as a political theorist rather than political philosopher, and I work in a politics department rather than a philosophy one. But looking back to my early career moves, I do wonder if these choices also reflected my perception, as an undergraduate, that you had to be amazingly clever to be a philosopher and that, as a female undergraduate, I just wasn't clever enough. No one ever told me that philosophy wasn't for women, but some things you pick up without anyone actually saying it!

Rebecca Roache: Philosophy remains a male-dominated discipline, and many undergraduate courses still spotlight testosterone-fuelled musings through the years. But progress is happening: there is increasing recognition that we need diversity. All-male reading lists are frowned upon where they would have gone unnoticed a decade ago. There are many smart and exciting women philosophers around today, and social media make it easier than ever to share support, resources, and ideas about how to make our teaching more inclusive and more representative of the students who come to us from a wide variety of backgrounds. I hope we'll see a much more diverse discipline a decade or so from now.

Jennifer Saul: Well, I run a blog devoted to this topic so I know that it varies a lot. For some of us (myself included), it's pretty good. But for far too many it's really awful. To learn more, check out http://beingawomaninphilosophy.wordpress.com.

Elisabeth Schellekens: Ask this question in the past tense and you realize how much has changed. Numerous behaviours and modes of communication—sometimes benevolently conceived, often not—which just a decade ago passed as normal daily occurrences would today be classed as acts of sexual harassment or discrimination that (in many but not all cases) can be called out as such without fear of destroying one's career. There is still a long way to go, but male entitlement to exercise power over the careers and bodies of their female colleagues in our academic discipline is now reduced and female agency is greatly increased.

Two personal milestones: eleven years ago I was the first member of my then department to apply for maternity leave (in response to which several well-meaning colleagues wondered why I would want to sabotage my career thus and if I ever intended to return to work); it took ten years after my PhD to experience for the first time a formal academic meeting at which only women were present.

The problems for today's young women philosophers remain, but I think real progress has been made. Although I would consider myself first and foremost a philosopher rather than an activist, I will fight tooth and nail to ensure that my graduate students don't experience what I experienced. I am immensely proud of the way all my PhD students, women and other, show an awareness of these questions. Fundamentally, we should all be united not just by our love of philosophy but also our commitment to notions such as fairness, tolerance, and equality.

Amia Srinivasan: The French philosopher Michèle Le Doeuff wrote: 'When you are a woman and a philosopher, it is useful to be a feminist in order to understand what is happening to you'.

Ashwini Vasanthakumar: Worthwhile, thanks to the other women in philosophy.

INTERVIEWS

I

AMIA SRINIVASAN
What Is a Woman?

David Edmonds: *What is a woman? That's not a question that has puzzled people for much of human history. But in the twentieth century, some feminists, most notably the French philosopher Simone de Beauvoir, drew a distinction between female biology, and what it is to be a woman. Women are not born women, thought Beauvoir, society makes them so. But this issue has been further complicated by a relatively new debate. How should we categorize trans people, those who have a gender identity that differs from their sex? It's a question that has caused a bitter rift among feminists, with one faction arguing that just identifying as a woman is not enough to make you a woman. Here is Amia Srinivasan.*

Nigel Warburton: *Amia Srinivasan, welcome to Philosophy Bites. The topic we're going to focus on is 'What is a woman?'. Well, for many people, it is fairly obvious what a woman is. So, what is the philosophical question here?*

Amia Srinivasan: It's fair to say that for most of human history, the question 'What is a woman?' would just seem like a silly question, because the answer would have seemed very obvious: a woman is an adult, human, female; a woman is the member of the human species who has ovaries, who produces eggs, who nurses young, who gives birth to young, and so on. The reigning assumption had been that 'woman' is a biological category. In 1949, the French philosopher Simone de Beauvoir published a book called *The Second Sex*, in which she proposed that, while being female is a biological category, being a woman is not. She famously said that 'one is not born, but rather becomes, a woman'. The idea here is that a human can be born female or born male, but they have to somehow become, through a process of socialization, a particular gender: namely, a girl or a boy, and then a woman or a man. And so while sex, for Beauvoir, is a natural thing, gender is a socially constructed thing.

NW: *What does it mean for gender to be socially constructed? Does it mean that society imposes a role upon a woman? Or does it mean that different societies impose different roles on women?*

AS: That's a very good question, and feminists since Beauvoir have disagreed over the question of just what kind of socialization is involved in becoming a woman. But the general view has been that there is some kind of coercive process at work, whereby biologically female humans are forced to act in particular, stereotypically feminine, ways. This might include a certain way of dressing, speaking, acting, and a whole host of other things that we associate with femininity.

NW: *Does that mean that all women are constructed in the same way, and thus are connected to other women in virtue of having the same kind of view of femininity thrust upon them?*

AS: That question has been at the heart of feminism over the last few decades. For someone like Beauvoir, the answer is largely 'yes'. She thought that there was something that all women shared in virtue of going through a common process of socialization. Specifically, she thought one becomes a woman by being 'othered' by men. She argued that for men, in order to achieve a sense of their own selves—their own subjecthood—it is required that they posit women as the 'other', as secondary. Hence the title of her book, *The Second Sex*. And, I think it's fair to say that Beauvoir thought that general experience was pretty uniform across women, although, of course, she recognizes differences between particular women. All women, for Beauvoir, are assigned the social status and function of being the Other in relation to men's Subject.

NW: *Beauvoir was famously an existentialist, and so presumably she believed that whether you accept the role that other people put upon you is an individual choice. Is that right?*

AS: Yes, Beauvoir was an existentialist and, as such, believed in a profound ability for humans to act freely, even in a context of social coercion and oppression. And so, while women were forced to become women and therefore act in certain ways, she also thought that women could liberate themselves from this and could achieve their own sense of subjecthood.

NW: *That is interesting in comparison with another existentialist, Jean-Paul Sartre, because he tended to underplay such social factors,* *whereas Beauvoir was much more sensitive to the ways in which society shapes who we are.*

AS: That's a great observation, and I also think any feminist would tell you that such a contrast is unsurprising. It's easy for someone in a dominant position, like a rich white man such as Sartre, to think of himself as purely free and unconstrained by society. Whereas someone like Beauvoir, who, although privileged in many ways, was shackled by her gender, will always include in her analysis a theory of social constraint.

NW: *Since* The Second Sex *there has been a lot of feminist writing on the topic of 'What is a woman?'. What in particular do you think has importantly followed on from Beauvoir's work?*

AS: Yes, there has been a huge amount of writing in feminism on the question of the social construction of gender. Most feminists have accepted Beauvoir's distinction between sex and gender, and, along with Beauvoir, think of gender as something socially constructed. There is a lot of disagreement within feminism about whether gender is something that we would ideally abolish. Beauvoir thinks that gender really exists, but she thinks it only exists because we perpetuate the system that brings it into existence. This theoretically opens up the possibility of abolishing gender altogether. As such, an important question in feminism has been this: should we seek ultimately to abolish gender, to make it the case that there are no longer men and women, or is there some reason to keep the categories of 'woman' and 'man' around?

NW: *But how could somebody seriously get away from gender? It's such a dominant aspect of human life across the world. It would be very strange to just abolish gender altogether.*

AS: No doubt it would seem strange to many of us to abolish gender. And the world without gender would be profoundly different from our world. But so would a world without racism, and so would a world without economic oppression. The sort of feminism that seeks to abolish gender sees the abolition of gender as a regulative ideal: something we should aspire to, but that we are probably quite far away from still.

NW: *Another very prominent thinker in the area of gender is Judith Butler. Where does she stand on some of these issues?*

AS: In 1990, Judith Butler wrote a very important book called *Gender Trouble*, in which she proposed that gender isn't something we have, but something we do. It sounds strange to say, but Butler essentially thinks that I *do* woman, not that I *am* a woman. I do woman through a series of performative acts of femininity: how I dress, how I talk, how I relate to other people, how I think of myself in the world. Butler does not think that we are all aware that we are performing our gender; in fact, she thinks we are largely unaware. For most of us, it just feels like we *are* women, or we *are* men; gender doesn't feel like something we are actively constructing and doing. So, it's not that we are all consciously, voluntarily playing a role, it's that we find ourselves playing a particular gender role and indeed are compelled and coerced by society into playing that role. That said, for Butler, there is an element of voluntariness, just as there is on Beauvoir's account. Butler thinks there is the possibility of taking control, albeit some limited amount of control, over our own gender performativity. And specifically, she thinks that we can *subvert* the gender system by acting in ways that are unexpected, or that don't conform with the standard views of how a woman (or a man) should behave.

NW: *Does Butler actually advocate revolutionary acts—doing something unexpected in order to make people aware?*

AS: I think it's fair to say that Butler celebrates those kinds of revolutionary acts. She, of course, understands that such revolutionary and subversive acts come with different costs for different people. Therefore, she would be reluctant, I think, to say that everyone ought to try to subvert the gender system. A lot of people die when they try and subvert the gender system. But nonetheless, it seems that Butler takes hope from certain kinds of subversive gender acts and wants us to celebrate them.

NW: *Another really interesting development in feminism is the notion of intersectionality. That's something that is a result of the thinking in the 1980s and is quite different from Beauvoir's approach to what it is to be a woman.*

AS: Intersectionality is one of the most, if not the very most, significant development within feminism of the last forty years. You see an intersectional turn within feminism happening, as you said, in the 1980s and the 1990s, mostly thanks to Black and Latina feminists. Kimberlé Crenshaw, a Black feminist, coined the term 'intersectionality', though you find the concept in the earlier work of feminists like bell hooks, Angela Davis, and the Combahee River Collective. So, what does it mean? An intersectional approach to feminism attends to the multiple axes of oppression or privilege that an individual person can instantiate. Thus, women aren't all the same, because women vary by class, ethnicity, race, disability status, and so on. A common trope in second-wave feminism—the feminism that was dominant in the 1960s and the 1970s—is that women didn't have access to the workplace and that working was to be an essential part of the emancipation of women. But this implicitly took for granted that the experience of white, middle-class women was the experience of all women. Because while it's true that white middle-class women didn't have access to the workplace, working-class white women and Black women were already in the workforce. Intersectional feminism draws attention to the ways in which one's particular experience of being a woman is going to be inflected by one's race, ethnicity, class, disability status, and so on. Specifically, if one is oppressed as a Black woman, one isn't simply oppressed as a woman and as a Black person; one can also have a particular experience of oppression as a *Black woman*. A feminism that focuses on what all women have in common is a feminism that will thus neglect the experiences and needs not just of women at the intersection of multiple axes of oppression, like race and class, but also the women who are *most* marginalized. That's the key intersectional insight. Now, intersectionality poses a certain kind of problem for thinking about the social construction of womanhood, because on an orthodox feminist way of thinking, women had a common social experience that made them into women—for example, the experience of being 'othered' by men. But once you start recognizing the diversity of women's experiences, it's not clear that you can identify a common social process that produces women. And you might think that the drive to do so will inevitably exclude some of the most marginalized women.

NW: *Does that mean we should revert to a kind of feminism with many sub-divisions? So, you have a feminism of a Black working-class woman, and so on. Does that result in a multi-faceted feminism, rather than a feminism that says there is a condition shared by all women?*

AS: Indeed—in other words, how can we take very seriously the diversity of women's experience while having a feminism that is supposed to speak for and to advocate on behalf of all women? Well, some feminists would simply say that you need a more fractured feminism with shifting coalitions and solidarities. That's the sort of response you find in feminists like Judith Butler, Bernice Johnson Reagon, or Chandra Mohanty. Another approach would hope to identify something that all women share regardless of the diversity of their experiences.

NW: *Presumably this is being complicated, recently, by the increasing visibility of trans women and trans men and the difficulty of fitting people into simple categories when the categories seem to be multiplied.*

AS: Trans women and trans men have, of course, existed for a long time. But feminism has recently been under pressure to politically accommodate and vindicate their reality—especially of trans women. A trans woman is a woman—someone who identifies as a woman, who feels herself really to be a woman, just as I feel myself to be a woman—but who at birth, and perhaps for a long time after that, was identified by those people around her as a boy or man, usually on the basis of what might be called 'male biology'. So, on the orthodox feminist view of gender as a social construction, the kind of view that Beauvoir put forward, women are women in virtue of a shared experience of a certain kind of social process, namely socialization as women. Now, this thesis stands in some tension with the idea that trans women are really

8

women. For a trans woman who has only recently transitioned, how can it be that she was *always* a woman?

NW: *Is there a way to argue that trans women really are women and always have been?*

AS: Yes, and I think it's very important for feminism to rethink the question of 'What is a woman?' in light of the experience of trans women. I'd like to offer two different ways of addressing that challenge, namely the challenge of vindicating the reality of trans women as women while holding on to a constructivist notion of gender. The first way is to draw on intersectionality. An intersectional analysis tells us that the experience of women is really diverse. Not all women will have gone through, for example, the experience of getting their periods, or having been cat-called, or having given birth, although these might be true for many women. Once we recognize that women can have really diverse experiences, we can think of the childhood of a trans woman, a childhood in which she was mis-gendered as a boy and treated as a boy, as just another kind of girlhood. The second way has to do with rethinking what it is we're asking when we ask the question 'What is a woman?'. So, when Beauvoir or Butler ask that question, they're asking it as a metaphysical question. What sort of thing, metaphysically speaking, is a woman? What sort of thing in the world does the concept 'woman' pick out? That's to ask a descriptive question. But we can also ask a prescriptive question. What sort of concept of woman *should* we have, politically and morally speaking? And you might think, and I do think, that the category of woman we should have is a very inclusive category and should include all of those people who identify as women.

NW: *So, you're saying that the category of womanhood is actually a kind of call to solidarity and it's almost self-defining. If you think of yourself as a woman, then you are, by definition, a woman?*

AS: I think that's exactly right. Feminism is a political movement, and political movements need to think about who they're including and who they're excluding, with whom they want and do not want to create solidarity. A feminism that isn't inclusive is just not a very good feminism, politically or morally speaking. I think that, for political purposes, for the very central purposes of feminism, we should think about the question 'What is a woman?' in terms of what our solidarities should be—who do we want to include in our fight against the patriarchy? And I think it's very clear that trans women should be centrally involved in that fight—indeed, that they already are.

Further Resources

Simone de Beauvoir (2015) *The Second Sex*, translated by C. Borde and S. Malovany-Chevallier, Penguin.

Talia Mae Bettcher (2014) 'Trapped in the Wrong Theory: Rethinking Trans Oppression and Resistance', *Signs*, 39:2.

Judith Butler (1990) *Gender Trouble*, Routledge.

Mari Mikkola (2019) 'Feminist Perspectives on Sex and Gender', *The Stanford Encyclopedia of Philosophy*, ed. Edward N. Zalta: http:// plato.stanford.edu/archives/fall2019/entries/feminism-gender.

2

JANET RADCLIFFE RICHARDS
Men's and Women's Natures

Nigel Warburton: *Are men different from women by nature? If so, what follows? Does it follow that women and men should be pushed or encouraged into different spheres, such as different types of jobs, or different roles in the family? In his ground-breaking book* The Subjection of Women, *the nineteenth-century philosopher John Stuart Mill developed a sustained argument against established views about the natures and appropriate situation of women and men. Janet Radcliffe Richards, author of* Human Nature After Darwin *and* The Sceptical Feminist, *explores the ideas of Mill and his opponents about the natures of the sexes, and what they imply about their position in society.*

David Edmonds: *Janet Radcliffe Richards, welcome to Philosophy Bites. The topic we're going to talk about is human nature—whether men and women have different natures, and if so, so what? One place to start would be the historical context of Mill.*

Janet Radcliffe Richards: At the time when Mill was writing, in the second half of the nineteenth century, the law and most social institutions treated men and women quite differently. Women were systematically excluded from areas regarded as the preserve of men, such as higher education, the professions, and the franchise. Married women were also legally subordinate to their husbands, to an extent that Mill argued amounted to slavery. Mill thought that this was quite wrong, and that the law should treat women and men according to what he called 'a principle of perfect equality'.

DE: *What was the argument of Mill's opponents? Was it that it was women's nature to be in the kitchen, i.e. to be domesticated creatures?*

JRR: Yes, most of their arguments were based in the deeply rooted idea that men and women were quite different by nature. Some of them tried to make out that their claims were simply about differences, rather than inequality. But most of the time it was clear that the idea was that women were naturally weaker and inferior in all respects—intellectual as well as physical—and the excuse for differential treatment was that it would be inappropriate and cruel to treat them as if they were the same. They were incapable of doing what was recognized as the preserve of men, and were naturally suited to their position of supporting their husbands and caring for their families. This was their proper role in the scheme of things, and where they should look for true fulfilment.

DE: *And what was Mill's view? Did he believe that men and women were fundamentally the same?*

JRR: He obviously thought, from his own experience, that it was absurd to regard women as inferior to men in any respect other than brute physical strength. But what he actually said was that at the present time it was impossible to know how different the sexes were by nature, because for the whole of history they had been treated in systematically different ways. They had had different educations, and had been in different social and legal positions, so it was impossible to know how many of the apparent differences between the sexes came from their natures and how many from their environments. But even so, he said, everyone already knew that the claims made about women were nothing like universally true. Everything women were said to be incapable of doing, at least some women had already done, and done well. Everyone also knew that women had always been disadvantaged in education and opportunity, so any reasonable person should recognize that without those drawbacks many more of them could be expected to show these abilities. And the same applied to the idea that women were happy in their situation of domestic subordination. It was well known that some women had already complained through their writing—the only means of protest available to them—about this situation. And, again, it was reasonable to suspect that if women hadn't been so assiduously educated to fit their role, many more of them would object. Furthermore, since women were dependent on their husbands, they knew how dangerous dissent and disobedience could be. So, all in all, he said we already knew that these sweeping claims about the different natures of the sexes were not true.

DE: *Had you been able to show to John Stuart Mill that in fact women and men were different, would that have persuaded him that separate laws would be appropriate for men and women?*

JRR: No, because he thought that even if you granted the premise about sex differences, the arguments still didn't work.

They ran straight into logical difficulties. So, it was said that women were excluded from men's terrain because they were incapable of fulfilling male functions; but as Mill said, 'what women cannot do it is quite superfluous to forbid them from doing'. If some job needs to be done, there are always standards for selecting suitable people and excluding others, so if women turn out not to be suitable, the existing criteria will exclude them automatically. You don't need an extra rule excluding women. Conversely, if you do have an extra no-women rule, precisely what it does is exclude women who would otherwise have to be let in because they were suitable. Either way, you can't use alleged differences between the sexes to justify unequal laws. And similar arguments apply to the idea that women happily choose their situation in marriage. If you really thought women would voluntarily choose their situation in marriage, it wouldn't be necessary to force them into it by closing everything else to them. We should have impartial laws, and then see what happened when people made their own choices.

DE: *That argument sounds pretty watertight. Did it convince Mill's opponents?*

JRR: No, it didn't. For instance, Mill was at the time an MP, in the thick of the debates about suffrage that were leading up to the 1867 Reform Act. Suffrage was not universal at the time, even for men, and Parliament was trying to decide what criteria should determine eligibility for the vote. Mill wanted to put 'person' instead of 'man' in the text of the bill, pointing out that whatever criteria were chosen, criteria that excluded unfit men would automatically exclude unfit women. But there wasn't a chance of its being accepted at the time.

DE: *Why were his opponents not convinced?*

JRR: The usual feminist reply is that it was because the men didn't want to give up their power, and of course that's no doubt true. But I think there was more to it than that. As a philosopher, I am interested less in speculations about psychology and motives than in how the arguments on the opposing sides worked. In particular, they often seemed to pass each other by without engaging at all. For instance, consider one of Mill's critics, a conservative judge by the name of James Fitzjames Stephen. Mill had pointed out that we could not know how different the sexes were by nature, since they had always been treated differently. Stephen's reply, if you can call it a reply, was simply to assert that 'all the talk in the world' could not change the fact that men and women were different 'from the crown of their head to the soles of their feet', and that men were 'stronger in every shape'. But he knew perfectly well that thze sexes had different educations and opportunities, since that was exactly the situation he was defending. So how could he regard this as a reply to Mill's argument that we couldn't tell what came from nature and what from differential treatment? Mill had also said that we couldn't know existing arrangements between men and women were best, because we'd never tried anything else. Stephen's reply was again just a reassertion of the claim Mill had argued against, without any reply to the argument itself. He just said it must be the best way, because all societies in history had worked that way. He also said that the purpose of laws was to maintain society in the form it naturally assumed, without replying to Mill's arguments that you don't need laws to bring about what will happen naturally. So, there was something puzzling going on here, and it wasn't until years later, when I'd been working on the implications of Darwinian theory, that I began to realize what was going on.

DE: *So what was it?*

JRR: I think they were working on the basis of completely different conceptions about the fundamental nature of the world. A lot of people at the time explicitly appealed to religion in political arguments. But many of the ones who didn't actually mention religion, like Stephen, still seemed to be presupposing an essentially religious view of the world. This is complicated and takes a lot of explaining, but the essence is that Stephen and most of his contemporaries seemed to take it for granted that the world as a whole was designed to work in a particular way, rather like an organism, in which different parts had different functions which worked in harmony for the good of the whole. The only way to get everything to work well was therefore for the different parts to fulfil their natural functions in their proper places. It's what you'd expect from the Christian tradition, with God designing everything and seeing that it was good. To make things work as they should, you had to go along with its design.

DE: *Give me a concrete example.*

JRR: Well, Stephen said that the two sexes could no more have different interests than different parts of the same body could. Obviously, in a body you can't have different parts changing places with each other; each must fulfil its own function. And each must fulfil that function well. If you try to make clumsy feet look better by cramming them into tight boots, you harm both the feet and the body as a whole.

And when something does go wrong, you should try to correct it, in the way that you may try to straighten bent legs with irons. So, he implies, the relationship between husband and wife in marriage must involve a division of labour that is fixed by nature, and the wife must defer to the husband because men are naturally stronger and therefore meant to be in the superior position. Stephen says the relationship is like the one between the captain and first mate of a ship: even though the first mate may occasionally make better judgements, he must always obey the captain. And, he says, to object to the arrangement is to show 'a base, unworthy, mutinous disposition'. A wife who does not act appropriately to her natural position is working against her own interests as well as those of the family, and of society as a whole. I think that's how Stephen and all the other people who agreed with him were seeing it. He was seeing the world as designed with a certain natural order, and our job was to maintain that order.

DE: *Why would that be our job? What would be wrong in having a few aberrations, as Stephen would have seen the women who wanted to enter men's domain?*

JRR: Well, with this view of things he would say every aberrant individual would do some harm to the whole. But don't forget that the point isn't primarily about the odd individual. The debate at this time was about the social framework: in particular laws, but also such things as policies for education and social organization. If you think women's natural place in a complex social structure—designed for the good of all—is different from men's, then it will seem to you that education and institutions should reinforce that structure.

If things get out of the place they are supposed to be in, you get disorder and chaos.

DE: *Was Stephen worried about anarchy breaking out?*

JRR: I'm sure he and many others were appalled at the thought of what would happen if women started questioning their traditional role. But the real point of explaining the presuppositions that underlie traditional thinking, like Stephen's, is to contrast it with Mill's, and show why their arguments simply failed to mesh. Stephen's arguments presuppose the essentially religious idea that the world was designed rather like an organism, to work for the good of all as long as all the component parts contributed in the way they were designed to by nature. But Mill was in a different intellectual tradition—that of the Enlightenment. This grew out of the development and increasing success of natural science, and the Enlightenment view was essentially that the natural order of the world—the workings of mechanical causes and effects—had in itself nothing to do with anything we would recognize as a moral order or plan. The natural world was morally indifferent and often bad. As Mill said in another essay, 'all the things that men are hanged or imprisoned for are nature's everyday occurrences'. So if we want to make the world better, it's no good just going along with nature. We need to understand how the world works, through science, and then manipulate it ourselves to bring about what we recognize as good. Of course, a lot of people doubted—and still doubt—that the world can be like this, without underlying purpose. Most people intuitively accepted what is known as 'The Argument from Design', one of the traditional arguments for the existence of God. The idea was that the amazing intricacy and coordination of nature could not have come about by chance without there being a designer and an underlying plan for the whole. But at the same time as Mill was writing, Darwin was also working; and the great Darwinian breakthrough was the theory of evolution by natural selection, which showed for the first time how order could come out of chaos without there being an underlying plan. This is essentially what Mill and the Utilitarian philosophers were recognizing: that the natural order and moral purpose were completely different things.

DE: *Do you think Darwinism can give us some insight into whether men and women do have different natures?*

JRR: Yes. Mill had pointed out that observing men and women as they now were couldn't show how many of the differences between them came from their nature and how many from their systematically different situation. As a philosopher of science, he recognized that we hadn't any controlled experiments. Now we have made enormous headway in equalizing opportunity, and, as Mill predicted, women's abilities have been shown to be quite equal to men's. But quite a lot of differences between the sexes still persist, and a lot of feminists insist that all of these are socially constructed: produced in girls from infancy by aeons of habit and expectation. But what Darwin did was show a quite different direction from which to approach the whole question. What he did was show that where males and females of a species have significantly different functions in reproduction, they will inevitably be different in other ways as well. What natural selection does is favour characteristics—mental, emotional, or physical—that have made the species reproductively successful; and since males and females have different reproductive functions, selection will inevitably favour different characteristics in the sexes. What these are will depend on the reproductive strategy of the species, but consider ours. Females can produce only—at most—a child a year; far less in practice. Males' reproductive capacity, on the other hand, is limited only, but of course entirely, by their ability to get females to do the work of producing and nurturing those children. This difference means that natural selection should favour quite different characteristics in the sexes. Men who can get more than their fair share of women will be the ones whose characteristics get passed on. If some men get more than their share, others will inevitably get none, and their attributes will be lost. Women, on the other hand, have nothing to gain by getting large numbers of men, since that can't increase their reproductive capacity. What they need is to find a good-quality father for their children, who can command a large range of resources to invest in them. This suggests that natural selection should favour very different characteristics in men and women.

DE: *One can see why men would be more promiscuous, but people often say that men are more aggressive, or that men are more dominant. What's that got to do with reproduction?*

JRR: You have to distinguish between being aggressive to other males and dominating females, but both phenomena are what you'd expect of males with our kind of reproductive strategy. Since a male who doesn't get any females will not reproduce, you'd expect natural selection to favour men who could successfully compete with other men for power and status that enabled them to get access to females and keep other men away, and also to make them attractive to females. Dominance over women is also understandable. In a species like ours, where males invest in their offspring, it is of crucial importance that they should be concerned to watch and control their women, to make sure they are not inadvertently investing in some other man's offspring. So reasoning of this kind opens up a quite different direction of enquiry from traditional controlled experiments—which are very hard to conduct among humans.

DE: *So some might say, if men are perhaps more ambitious and competitive by nature, that offers one explanation for why, say, there were more male chief executives in business than women. Whereas a feminist might say it's nothing to do with that. It's explained entirely by discrimination or culture.*

JRR: Of course there is still discrimination, and there are lots of long-standing habits and cultural assumptions. But evolutionary thinking does give us good reason for thinking that male competitiveness goes much deeper than social pressures, while women have far fewer reasons to have evolved this kind of competitiveness and status seeking. So that is indeed likely to be part of the reasons for men's getting to the top more than women. But why do feminists feel they should deny this? If it's true, we need to know it, so that we can think about what to do about it. If we value certain abilities and aptitudes, and think that people who have these are being elbowed out of the way by naturally pushy men—or indeed pushy women—then what we need to do is concentrate on finding ways to make sure the people who have the abilities we want are in a position to use them. As Plato said, the people most suited to be his Guardians will be people who don't want the position, and will have to be put there by others. And I think this is what essentially Darwin and the Utilitarian philosophers were recognizing—that the natural order and the moral order were completely different things. You need to understand what things are like if you are to make them better, but deciding what would count as better is a quite different thing.

DE: *So even if we accept that there are these average differences, should a feminist be threatened by this argument?*

JRR: I don't think so. I must admit I'd be disappointed if science were showing that women were on average inferior to men in intelligence or capacity for various other kinds of achievement, but fortunately it shows nothing of the kind. There is absolutely nothing in evolutionary reasoning, or in direct scientific research, to suggest it. There are some variations of detail, but nothing significant. The differences evolutionary reasoning would lead you to expect are mainly in the area of emotions and temperament and preferences and interests, which is exactly what we find. And if that's true, it's something feminists need to know. There's no point in pursuing the kind of sex equality that has as its aim an equal sharing between women and men of all kinds of activity and profession, if that would suit neither.

DE: *It sounds like quite a dangerous idea because some people might say, well, we now have the explanation for why men are paid more, or why women choose to spend more time with their families. We do not need to work hard at making, let's say, the workplace more equal between the sexes.*

JRR: No—I think it's just the opposite. It means we need to work harder, and think much more radically. Don't forget that all our current working arrangements developed at a time when men went to work, and household and children were the responsibility of women. This meant that the workplace developed without any need to accommodate the care of children on a day-to-day basis, or for careers that seamlessly allowed for interruptions. Women may on average be more inclined to spend time on care of children and domestic matters than men are, but that certainly doesn't mean that is all they want to do, or can do. So we need to find quite different ways of organizing things. We're making some adjustments, but it's hard to make real changes in a complex society where everything is linked to everything else. Seriously radical thinking, no doubt propelled mainly by women, is needed. And quite apart from that, we also have to allow for the fact that the detailed structures and patterns of work have been developed by men. If women are significantly different in tastes, preferences, and emotions, they might find quite other arrangements more congenial. We still have no real idea about what kinds of arrangements might be best. So if women do tend to make different choices from men, as it seems they do, that is all the more reason for making sure those choices aren't limited to the ones arising naturally in a framework developed by men.

DE: *So feminists who worry about these kinds of arguments—who worry about any evidence showing that men and women have different natures—are showing a misplaced anxiety?*

JRR: Well, I can see why they are anxious. When people make claims about sex differences, especially if they involve claims such as that women are not as status seeking as men and are more interested than men in domestic matters and looking after small children, it sounds ominously like the kind of thing

James Fitzjames Stephen and his fellow conservatives were saying. It's no wonder that feminists want to deny the whole idea, because the claims about different natures are taken to be intrinsically bound up with ideas of traditional roles.

But this is a mistake, because even if some of the claims from evolutionary scientists sound rather like the traditional ones about men and women, they are really quite different, and have nothing like the traditional implications. They are not about unchangeable essences of maleness and femaleness. They are not claims that all women differ from all men, or that all men and all women have certain characteristics; they are just about tendencies and averages. They have in themselves no implications at all for policies about who should be doing what, and certainly do not imply that men and women should be treated differently.

Understanding the differences between traditional and modern scientific claims is absolutely essential. Whatever changes feminists want to make, they cannot afford to resist or ignore biology. What they need to resist are the widespread caricatures of its claims, and equally widespread mistaken inferences from them.

Further Resources

Martin Daly and Margo Wilson (1988) *Homicide*, Aldine de Gruyter.

Janet Radcliffe Richards (2000) *Human Nature After Darwin: A Philosophical Introduction*, Routledge.

Robert Wright (1994) *The Moral Animal: Why We Are the Way We Are*, Pantheon.

3

PATRICIA SMITH
CHURCHLAND
What Neuroscience Can Teach
Us about Morality

David Edmonds: *What can science tell us about morality? Many philosophers would say, nothing at all. Facts don't imply values, they say. You need further argument to move from facts about us and about the world, to conclusions about what we ought to do. For example, most humans are altruistic. They genuinely care about the well-being of friends and family, and to a lesser extent even of strangers. They'll give money to charity to help people they've never even met. Suppose science gives us a compelling scientific explanation for why we are altruistic. Does that tell us whether we should be altruistic? Patricia Smith Churchland is well known for her work at the intersection of neuroscience and philosophy.*

Nigel Warburton: *The topic we're going to focus on is what neuroscience can tell us about morality. I wonder if we could just begin by sketching your view of the neural basis of morality.*

Patricia Smith Churchland: It's a bit of a story. There was a major shift in brain organization and structure as mammals evolved, and there were a number of changes that were really important in the mammalian brain—one of which was that mothers were motivated to care for and nurture offspring. In the case of reptiles or frogs or snakes, by contrast, basically what happens is that the female lays the eggs and goes on with her life. Because mammalian babies are born very immature, evolution favoured circuitry for other-care, i.e. the care of others. Pain and pleasure wiring ensured that when there was separation of the infant from the mother, the mother felt pain and so did the infant. They felt pleasure and well-being when they reconnected. We know something about that circuitry and we know that oxytocin (although not by any means the only important molecule) is in a certain sense at the hub of all that. The endocannabinoids are also important as they modulate pleasure.

NW: *Just to clarify, what is oxytocin? What does it do?*

PSC: Oxytocin is a very ancient molecule and it's found in all reptiles and probably almost all animals. In reptiles, oxytocin functions in smooth muscle contraction for the release of eggs. In mammals, it was put to rather different uses, and its new role in the brain was to regulate attachment between parent and offspring. This shift in the mammalian brain for attachment to others was essentially an extension of self-care (seeing to one's own temperature and safety and food) to other-care (seeing to the temperature and safety and food of others). The flexibility in care of others that distinguishes mammals from social insects has to do with the mammalian cortex. All mammals have cortex; no non-mammals do. Birds do have wiring comparable in functionality to mammalian cortex, but to the eye, it looks different from cortex.

NW: *I can see how that works with the care of one's own offspring, and there's obviously a genetic component to that in terms of looking after one's genes and so on. But how does that extend to others who aren't related?*

PSC: Essentially, small genetic tweaks modify the range of others whom one can bond with and hence care about. A discovery about ten years ago with regard to mate attachment suggested a mechanism that gave us insight into how care and attachment can extend beyond offspring to unrelated others, to friends and so forth. The story involved oxytocin and its distribution of receptors, and the species studied were voles. I'm going to contrast for you two species of voles—prairie voles and montane voles. The behaviour of prairie voles revealed something very surprising. After the first mating, the male and the female bond for life. Thus the male guards the nest, the male helps take care of the offspring, and they just like to hang out together. They suffer if they are separated and they recognize when the other is stressed and begin to cuddle and groom the stressed mate. By contrast, consider the montane voles. They do not form attachment to mates, and the female raises the pups on her own. So when the contrasting behaviours were observed, a number of neurobiologists asked this question: what's the difference in the brain that explains the difference in social behaviour? The answer mainly concerned the receptors to which oxytocin binds, or the receptors to which a very similar molecule, vasopressin, binds. More exactly, the *density* of receptors in very specific places in the prairie vole brain were much greater than receptor density in the montane vole brain. Researchers found that when they blocked oxytocin or vasopressin receptors, the social behaviour completely changed. The prairie voles no longer formed strong mate attachment. Likely the genetic differences between prairie and montane voles are quite minor, and mainly concern the gene expression of the proteins that make the receptors for oxytocin and vasopressin. Why are prairie voles long-term pair bonders? Given the particular ecology for prairie voles—they live out in the open prairie where they are susceptible to predation by kestrels—evolution likely favoured the animals who formed strong social bonds with their mates and who liked to live in communities. Changing circuitry to modify or extend those to whom individuals form strong attachments yields different social patterns—wolves and beavers are long-term pair bonders, but baboons are not (though they form strong bonds with female kin). Animals who are highly social, such as wolves and dogs, form bonds with conspecifics but also with individuals of other species, such as humans and ravens. This is because bonding and cuddling feel good. To simplify somewhat the story of moral motivation, *attachment begets caring, and caring begets morality.* This does not tell us what specific actions a species will evaluate as socially important. That will depend on the ecology of the group, on its cultural traditions, and the particular circumstances an individual finds itself in.

NW: *What would be the advantage of an individual cooperating with people who aren't close relatives?*

PSC: Safety, defence, offspring care, foraging, and hunting can be more successful in a group, meaning more offspring survive and reproduce, though much depends on how the species makes its living. Consider wolves, for example. A wolf pack can more easily bring down major game, such as a

caribou or a moose; a lone wolf has little chance of success.
A wolf pack jointly can drive a grizzly bear off a kill. The pack
can also engage in defence against predators. A lone wolf, or a
lone coyote, a lone baboon, a lone chimpanzee, doesn't last
very long—they can't get the food resources and they're much
more vulnerable to predation. Darwin clearly understood
these points, and discusses them in his 1871 book, *The Descent
of Man*. Hume and Smith also recognized the advantages for
humans of living in a community. When Aristotle observes
that humans are *social by nature*, he remarks on the advantages.
What is kind of satisfying about recent neurobiological
discoveries concerning sociality is that they link rather well to
these earlier observations about the advantages of a social life.

NW: *I can imagine someone reading this and asking why you are
talking about animals. Human morality isn't simply a matter of group
cooperation in the way it is with chimpanzees. It has got a self-reflective
aspect to it and a cultural aspect to it. What you are describing isn't
morality, this is a long way back in the past—rather, these are all the
precursors of morality.*

PSC: The evolutionary perspective, along with good studies
of nonhuman mammals, shows many examples of cooperation,
food sharing, consolation, third-party punishment, and a sense
of fairness in nonhuman animals. This looks a lot like
morality to me. Notice that the brains of all mammals are
remarkably similar in structure and organization. We all have
cortex. Mammalian brains vary mostly in numbers of
neurons, and humans have very big brains. True enough, as
you say, in the case of humans living in the last 2,000 years,
complex culture is hugely important. Nevertheless, broaden
your focus beyond culture as it is right now. Consider Homo

sapiens as they emerged in Africa about 300,000 years ago or Homo erectus who emerged about 1.8 million years ago and who had fire and made stone tools. These early hominins lived in groups of about twenty to thirty individuals and their social life and social organization were probably pretty similar to that of chimpanzees and baboons as we can observe them now. Bear in mind that only since the advent of agriculture about 10,000 years ago have Homo sapiens begun to reflect on contracts and social hierarchies and private property. In other words, for most of our history, morality was the morality of small groups, and as we know from the Inuit, for example, their social practices served them very well. Once humans began to congregate in very large groups—largely made possible by the advent of agricultural techniques such as herding and cultivating—then a new level of problem-solving emerged to deal with new kinds of problem, problem-solving having to do with resource distribution, private property, how to deal with miscreants, how to deal with inheritance, and so forth. But those institutions were forged in a highly pragmatic context, as a result of collective problem-solving about what will work and what won't work.

NW: *You've told a story about the origins of what I called the precursors of morality. You seem to be saying that's what morality now is. So you're moving from a description of facts about the past and facts about neuroscience, to saying how we engage with each other now, and how we ought to engage with each other now.*

PSC: Well, not exactly. First, I may have a slightly broader conception of morality than you do. Thus I think that indigenous people, such as the Inuit or the Cheyenne or the Haida, certainly had social practices that I call moral, whether or not they had a written language, and whether or not they spent much time in self-reflection. Incurring a cost to oneself to help another is a basic feature of morality, and you see that in the Inuit and the Hadza as well as in wolves and baboons and capuchin monkeys. Social behaviour in mammals and birds can be seen to fall along a spectrum of 'serious cost'. At one end is social behaviour that concerns etiquette and manners—matters that help grease the wheels of sociality but which do not implicate serious issues of life and limb. At the other end are social practices that bear upon really serious aspects of social life. The boundary between where morality begins and etiquette and manners shades off is just plain fuzzy. The fact is, we recognize the prototypical cases of serious moral issues and what are prototypical cases of etiquette. This structure is by no means unique to moral concepts. As experimental psychology has shown, workaday categories in general, such as vegetable, river, bald, friend, are radially structured. This means that the categories have prototypes at the centre where we all pretty much agree upon what counts as an instance of that category, and with declining similarities the prototype shades off to a fuzzy boundary. Carrots and potatoes are prototypical vegetables, whereas mushrooms and parsley are out at the fuzzy boundary. Squash is somewhere in between. These categories are radial; they do not have necessary and sufficient conditions of category membership, and they do not have essences. The same is true of many concepts that we use in the social domain such as honesty or fairness. Normal speakers understand these categories in terms of prototypical cases, roughly speaking. Individuals will disagree at the boundaries, but it often does not matter to communication. Thus there may be no right answer as to whether a case counts as an instance of moral behaviour or whether it's merely social and conventional. Moreover, no amount of conceptual analysis is going to solve that. If you consider the concept of morality as having to do with matters of serious social cost and as being a workaday concept with fuzzy boundaries at the edge and prototypes at the centre, we begin to understand differences amongst groups regarding how they handle matters such as fairness. It also helps us see the important role that social problem-solving has in actual, as opposed to idealized, groups.

NW: *Right at the heart of morality is this notion that we have a concern for other people's interests, yet the way you described it, that concern is really just a concern for our own genes. So for many people that wouldn't be morality at all.*

PSC: At the heart of mammalian social instinct is the concern for offspring, family, kin, and friends, in expanding circles. The instinct can exist as an instinct only if evolution favoured the wiring that enables the expression of the instinct. Morality does not arise from pure reason, Kantians notwithstanding. It's not that an individual is maximizing their self-interest in anything like a straightforward conscious way as when we play Monopoly, for example. When we fall in love, it's not because we explicitly say to ourselves, 'oh, gosh, I must get on with spreading my genes'. When we enter puberty, we are motivated to engage in certain kinds of social interactions that hitherto we likely found silly. Our genes see to it that our brains are wired to make this happen. We fall in love and this is evolution's way of motivating us to mate and have babies. It does not feel like that at the time. It just feels like love. Sex is pleasurable because evolution made darned sure that it is. In the case of morality, the evolution of the brain did this really interesting thing—it took the circuitry for self-interest and it expanded it so you genuinely do care for others. You absolutely do incur a cost to benefit others. Your genes never figure in the conscious calculation. For virtually all of human history, humans had babies without knowing one single thing about 'genes'. So you need to distinguish between the background ultimate cause and the proximal cause that motivates people in the here and now. If being social by nature does not mean this, what else could it mean?

NW: *You've mentioned David Hume. David Hume famously said that you cannot move straightforwardly from a description of the world (the way the world is) to the way it ought to be. There has to be some kind of implied evaluative premise to get from any descriptive account to a moral account.*

PSC: As the philosopher Owen Flanagan has pointed out, Hume is a lot more subtle than you might imagine based on that famous is–ought passage. Read that passage carefully, and you will see that Hume is actually lambasting clerics who think that there is a *simple* inference that takes you from something that is the case to something that ought to be the case, such as (let's just take a hypothetical example) 'small boys work as chimney sweeps, therefore small boys ought to work as chimney sweeps'. And Hume thought that any kind of inference that was *simple* and *direct* like that was stupid. On the other hand, remember that Hume was a thoroughgoing naturalist about ethics. In Hume's view, the moral sentiment (aka 'social instinct'), along with self-care and prudence, are motivating. In short, the moral sentiment is a feature of the nature of the species in virtue of which certain things ought to happen—we ought to be social beings who enjoy each other's company and benefit from it. Exactly *what* things ought to be done depends on many facts and circumstances—not simple, not reducible to a handy rule. Still, the moral sentiment and prudence are motivating in a social context; cultural norms as well as problem-solving help us figure out what we ought to do. As a naturalist, Hume was quite willing to recognize that, circumstance by richly embedded circumstance, there is a way of getting from what is—our social nature—to what I ought to do.

NW: *If Hume had been alive today, he would very likely have been fascinated by the developments in neuroscience, but I'm still intrigued to know which developments can actually shed light on morality—namely, which can reflect on our understanding of what we are in relation to how we ought to be?*

PSC: It has long been known that loneliness is typically very painful, and science has now shown that social isolation has significant costs in mental and physical health. For example, it affects the immune system, rendering the lonely person more vulnerable to infections. As well, one might draw some conclusions about certain forms of punishment. So, for example, the discovery that the prefrontal neurons are not well myelinated in adolescents, and aren't really well developed until early adulthood, has had an impact on the court's decision about trying capital crimes in children. The frontal structures are known to be very important in executive control in general, and that means they are important in impulse control and evaluating the consequences of one option versus another, of not being overwhelmed by your passions. And in the case of youthful offenders, aged eighteen and under, their brain lacks the maturity to be able to manage impulse control in quite the same way that an adult can. In the USA, this is now taken into account in sentencing. Difficult questions about the fairness of an inheritance tax or about the obligation to donate an organ, or when a war is a just war, and so forth—these, I think, are questions where neuroscience (certainly today, but also in the foreseeable future) is really not going to have anything specific to say. But it does tell us that early attachment of babies to caregivers is crucially important in their social development. Neglect damages the baby brain.

NW: *Do you think that neuroscience could ever have an impact on our understanding of specific moral issues?*

PSC: We might try this on for size, just to get started: recent research from Columbia University has shown that family income is significantly correlated with a child's brain size, but that increases in family income are associated with the greatest increases in brain size among the poorest children. That seems a morally important fact bearing on ideas about what *ought* to be done (assuming it is indeed a fact). But some philosophers who want to dismiss the relevance of neuroscience in moral thinking will try to trap me into making a simple-minded is–ought inference, and I learned from Hume not to be trapped like that. It's hard for me to see that neuroscience can weigh in strongly because many of the problems that we deal with in the existing moral domain involve incredibly complex social problems. And so for something like 'When is a war a just war?', it does not seem likely that there would be any discovery about the neurobiology of humans that would help us to answer that question. Similarly for whether organ donation ought to be

35

the default in terminal patients or whether Amazon should be downsized. On the other hand, neurobiology may deepen our understanding of anti-social behaviour or fanatical behaviour so that we could respond more effectively to its origin. I also think that understanding the origin of moral motivation gives people a much deeper and broader perspective on the nature of moral decision-making. The traditional ideas that moral rules are divinely handed down or produced by pure reason have both been rather unfortunate socially. Some Kantians insist we cannot claim to have done the morally right thing if we took any satisfaction or pride in our self-sacrifice; our reasons have to be pure as the driven snow. That seems to me biologically rather bizarre.

NW: *Imagine we could put oxytocin in the food supply somehow, and it produced a big effect on people—that they're much more likely to cooperate, much less likely to be violent to each other—that would seem to be the direction that this sort of discussion of neuroscience is going in. Should we do it?*

PSC: Well, that is just a fantasy. One problem is that oxytocin plays an important role in many aspects of the body function; in females it regulates oestrus and in males it regulates sperm ejaculation. I would not mess with those functions if I were you. There are experimental procedures where researchers administered oxytocin in a nasal spray, expecting it would get into the brain as cocaine does. The results so far are unimpressive. One problem is the experiments are largely underpowered and hence not very meaningful. Additionally, there does not seem to be a way for oxytocin, as opposed to cocaine, to cross the blood–brain barrier, so the nasal spray may not be getting any oxytocin in the brain anyhow. The other more simple point is that we have some fairly good ideas of how to enhance cooperation and to reduce violence behaviourally. The shortcut through a particular molecule is unrealistic, technically and in terms of our neurobiology.

Further Resources

Patricia Smith Churchland (2011) *Braintrust: What Neuroscience Tells Us about Morality*, Princeton University Press.

Patricia Smith Churchland (2015) 'Neurophilosophy and Moral Values', *Serious Science*: http://serious-science.org/neurophilosophy-and-moral-values-4953.

Adina Roskies (2016) 'Neuroethics', *The Stanford Encyclopedia of Philosophy*, ed. Edward N. Zalta: http://plato.stanford.edu/archives/spr2016/entries/neuroethics.

4

CHRISTINE M. KORSGAARD
The Status of Animals

David Edmonds: *Many moral philosophers argue that it really matters how we treat animals. We can't justify factory farms, or much of our experimentation on animals, and so forth. Christine Korsgaard agrees, but not for the usual reasons.*

Nigel Warburton: *The topic we're going to focus on is the moral status of animals. Now, post-Darwin, we know that biologically nonhuman animals are very closely related to us. Yet we're still developing a clear notion of what the moral status of nonhuman animals is. What's your main stance on this?*

Christine M. Korsgaard: Well, unlike many defenders of animal rights, I do think there are strong and distinctive differences between human beings and the other animals. I use the traditional word 'rational' to describe these differences, but I don't think it follows from those differences that human beings have a superior moral status to animals.

NW: *What does it mean to be rational in this context?*

CMK: To be rational is to have a certain form of self-consciousness, namely consciousness of the grounds of your beliefs and actions, so that you're aware of the things that prompt you to believe and act as you do, and therefore have the capacity to evaluate those grounds and assess them and decide whether they're good reasons or not.

NW: *Now, in the area of animal rights and considerations about animal welfare, I think it's fair to say that Utilitarianism dominates the field. There's a sense that what makes it wrong to harm an animal is a matter of the consequences—the pain that the animal feels—namely that more suffering is brought into the world than would otherwise be the case.*

CMK: I hold a view in general about good and bad, which is that nothing is good unless it's good for *someone*, or bad unless it's bad for *someone*, and that the value actually attaches to the 'someone', not to the pleasure and pain themselves. And Utilitarianism misconceives consciousness as the place where value happens, whereas the Kantian focus is on the creatures themselves and their value as ends in themselves.

NW: *What is it to be an end in yourself?*

CMK: To be an end in yourself is to have a sort of value for your own sake, and not to be something that's appropriate to use as a mere means to someone else's ends. That's the main part of it. It leads to various duties in the human case—it means that you get to make your own choices, that you shouldn't be coerced or deceived or forced to pursue someone else's ends, that you shouldn't be abused in various ways, and that your rights should be respected. In the animal case, it means that the way in which the animal is used should always be compatible with the animal's own good.

NW: *Now, Kant himself didn't extend this notion of having a right to be treated in a certain way to other animals. And yet you want to ground respect for animals in this Kantian terminology and in this Kantian stance.*

CMK: That's right. Kant formulates the Categorical Imperative in various ways. One of them is the formula of humanity as an end in itself. And in making the argument for the formula of humanity as an end in itself, I think Kant overlooked something important about the implications of that argument. Kant said that it's a feature of human choice that we represent ourselves as ends in ourselves—that this is a subjective principle, he called it, of human action. I take it that what he means is something like this: what we know, ordinarily when we make a choice, is that something is good for us. As rational beings, though, we only actually pursue an end if we think it's something good absolutely. So it's built into the nature of choice that we take the things that are good for us to be good absolutely—that is, they are things that anyone has to view as good and as reason-giving. The side of that which Kant focused on was that in doing that, we in effect make laws for each other. Because if I choose something and I say, 'Okay, I choose this now, it's good absolutely', it's now something that you have to regard as a source of reasons. So I made a law for you by making a choice. Kant thought of making choices as involving all beings who could follow laws, and our status as beings who make laws for each other. But there's something else going on when you make a choice of that kind, which is not between you and the other fellow, but between you and yourself, which is just that you are taking what's good for you to be good absolutely, and therefore declaring yourself to be an end in yourself. In this sense, you are an end in yourself just as a being who has 'a good', and I take that to have the implication that all beings who have 'a good' are ends in themselves.

NW: *So rationality isn't a prerequisite for having 'a good' for yourself?*

CMK: Ah, no, rationality is certainly not a prerequisite of having 'a good' for yourself. The prerequisite of having 'a good' for yourself is just that you are the kind of organism that pursues its own good in the functional sense of good—health and welfare—through action; that is, by finding the things that are good for you attractive and the things that are bad for you aversive. That's what gives you 'a good'.

NW: *How do you determine what the good for an animal is, though, beyond its mere health interests? Because there are many different ways any particular member of a species could live and survive in a reasonably healthy way. But what is the good for a cat, for instance?*

CMK: I don't have detailed views about that, ordinarily. I think an animal's good is, really, just to lead some kind of healthy life in an environment that's conducive to her leading a healthy life. There are particular complications in the cases of animals that are out of place in some way. So, determining the good for a pet animal, for instance, is a little bit challenging, because ordinarily for an animal in the wild, its good is to survive and reproduce. That's what animals like to do—they like to survive and reproduce. But when you bring an animal into the human world, one of the first things you're told when you become a pet owner is 'get your pet fixed—it's the best thing for her'. So the pet is not allowed to reproduce anymore, because she fits into the human world better that way. Therefore, there are some differences when you take an animal out of its natural environment and ask what is good for it.

NW: *It's interesting what you're saying about fitting into the human world, because on many versions of our relations with animals, what matters is what they are to us, not what they are to themselves.*

CMK: And I think that's wrong. I do think it is possible to have an animal as a companion and be just as concerned with the shape of her life as with the shape of your own.

NW: *Does your approach end up with different conclusions from, say, a Utilitarian like Peter Singer, a very famous exponent of animal welfare? Do we get a different conclusion from treating animals as ends in themselves, as opposed to treating their interests as just as relevant as our own?*

CMK: You do get different conclusions in some cases. In particular, Peter Singer has, on some occasions, said that he thinks it's all right to kill an animal as long as you do so humanely. He imagines a scene where he's talking to his daughter about their dog Max, and the daughter is wondering about Max's life and its value, and Singer says, well, you know, if Max died, we could breed another dog and put the dog in Max's place, and then that dog would have dog pleasures, and there would still be dog pleasures going on in the world... That sort of thing is not permitted on the Kantian account, because the animal is an end in itself, not just a place where there are pleasures happening.

NW: *Does this have difficult implications in terms of dealing with animals which are pests? For instance, in order to grow food on an allotment, you're going to have to probably kill some rats and then some slugs in order to produce food for us to eat.*

CMK: Yes, it has very difficult implications for that. In fact, generally speaking, it seems to me important to acknowledge that human moral standards and nature are, to this extent, at odds with each other. Human moral standards demand that we look for solutions to our problems that are, as far as possible, good for all concerned, and nature sets us at odds with each other in terms of our interests. I think we just have to do the best we can about that. In order to think that there wouldn't be grave difficulties, you have to think the natural world has a moral structure already—and I *don't* think *that*.

NW: *Some people might see keeping a cow as a source of milk as a fairly obvious case of using an animal as a means to an end. Would that use be prohibited by your outlook?*

CMK: Well, you can even use people as a means to ends, as long as you act in such a way that they could consent to what you're doing. We can't use quite the same criterion for an animal because animals are not capable of consenting in the relevant sense. But I do think that you can use an animal as a means, if you can do it in a way that's compatible with the animal's own good. Now, whether things like keeping cows for their milk, or sheep for their wool, chickens for eggs, etc. are compatible with the animal's own good is kind of an empirical question that people hotly disagree about nowadays and I don't feel like I know the answer. But the one thing I'm pretty sure of is that if we kept animals for those purposes in ways that were compatible with their own good, then milk and eggs and wool would be a lot more expensive than they are now.

NW: *I could imagine somebody wanting to extend your argument beyond animals to plants, and to environments as well. Is there any reason why we shouldn't treat a forest as an end in itself in the same sense?*

CMK: I think to have 'a good' in the sense that's relevant to morality involves consciousness and experience. Basically, I think the good is something like 'life's positive experience of itself'. Plants have 'a good' in a functional sense; that is, the things that are good for them are the things that enable them to survive and reproduce, but they don't have 'a good' in what I call the 'final sense', the moral sense, because they don't experience their own good as a positive thing for themselves.

NW: *When we're talking about the good for human beings, that does involve rationality, unlike nonhuman animals, and yet we know that some human beings lack the capacity for rational thought, sometimes through tragedy, or through some kind of genetic defects, or whatever. What status do such human beings have in your view?*

CMK: I think those human beings may lack the capacity for rational thought in the sense of the capacity to get rational thought 'right', but they don't lack the capacity for rational thought in the most fundamental sense, which involves having the capacity to be aware of the reasons for what you do. That is a certain kind of self-consciousness that makes you aware of the grounds on which you believe or act. So rationality has more to do, fundamentally, with the ability to ask a certain kind of question rather than to answer it correctly. As a result, I think that rational beings who, in various ways, are unable to reason well nevertheless are still rational beings. They're rational beings in a defective condition—their condition gives us obligations of care. But I think it's important always to keep in mind that any kind of organism is a functional unity—its parts and its systems work together to enable it to lead whatever life is characteristic of its kind. It's not just a heap of capacities. So it's not like you can just remove one capacity and have a different kind of being altogether. Frankly, it is not like you can subtract rationality from a human being and what's left is a dog. I think there's an important metaphysical difference between a defectively rational human being and a nonhuman animal.

NW: *That seems to undermine the kind of argument which says, well, look, there are some apes who are more intelligent, more capable of using language, better at solving puzzles, etc. than, say, some unfortunate young children who've got brain damage.*

CMK: It *does* undermine that kind of argument. I think that kind of argument is not a good way of thinking about the subject.

NW: *Would it be fair to characterize what you were saying as that we do need to get back to a notion of animal rights, not just animal welfare, and that should be grounded on a recognition that all animals, or nearly all animals, are ends in themselves and shouldn't be used by human beings in any way without recognizing the good for that particular animal?*

CMK: I do think that's right. I also think there are good grounds for animal rights in the more specific sense of 'right', where a 'right' means a claim that should be upheld by the law. I think they're rights of a peculiar kind. Most of the rights that we ordinarily think about are either held by every individual against every individual (like your civil rights), or by specific individuals against specific individuals (like when you've made a contract or a promise). I think that animals have rights that are held against the human species collectively on the grounds that we have, in effect, taken over the world and taken control of their lives, and now exercise an authority over them which we can't legitimately exercise unless we also protect them.

NW: *And protect them by the law, not just by the moral law?*

CMK: Yes, to protect them by the law, not just by the moral law. There's really no other effective way to protect them. I mean, it's not like we're going to wait around until everyone gets humane impulses after all.

Further Resources

J. M. Coetzee (1999) *The Lives of Animals*, Princeton University Press.

Christine M. Korsgaard (2018) *Fellow Creatures: Our Obligations to the Other Animals*, Oxford University Press.

Lori Gruen (2011) *Ethics and Animals: An Introduction*, Cambridge University Press.

Peter Singer (2011) *Practical Ethics*, 3rd edition, Cambridge University Press.

5

ASHWINI VASANTHAKUMAR
Do Victims Have Obligations Too?

David Edmonds: *Do victims have obligations? If I see a woman drowning in a pond, I have an obligation to do something to help. If she'd fallen into the pond after I'd bumped into her, my obligation might be all the greater. We tend to think of bystanders having obligations and culprits, of course, too. But the issue of whether victims also have obligations and what they might be is not typically discussed. Ashwini Vasanthakumar, an obvious first question, then, is: what counts as a victim?*

Ashwini Vasanthakumar: The victims that I have in mind are the targets, explicitly or implicitly, of certain kinds of injustices—injustices that range from torture, for example, to the much more diffuse forms of structural injustice, like sexism and racism, that might manifest themselves in less obvious ways.

DE: *It seems obvious that torture is a worse crime than casual sexism, for example. You're not putting the two of those crimes on a par?*

AV: Let me say a bit more about the ways in which I am thinking about these injustices. Torture is obviously a vicious injustice—there is intentional wrongdoing, it is extremely harmful to the victim, and it seriously infringes on important values like autonomy and bodily integrity. You're correct to say that structural injustice, for example, casual sexism in the workplace, simply doesn't seem to involve the same kind of grave wrongdoing. I think, though, that if what we are worried about are values like autonomy, self-respect, and dignity, it's important to recognize that these can be infringed upon in ways that are also important in the casual sexism case. So I wouldn't necessarily say that they're of equal gravity, but that it's important to recognize that what look like everyday wrongs can actually be connected to structures of wrongdoing that can also inflict their own very serious violence.

DE: *Give me an example of that. What kind of effects can casual sexism have?*

AV: I would encourage us to think that what we're looking at when we see, say, casual sexism in the workplace is in many ways the tip of the iceberg. So, theories of structural injustice are also interested in the ways in which the everyday norms, institutions, and practices of society (where it doesn't actually look like there's any wrongdoing going on) can also mean, for example, that there is greater violence against women—there is less protection for women who are victims of violence, especially when it comes to intimate-partner violence. Death by a thousand cuts is still going to result in death, and the difficulty is in appreciating when one of those individual cuts is in fact contributing to overall harm.

DE: *So that does seem to be a distinction between torture and casual sexism, for example. There's an obvious causal link between the torturer and the harm of the victim, but it's never quite clear in those structural cases whether somebody who, let's say, interrupts a woman during a meeting is being sexist or is just engaged in normal 'banter'.*

AV: Absolutely. I think one of the reasons we have very strong intuitions in cases of deliberate wrongdoing is that you have a clear perpetrator who is intentionally harming someone who is clearly a victim. Everyone knows that grave injustice is occurring. In the case of being interrupted in a meeting, not only does that particular instance not seem to inflict harm at all on the same level as torture, but there is a great deal of uncertainty. It is uncertain, for example, whether in this particular case it is actually an instantiation of sexism; or, if it's just, perhaps, a really enthusiastic interlocutor; or, it might just be that you're in a meeting with somebody with very different cultural norms where people constantly interrupt each other. Therefore, it might be a case where gender isn't even at play. And then, the indeterminacy is even more acute as it is also not clear what the best response is. If what we are interested in is what would be effective in defeating injustice and bringing about more just practices, well, is it going to be more effective if you say something to the person immediately or afterwards, or is it better to start creating certain institutional norms without leaving it entirely to individuals' discretion?

DE: *And the person who is guilty of a sexist comment in a meeting at work doesn't feel he's part of a system that leads to somebody else's wife being beaten up in another part of town?*

AV: I think it's very important to highlight that, especially with structural injustice, the distinction between perpetrators, bystanders, and victims is blurred, and victims can themselves be complicit in their own victimhood. So, the argument here isn't that when my male colleague speaks over me at a meeting, he has blood on his hands. It's maybe more helpful to think about this in the following way: we all participate in a world that is heavily coloured by various forms of injustice that get perpetrated through these everyday practices. It isn't so much about pointing the finger at somebody, but thinking about what would be the most effective way that we can change certain practices; knowing that these practices contribute, in ways that we may never be able to measure, to very serious injustices. Iris Marion Young has very eloquently made this point in her work on structural injustice and political responsibility.

DE: *Normally when we talk about people having obligations when somebody is harmed, we talk about the culprit having the obligation, not the victim.*

AV: And I think that is for a very good reason, which is that morally blameworthy people typically should bear the heaviest responsibilities. By no means, when we talk about victims' duties, do we let anyone else off the hook. So the idea isn't that as a victim of injustice you also have the most onerous duties to resist or defeat those injustices. Rather, I think it is more helpful to think of victims as playing an essential role in resisting injustice, in, for example, alerting other bystanders to the fact that certain injustices are going on. The upshot of this would not be to say that victims bear the only duties, or even the most onerous duties. Rather, it is to point out that they have an important role to play in bringing about justice. One reason I think it is important to point this out is that often perpetrators are not morally motivated, as they are intentional wrongdoers—they are not going to suddenly stop and say, 'Oh, I have a duty not to commit injustices'.

DE: *So, the typical philosopher's example would be somebody who's being drowned in a pond and you're observing this as a bystander. You have an obligation to stop the person being drowned. But you're not the victim, you're the bystander—you're the observer.*

AV: I think this paradigm rescue case or paradigm assistance case is very helpful and it is one that certainly motivates my thinking. In many cases, victims were drowning, but have since come to safety, and are potentially now in a position where they can assist others. They are often the only people aware that there are other victims drowning, so they are the ones who are in the position now of having the duty to rescue.

DE: *I can see how that would work quite clearly in the torture case: so somebody is being tortured; they escape; they move to another country. They have an extra obligation to inform the world that there are others still back home who are suffering.*

AV: Well, I mention the torture case because a lot of reports that we have by Human Rights Watch or Amnesty International come out because we have survivors who have got to safety. So in the case you mention, it seems like they have fled torture, and that they now have a duty to alert others to the fact that there are other people who still need help. Then the question might be, how do we now extend this to cases that are more like structural injustice? By no means do I think the extension is easy or straightforward, but I think there is still a valuable insight here. As a victim of certain kinds of structural injustice, you might be in an epistemically privileged position. Structural injustice is injustice that is hiding in plain sight, and in virtue of your experience of it, you might actually sense that some practice is not everyday, benign behaviour, but that actually there is something morally infirm with it. So then you are in the position, many degrees removed (but I think in a way that is still morally relevant), of the victim who is aware that there is injustice going on.

DE: *And your special obligation is because you can see it—you know about it? Is that right? Is it because you are in a privileged position to identify when there is injustice?*

AV: Yes, you are epistemically privileged in virtue of your experience. In something like the torture case, it is clear that one way in which the epistemic privilege operates is that you have information that other people don't have. Perhaps you know that people in this country continue to be tortured in that particular way, which is something that others may simply not know. Whereas in the case of structural injustice, the knowledge is more about understanding that there is a practice that we all engage in, and you have the privilege of recognizing it as an injustice, or recognizing it as inflicting certain kinds of harms. So I use the interrupting case precisely because it seems so trivial. We think being interrupted is not that big of a deal. I do think, though, that it is women who called attention to the fact that women tend to get interrupted more often than men, and measured this. Maybe women sharing their experiences of being in a meeting where people seem to actually not hear you when you speak, or think that you can just be spoken over, could prove helpful in understanding whether and how this practice is harmful. If such experiences make women less interested in speaking, or make them feel like their contributions are not valid—that is just disrespectful. If the ultimate result of 'manterrupting' is that women simply speak less, well, then that seems like a paradigmatic example of structural injustice, and its mechanisms of self-perpetuation. And as I note, others have connected this erasure to other, more grave, injustices.

DE: *So the suggestion is that victims have special obligations because they have privileged knowledge. Do they also have a special obligation because they might be able to sense or feel the injustice to a greater degree? A torture victim understands quite how bad it is to be on the receiving end of various forms of torture, in a way that somebody who's never been through that kind of experience might find it difficult to imagine.*

AV: Yes, absolutely. There is information and then there is understanding. Even in the case where we might imagine the experience of physical violence as being unpleasant and harmful, it is only when we read accounts that we understand the experience better. And this isn't restricted to the example of torture; we could also think of everyday prison practices that have been normalized. I actually cannot imagine what solitary confinement would be like, because there is nothing in my experience that equips me to imagine what that is like. There are limits to the moral imagination, no matter how earnestly or empathetically it is deployed. It was only by reading testimony that I appreciated some of its effects, for example, on processing time, the loneliness. We do need those accounts, and that is simply because there are limits to how much we can imagine.

DE: *Are you not asking too much of victims? Take the most extreme case that we're talking about, the torture victim. The torture victim has had this incredibly life-changing experience, left the country, trying to rebuild their lives, and now you are expecting them to play a role in helping those back home suffering from the same thing. They may want to forget about their past experience—they may want to move on.*

AV: Thank you, that is a really central question. We don't expect people to harm themselves or to build their lives around discharging duties—that would be too demanding. But the fact that discharging a duty is painful or is just very demanding isn't necessarily or by itself going to limit the duty. I want to say that the victim has a role to play, but it isn't that, if you fled torture, you now have to dedicate your life to defeating torture in your home country or elsewhere. The duty is that you have to do something; for example, get help. If your duty arises from your epistemic privilege, well, the minute you share that knowledge with other people, you've lost that privilege—now you are just one of many bystanders. In an ideal world, if everyone does their duty, then the duty is that you testify, or that you tell other people. And that might be the limit of your duty. So that is one important restriction on it. The other restriction is that in many cases people are simply too traumatized to give testimony. And in that case, these are not individuals who are subject to duties. If the paradigm case is that you are the *capable* bystander, then in this situation they are *not* capable bystanders. As such, my account of duties is actually a lot more restrictive than it initially seems. There is a limit to your duty. So, say you alert the world and then Human Rights Watch writes a report. At that point, I think, as a survivor of torture, you can say, 'Surely now the duty falls on other people; I've done my part'. But it does mean that, even in the highly idealized case, there can be a duty to testify: if there is torture going on and I flee to safety, and I am the only person who has fled and nobody else in the world knows that there are people being tortured. This duty is onerous. It means telling people that very humiliating things have been done to you. It means reliving that for some time. If we keep in mind, though, in addition to how burdensome it is to the torture survivor, thinking about the people who are still being tortured, then I think it is difficult and it is demanding and maybe we don't condemn you if you can't do it, but it does not mean that you don't have the duty.

DE: *And at the other end of the spectrum—the much more complicated case where you're in that meeting and a woman is constantly talked over and you don't say anything—it's difficult to tell whether you're morally culpable or not, precisely because, as we mentioned, you're not sure whether this is an instantiation of sexism.*

AV: Absolutely. So, one way of thinking about this is: what would it be appropriate for you to say to the person that you think has failed to discharge your duty? In the case of the torture survivor, if one can say, 'Look, you're the only person who could alert the world, and you didn't,' then I think one can say that the survivor failed to do something that they clearly had a duty to do, whilst at the same time being very sympathetic to how difficult it would be. In the case of the meeting where I noticed that my female colleagues keep getting interrupted—if one of those colleagues were later to say to me, 'Why didn't you say something?' it is plausible for me to say, 'Well, I didn't know if James is interrupting you because you're a woman, or if it's just that James is a little hard of hearing, or James is just very excited about this faculty meeting topic—who knows, right?' So one plausible response is simply, 'I actually just didn't know that's what was going on.' But, even if I were to say, 'I know, can you believe it, everyone kept interrupting all the women!' there is still uncertainty about what would have been the appropriate thing for me to do. And by appropriate, here, I mean effective. It is not always the most effective thing to confront somebody in the midst of a meeting with the fact that maybe they should think about the practice of interrupting. Maybe I thought I would have a word with the interrupter or I thought I'd see if this is a regular occurrence before I said something to them. That seems like a second possible response. And then just finally, I think I could also say, well, I have a duty to assist other people insofar as it is not too onerous on me. Nobody says you should risk your life to save someone drowning. In a lot of these situations, it is not clear what kinds of retaliation someone will face and if the costs outweigh potential benefits—then I don't think the duty operates. Women and minorities certainly face a lot of retaliation when they point out, for example, implicit sexism, racism, and homophobia in the workplace.

DE: *But in the meeting case, that sounds like a call for inaction.*

AV: The worry is that it is often an *excuse* for inaction. And I think there *are* ways in which we can be alive to that worry and guard against it. But that does not diminish the fact that there is a real complexity there. If you speak to many people in workplaces, they are often thinking about what the best strategy is. Sometimes the best strategy is to try to create certain institutional norms, for example. One strategy is just to call it to people's attention, in general. So, you might say at the beginning of a meeting, 'Let's just try not to interrupt one another,' and that is a way in which you might remedy a situation without necessarily having to blame people who then get defensive. So, the fact that people often have good reasons for not acting should not be used as an excuse for inaction.

DE: *Do you find yourself stepping in more, now, when you notice a woman being talked over in a meeting?*

AV: Well, working on this topic was very helpful because it gave me a pretext for talking about this a lot. I think it is important for us to recognize, especially with structural injustice, that this is something that everyone struggles with. It is something that I struggle with. So, actually, what I worry about more is: when am I interrupting another woman?

Further Resources

Bernard Boxill (2010) 'The Responsibility of the Oppressed to Resist Their Own Oppression', *Journal of Social Philosophy*, 41, 1–12.

Jean Harvey (2010) 'Victims, Resistance, and Civilized Oppression', *Journal of Social Philosophy*, 41, 13–27.

Judith Shklar (1989) 'Giving Injustice Its Due', *Yale Law Journal*, 98, 1135–1151.

Ashwini Vasanthakumar (2020) 'Recent Debates on Victims' Duties to Resist their Oppression', *Philosophy Compass*, 15.

Ashwini Vasanthakumar (2019) ''Playing the victim' is politically vital and morally serious', *Aeon*: https://aeon.co/ideas/playing-the-victim-is-politically-vital-and-morally-serious.

Iris Marion Young (2006) 'Responsibility and Global Justice: A Social Connection Model', *Journal of Social Philosophy*, 23, 102–130.

6

MIRANDA FRICKER
Blame and Historic Injustice

David Edmonds: *There are many practices that today we condemn as ludicrous, barbaric, or abhorrent, which in the past were considered by the vast majority to be acceptable. In Ancient Greece, slavery was widely regarded as entirely natural. Not many people in the early eighteenth century believed that women should be entitled to vote. Until very recently, it was thought perfectly okay for schoolteachers to cane their pupils when they misbehaved. So, given that we're prisoners of our time, should we blame the culprits, the slave-owners, the children-floggers—after all, they surely couldn't have been expected to know any better (even though we now do)? And does the answer to this blame question have implications for how we should handle alien cultures today—cultures operating by principles or practices to which we might take strong exception?*

These are questions for Miranda Fricker.

Nigel Warburton: *Miranda Fricker, the topic we want to talk about is the relativity of blame. Could you outline what the moral problem is there?*

Miranda Fricker: Yes. One might think that moral blame can apply over any amount of cultural or historical distance. But some philosophers have thought that a certain sort of

cultural or historical distance can make moral judgements in
general—and I particularly want to focus on judgements of
blame—lapse. The core argument here is often put in terms
of our moral concepts becoming inapplicable over sufficient
historic distance. If you take a classic example like a medieval
English knight, the knight's code of honour simply doesn't
seem to have any analogue today. So if we look back and see
some of the dreadful things he might have done in the name
of honour, and we disapprove, it would be absurd, some have
argued, moralistic, closed-minded, and historically insensitive
to blame him for those acts. The relativist impulse in ethics
comes from wanting to respect that historical distance and
allow that this knight, although he will have acted in terms of
his code of honour in ways which we may now find appalling,
should not be blamed, and should not even be morally
disapproved of in any way.

NW: *We don't have to go back all the way to medieval knights. When I
was at school, which wasn't all that long ago, we had the cane. It seems to
me quite barbarous now, but at the time it was an accepted pedagogic tool.*

MF: Yes, that's right. And what interests me about moral
relativism is that a lot of the argument for it ought to be
contained in a thesis about the relativity specifically of blame,
and not moral appraisal more generally—certainly not moral
appraisal of *acts*. Relativism needs to be confined to certain
kinds of moral judgement, and I think blame is the obvious
case. Now in this nice example you raise of corporal
punishment against children, moral sensibilities have moved
on. And we now regard hitting children, smacking children,
caning them, depriving them of food as utterly morally

unacceptable and vicious practices which we now bring under quite different moral concepts—not of discipline or something 'character-building', but rather of child abuse, domestic violence, assault, and so on. You have school teachers who used to go in for some of these practices, who understood them as a normal part of disciplining children. It would be moralistic to think we can stand here and blame them for engaging in these practices when they were thought of as a proper part of a morally good way of treating children at the time. So I think even over a very little cultural and historic distance, we can look back and find judgements of blame do run out. And I think that's explained by the fact that it's really a condition of blame that we have to be able to see people as being in a position to have known better. And if people aren't or weren't in a position to have known better, then we can't blame them. But we can regard their *actions* as morally abhorrent, and I think we probably ought to be able to say something critical about the agents too, in terms of their character, but which falls short of blame. But it's obscure exactly what we can say.

NW: *So how does that fall short of relativism where you say there are just these compartmentalized different ways that people behave? And we're not in a position to judge at all what somebody did at a different time or in a different culture?*

MF: Well, it will seem to be the same thing as relativism so long as we assume that blame exhausts our negative moral judgements. But I think in our ordinary moral reflection, though we may lack a vocabulary, we have lots of room for judgements that fall short of moral blame but which are still critical judgements directed at the individual agent for what they did. And I think we could usefully coin a term that I call 'historical or moral disappointment' to use in respect of people who fail to come to a moral insight that contemporaries of theirs did succeed in making. I need to explain this a little more because I think we need to distinguish 'routine' moral judgements—routine moral interpretations, if you like—and, at the times that we're envisaging, where children were standardly beaten as a form of discipline, the routine moral moves would have been in terms of 'did this child deserve such a severe punishment?', and there might have been a 'yes' or 'no' answer. Those would have been routine moral judgements. But there would have been people around that teacher at a certain point in history where we see a kind of moral transition who were able to make a different sort of move, a more 'exceptional' moral judgement, as I would call it, to see that and say, 'no, wait a minute, this is what you call "cruelty"'. They were able then to start bringing these activities, these standard practices, under different moral concepts, and come to see things in a more enlightened way, and you can see I'm assuming a fairly strong moral realism or moral objectivity about these things here. The important point is that the relativity of blame can fit into a framework not of moral relativism at all, but on the contrary, of moral objectivity.

NW: *So some people are just exceptional and see beyond the limitations of their time?*

MF: Yes, that's right. I think we have to see collective moral sensibility as growing and progressing and evolving through time. That's to say I don't assume that we're heading closer and closer to any notional perfect moral vision. Sometimes we go backwards. But in a particular case I think we can look back and see that we've made moral progress about certain sorts of subject areas, and the reassessment of the corporal punishment of children seems to be one of them. So if we regard morality as this rolling, self-correcting, organic enterprise, in sensitivity to others and to moral realities of various sorts, we might expect that some people are pushing that process ahead while others are lagging behind. When we look at historical change, while we may acknowledge that very often there's a certain sort of structural luck in what makes attitudes change, very often, for instance after a war or some other kind of major social upheaval, you find that there are leaps in moral attitudes, still we also expect to see that certain people's reflective capacities are also forcing change. People lobby for different attitudes and that means that at any given time of social transition there will be some people who, for whatever reason, are able to come to see smacking children as a form of violence instead of a form of appropriate discipline. And they're the people who move the collective moral consciousness on. They're the people who make judgements that I'm calling 'exceptional judgements', by contrast with the merely 'routine judgements' of the others who are carrying on thinking in the old ways.

NW: *Now, you've talked about disappointment as the appropriate attitude towards some people's behaviour and feelings in the past. How does that differ from regret?*

MF: Regret, taken absolutely generally, needn't be a moral attitude at all. The bank robber can regret that he left his fingerprints all over the safe. And one can regret that one missed the bus. Neither of these is a moral attitude. But forms of moral regret can be differently focused. There can be shame, which, I take it, is basically a desire to hide from disapproving eyes, which might be others' eyes or, indeed, internalized—it might be one's own. There's guilt, which is normally associated with a heavy conscience which you might be able to offload through some process of atonement or confession. And remorse is perhaps the most important of all, which is characterized fundamentally with a sympathetic grasp of the wrong one has done—a pained awareness of the hurt one has caused. Now, those different forms of moral regret are essentially self-focused. It's significant that it's *me* that did it. And that's why I'm feeling the regret, the remorse, the guilt, the shame that I'm feeling. Moral disappointment cannot easily be directed at oneself—though over a lifespan it's perfectly possible. More usually, however, it will be an attitude we have towards other agents in history, and it's a kind of disapproval we have towards them for a failure to bring their practices under a concept that was available to them, even in their time, because other people were just beginning to use it and to achieve a new moral interpretation.

NW: *So far we've been talking about historical distance. But actually geographically there are presumably tribes which haven't yet encountered people from technologically sophisticated societies who have practices we might find morally abhorrent. Let's imagine there is such a tribe and they standardly kill their third child in a cruel way. How should we treat them because they're contemporaneous with us—there's no distance of time—so should we just feel disappointed with them, or should we prosecute when we discover them?*

MF: Well, some of the general arguments for moral relativism look for very grand kinds of cultural difference to discover that our moral values in general simply don't apply. But, actually, if we've narrowed it down simply to judgements of blame that we're relativizing, I think judgements of blame run out pretty quickly. We've suggested already that they run out pretty quickly over historical distance, and the condition that's governing whether or not judgements of blame apply is the question whether the agent is in a position to have *thought differently*—to have known better—if you like. And I think *that* condition applies over cultural distance as well as historical distance. It applies within a culture too, across generations, for instance. So if we look at any other person who behaves in a manner we judge negatively morally speaking, before we blame we must ask ourselves whether or not they're in a position to think differently—to know differently, to know better, as we might put it from our own point of view—and if they are, we may blame them, but if they're not, then blame seems overly moralistic, and sometimes positively absurd.

NW: *Can you imagine anything that we do now, or that you do now, that in twenty years' time people will look back at and feel deeply disappointed in?*

MF: Quite possibly, yes. And I suppose this is an example of how one could almost, in advance of oneself, be disappointed in one's current practices, as it were. I eat meat but only in semi-good conscience. And I sometimes imagine if we were heading towards a more fully vegetarian or vegan future, those future-others would look back on people like me with some real moral disapproval. They would look at my attitudes towards pets, for instance, and wonder why on earth I didn't manage to bring my treatment of other sorts of animals under the same concept that I use for pets. And they would see incoherence in my thinking and all the sorts of things that we look back on when considering other people's attitudes towards beating children, say, and wonder why they didn't manage to see the light sooner. I don't know if that's what future generations are going to think, but I can see that it might be. And if so, clearly someone like me is in a position to be thinking differently, to be making more exceptional moral moves than I now do, for I am surrounded by vegetarians who have indeed made that sort of exceptional moral move in their ethical thinking. But I haven't, and I remain in a grey area. Now, I think that the worst judgement to be made of someone like me at this point would be historical moral disappointment—disappointment in my failing to make that more exceptional moral move in my current thinking. But eating meat is sufficiently normal—sufficiently routine around here, anyway—that I would not in fact be regarded as blameworthy. So I can imagine myself from a future perspective as now situated in this moral grey area that I'm naming 'moral disappointment'. I'm afraid it's a case of 'could do better'.

Further Resources

Miranda Fricker (2010) 'The Relativism of Blame and Williams's Relativism of Distance', *Proceedings of the Aristotelian Society Supp.*, LXXXIV, 151–177.

Miranda Fricker (2013) 'Styles of Moral Relativism: A Critical Family Tree', in R. Crisp (ed.) *Oxford Handbook of the History of Ethics*, Oxford University Press.

Mary Midgley (1981) 'On Trying Out One's New Sword', in her *Heart and Mind: The Varieties of Moral Experience*, St. Martin's Press.

Michele Moody-Adams (1997) *Fieldwork in Familiar Places: Morality, Culture, and Philosophy*, Harvard University Press.

Neal Tognazzini and Justin D. Coates (2018) 'Blame', *The Stanford Encyclopedia of Philosophy*, ed. Edward N. Zalta: http://plato.stanford.edu/archives/fall2018/entries/blame.

7

KIMBERLEY BROWNLEE
Social Deprivation

David Edmonds: *Sending someone to Coventry means, in English idiom, refusing to speak to them, pretending they don't exist. The origins of the phrase are disputed, but it's clear that cutting someone off entirely from the social world is a particularly cruel punishment. Not all people who lack social contact have been deliberately ostracized as punishment, however. Some are just lonely. But that can be a devastating condition nonetheless. There's an interesting question lurking here. Do we all have a right to social contact? Kimberley Brownlee believes we do.*

Nigel Warburton: *The topic we're going to focus on is social deprivation. What is social deprivation?*

Kimberley Brownlee: I define *social deprivation* as lacking minimally adequate access to decent human contact. So, someone who's put in solitary confinement in prison, or someone who's held in long-term medical quarantine, or even someone who's incidentally isolated—like the elderly person who is unable to get out of the house to seek social contact—would be experiencing social deprivation.

NW: *And do you have to actually feel deprived, or is it just that there's a basic need, whether you realize it or not, that you have as a human being?*

KB: That's an interesting question. We are highly likely to feel the effects of being isolated. It isn't a state we can typically go through and not register it psychologically and physically. In isolation, we are likely to feel intense chronic loneliness. Indeed, during a long period of isolation, we tend to break down—we experience unwanted isolation and loneliness in the same way that we experience pain, thirst, hunger, and fear. It triggers the fight-or-flight response, so it's an anxiety-inducing experience. And it's linked to a host of health risks. There may be some exceptional human beings who could endure isolation with equanimity in the same way that some people can fast for extended periods of time and manage to endure it. But the vast majority of us will experience social deprivation as an extremely negative experience.

NW: *And this is presumably why solitary confinement is a form of torture?*

KB: Solitary confinement not only comes with the ordinary health risks of unwanted isolation and acute loneliness, but it also has additional negative effects on people's psychological and physical well-being. Some people begin to hallucinate, some people become self-abusive, some people even become semi-catatonic. People really do break down mentally and physically in solitary confinement. The anecdotal evidence confirms this; journalists who've been held in isolation as prisoners of war say things like 'my mind's gone blank, it's just horror'. One journalist, Shane Bauer, who ended up in prison in Iran, said that he craved human contact so badly that he hoped each morning he would be interrogated. He woke up wanting to be questioned just so that he could talk to somebody.

NW: *Now, it's fairly clear that, for most people at least, even the people who say they want to be alone, some social contact is a condition of a reasonable life. Does it follow that we have any right to social connection with other people?*

KB: The evidence from psychology is that we are a deeply social species. There are many other social species, but none as hyper-social as us, it seems. We're highly dependent on other people when we're babies, children, and teenagers. We have the longest period of abject juvenile dependency of any species. We also spend reportedly 80 per cent of our waking hours in the company of other people, and we apparently prefer that time to the time we spend alone. (Philosophers might be an exception to this, or maybe even academics in general.) We not only flourish with other people, we need other people in order to survive and lead a minimally decent human life. And for many of us, talking about human rights is the reference point: what kinds of conditions have to be met for us to lead minimally decent human lives? I argue that we have a human right against social deprivation. It's a right in its own right, but it's also a right that has to be protected in order for many other human rights to be meaningfully available to us. If we are socially deprived and break down as a result, then any other rights that depend on the protection of our cognitive competence need this social right to be protected. For example, the right to vote, the right to stand for office, the right to education, the right to health, the right to meet our basic needs with some degree of self-sufficiency all require cognitive competence and, hence, all depend on our core social needs—our right against social deprivation—being met.

NW: *The right that we are talking about here, is it a legal right, a human right, or something else?*

KB: The picture I have focused on up to this point is about moral rights, which means justified moral claims. On this view, human rights are the justified moral claims that a person has as a human being in virtue of having certain fundamental needs and interests. The standard of a minimally decent human life is a moral standard. And so we must ask what the 'brute moral minimum' is in terms of how we can treat a person. This account of human rights does have legal implications, but what's interesting is that you won't find the human right against social deprivation in the *Universal Declaration of Human Rights* (UDHR) or the international covenants. You will find, however, many rights that presume that we are adequately socially included. For example, the UDHR includes a right to have an adequate standard of living to meet the needs of you and your family—and that presumes that you have access to a family. Similarly, you have a right to participate in the cultural and scientific development of your community—the presumption being that you are an accepted member of a community. For those rights to have teeth, we must acknowledge that you have a more foundational right to have minimally adequate access to social contact in general. It underlies those other rights, but is too often taken for granted.

NW: *If I've understood you correctly, what you are saying is that the need for social contact is so great in our species that depriving someone of it is almost as bad as depriving them of water.*

KB: That's right. When we punish people for criminal offences, we tend to deny them standing, we deny them respect, and we often deny them access to society. When we put someone in solitary confinement, we render them abjectly dependent on other people to come to them to provide some social contact. But there are other things that we might do to people as punishments which we don't do (or at least don't do anymore) because we think they're too extreme, beyond the pale. For example, we could not pump dirty air into someone's prison cell and justify it by saying that punishment should be burdensome. Likewise, we could not deny a person water or food and justify it by saying that punishment should be burdensome. So too, I'm arguing, we could not deny someone minimally adequate access to decent human contact, because it is too fundamental.

NW: *Now, we live in the age of social media. Do things like Facebook, Skype, or email constitute social contact?*

KB: That's a tricky question because, to some extent, forms of social media provide social surrogates. When we are away from our friends and family, video chats help us a lot to stay in touch. And, when a person's needs cannot be met in other ways (for instance, if she is ill and highly contagious and people cannot be around her directly), then we might have to rely on surrogates and mediated forms of contact to ensure she has some kind of social contact. Indeed, people who are put in isolation often talk to the TV, or talk to a plant—they'll find *some* sort of surrogate for social contact. But there's so much that's missing from social surrogates. They are unavoidably imperfect and do not meet our social needs in the paradigmatic sense. Direct human contact with the full context of the person you're engaging with brings an element of persistence: human connections are not one-off moments of contact—they're rich in detail and diachronic in that they persist over time. We build up joint narratives with each other. Therefore, a perverse way to punish someone would be to provide them with minimally adequate contact in terms of number of hours, but to have a different person provide that contact each time, thereby forcing the recipient to start over socially again and again. Given this fact, the way we provide healthcare service to people can actually be quite disruptive to their social connections because the social care often doesn't come consistently from the same person. Caregivers and receivers don't get to develop a joint narrative together; they don't get to show that they are trustworthy or that they can give their trust to each other. So, there are two important aspects of the required social contact that we can derive from this—one is the value of it being direct (ideally, the contact is direct contact), and the other is that the contact be in a form that is consistent with what it's like to experience an association. In other words, it's not just *mere* contact that matters. Rather, the social contact that is crucial has to develop a story.

NW: *Is this just a matter of some kind of contact, or does it have to be contact above a certain kind of threshold of engagement?*

KB: What counts as *decent* social contact will depend to some extent on the recipient. A very young child will require contact that is quite rich, which could indeed involve attitudes of love and care and commitment—for a child to thrive, they may need to be loved, not just cared for. For adults who are healthy and broadly self-sufficient, decent contact may meet a more minimal standard that includes merely opportunities to access human contact rather than the positive provision of contact. But even mature, healthy, self-sufficient adults will go through periods of dependency in their lives when facing significant moments like giving birth, facing death, or grieving for a loved one, for example. These are moments of dependency where we do need contact and where decency will be a core feature of that. And, for older adults, or people with certain impairments, those moments of dependency can be frequent, and then the necessary contact closely resembles that required for children.

NW: *I can imagine that, for a lot of adult listeners, some kind of sexual contact with other people of a reasonable quality is a condition of a good flourishing life. Yet they don't feel they have a right to that contact—they're lucky if they manage to achieve it, but it's not a right.*

KB: I think it's possible to lead a minimally decent human life without sexual intimacy. That said, for some people that life is not a choice. If you have a choice to lead such a life, it's consistent with minimally decent human existence. But if it's forced upon you—if you're severely physically impaired and unable to access sexual intimacy unless it's provided—then the interest starts to drift closer to rights territory. This raises issues about competing rights, which I think is a distinctive problem for social needs, as these needs are necessarily inter-subjective. It's not like the need for a material good. When we talk about freedom from poverty, we can send resources where they need to go (by providing food, for example), and that need not put pressure on individual persons' personal resources. By contrast, if we say that someone has social needs that are rights-protected, then someone else—family, friend, hired agent, public service employee—has to provide that contact. Another really interesting point about social resources is that the inter-subjectivity means that when you ask someone to provide social contact to you, you're also offering it to them. Social contact is a reciprocal type of resource.

NW: *It may be reciprocal, but it may also be asymmetrical in terms of what each partner gets out of the activity. Somebody who needs social contact and hasn't had it because there are things which are, let's say, unattractive about them in a serious way may benefit more from social contact than the person who gives it to them.*

KB: That's true. But I don't want to do a disservice to the contributions that some people can make. Someone who requires physical care can provide a social contribution in allowing someone else to have the opportunity to learn caring skills by caring for them. For example, there is a programme in the United States of America where older people who required physical care received some of that care from people with Asperger's Syndrome. The people with Asperger's were learning to make a social contribution through that relationship, and so there was an element of reciprocity between them.

NW: *There is a traditional liberal position that each of us should be free as adults to mix with whoever we want to—it's a matter of our own individual freedom.*

KB: That is related to an idea that we get from John Stuart Mill, namely that we have the right to choose the society that is most acceptable to us. But that idea is patently false. First, our society—our company—might not be most acceptable to the people whom we find most acceptable: they may not want to associate with us. Second, exercising that right to choose depends on our basic associative interests being protected when we were children. As babies and young children, we needed someone to privilege our associative needs. It doesn't make sense to talk about freedom of association in relation to babies or young children. In order for us to assert later in life that we have a preferred association, priority must be given to our associative claims when we're younger even if we weren't our caregiver's preferred associate. As such, we confront what philosophers call the 'What if everyone did that?' problem. What if everyone decided 'I'm not caring for this baby', or 'I'm not taking care of that older person', and justified it by saying, 'I'm asserting my Millian freedom not to associate'? That will pose not only a lot of problems for the person no one wants to associate with, but for the collective. We will all do less well if we assert this claim to not associate. Derek Parfit in his book *On What Matters* talks about 'each–we' dilemmas—these dilemmas are like the 'prisoner's dilemma' in which you have an option to do what's best for you individually or to try to do what's best for the group. And if you do what is best for you individually and everyone else does what's best for them individually, we will do less well as a group and as individuals than if we thought about the group. So, I might say, 'I don't want to associate with anyone', but if everyone else similarly says, 'I don't want to associate with anyone either', we will all do less well. All the things that we value about social connection—families, teams, societies, organizations, intellectual development, love, care, kindness—all depend on us thinking more about the associative interests of the group than about our individual freedom not to associate.

NW: *Does that mean that somebody who chooses to be a recluse is to some degree immoral?*

KB: Yes. We do not have a blanket moral permission not to associate. We romanticize the rugged individualist, the loner, the Thoreau at Walden Pond (who actually kept chairs reserved for company), the Robinson Crusoe. We respect and admire them. And I think the reason for this is that we hope that if we too were isolated, we could thrive. We also appreciate that being a social creature is stressful. On the one hand, we need each other, we get a lot of benefit and protection from each other, we can't survive without each other. But, on the other hand, we're also at each other's mercy. The whims of our family, the ideologies of our society, the shifts in perception are all indicators that we are vulnerable as social creatures. Hence, we romanticize the life of the hermit because we hope that we, too, could survive and thrive if we were isolated, if we were rejected. Someone who chooses to be a hermit has a conditional permission to live that way, provided first that there is no one who has legitimate expectations of them that they maintain an association. If that person has a partner, if they have children, if they have people with whom they are associated, then they do not have a moral permission simply to abandon those people. Second, a non-associated person only has a permission to withdraw provided that there aren't people in the world with whom they *could* associate and whose associative needs will go unmet if they don't. But the 'could' here is interesting.

We are not in close proximity with everybody. There's a practical limit on the people that we could help socially. We are also limited in the number of people we can be intimate with. But if there are people near us, that we could provide contact to, who are otherwise going to have their basic needs go unmet, then we have no moral permission to go off and be a hermit. Given the value of human communities, and given people's claims on others to meet their social needs, we have no moral permission—no blanket moral permission—to reject the human community, because we cannot have it be the case that everybody does that.

NW: *But isn't the solution to that problem that we have a division of labour, as it were? We can each choose things in relation to our own particular set of desires? It just so happens that there is quite a diversity of human life, and so that means there are different ways that people choose to live.*

KB: It will depend. If not many people desire the hermit's life, then our conditional moral permission is perhaps in good standing. If most people won't choose our lifestyle, it's not likely that there will be people whose social needs will go unmet. In our individualistic Western society, many people do favour a somewhat isolated, disconnected lifestyle. If that's the preference of most people, though, then it becomes morally problematic.

NW: *Is it fair to characterize your view as something like John Donne's 'no man is an island'?*

KB: That's right. Yes. We are inextricably bound up with each other as social creatures. We may not like it all the time, but we are interdependent.

Further Resources

Kimberley Brownlee (2016) 'The Self-Reliant Individual Is a Myth That Needs Updating', *Aeon*: http://aeon.co/ideas/what-lies-behind-the-myth-of-the-strong-self-reliant-loner.

Kimberley Brownlee (2020) *Being Sure of Each Other*, Oxford University Press.

Matthew S. Liao (2015) *The Right to Be Loved*, Oxford University Press.

Andrew Mason (2000) *Community, Solidarity, and Belonging*, Cambridge University Press.

Martha C. Nussbaum (2011) *Creating Capabilities*, Harvard University Press.

8

SARAH FINE
The Right to Exclude

David Edmonds: *States have borders, and they police who comes in. The ability to determine who is allowed into the country is, on the face of it, a fundamental right of the state. Indeed, around the world, politicians are often under pressure from citizens to tighten immigration control. But do states really have the right to keep people out? It's a widespread assumption, which Sarah Fine asks us to question.*

Nigel Warburton: *The topic we're going to talk about is 'the right to exclude'. What do you mean by the right to exclude?*

Sarah Fine: I'm interested in the question of whether states have something like a moral right to exclude people who want to come in, and in particular, non-citizens who want to enter their territory, potentially settle in that territory, and indeed eventually perhaps become citizens of that state.

NW: *Most people assume that states do have that right, in that they have some kind of moral authority to say 'you can't come in'.*

SF: I think you are correct that a lot of people do share that assumption, and states certainly act as though they have this right. But there is a question as to whether they *really* do have such a right. What might be the grounds for this kind of right? The way that I look at this particular question is to think about the kind of thing that the state is. I look at the idea of a liberal national democratic territorial state, and I ask whether any of the elements of that conceptual amalgam, either separately or together, might be doing the work to support the claim that this kind of entity has a right to exclude people who want to come in.

NW: *Just to get this clear, the claim you're interrogating is that for somewhere like the UK, or America, states that think of themselves as democratic and as liberal, certain things might follow from that framework which justify exclusion?*

SF: That's right. So somebody might say, for example, that a state just is the kind of thing that needs to have a right to exclude non-members. Or, they might think that a democratic people has the right to decide who may and may not become a member.

NW: *So I'm imagining that I'm coming to a country that I want to enter and I'm told I can't come in. I wouldn't be surprised by that, even if it was a liberal state. Rather, it seems to be quite a normal state of affairs that the state sets the parameters, and as such sets the criteria by which it determines who should be part of that state.*

SF: Whether or not you would be surprised doesn't seem to be that relevant, though, because somebody in the eighteenth century might not be that surprised by the institution of slavery, for instance. But the question is, by what right can the state make those kinds of decisions about you? Now, let's say, to add to your example, that the state refused to let you enter even though your spouse was a citizen of that state, or the state refused to let you enter even though you have some other special claims to enter, settle, and become a member of that state. Maybe then you'd be a little bit more surprised, or outraged, at the fact that you're not allowed to do those things. So we need to ask, by what *right* can the state claim to do these kinds of things?

NW: *And what's the usual answer to that question?*

SF: People do tend to use different sorts of arguments connected to the idea of the state itself. As I mentioned before, somebody might say a state is just the kind of entity that needs to have a right to exclude *because that's what sovereign states do*, or it's essential to the functions of states that they're permitted to exclude. And then we need to ask whether or not those things are true. Why do we think that this is part of the very concept of the state? In previous times, states have claimed other rights that we no longer consider to be part of the very concept of the state. For instance, states have claimed the right to control the exit of their own citizens, and states have claimed the right to control the movement of their own citizens within the state's borders. Those things are now no longer considered to be part of the legitimate package of state rights (apart from in exceptional circumstances). So why should we think that the right to exclude is one of those rights that states are able to claim with impunity? What kinds of things do we think states need to be able to do in order to be states, or in order to claim the authority that they claim for themselves? One obvious thing seems to be that states are really there to defend the people subject to their authority in some way. So we might think states have some kind of a right to self-defence, and that does seem to support the idea that certain forms of exclusion might be permissible under certain circumstances. If we think that states have a right to defend themselves against, for example, foreign terror threats, then we might think that states have at least a right to keep out those who present themselves as clear threats to the state's security. But that's far more limited than the idea of a *general* right to exclude people who want to come in—that states have a wide degree of discretion over these matters.

NW: *So are you suggesting that it's almost a sleight of hand when people assume that a state must, in order to be a state, have the right to exclude just about anybody who it wants to exclude?*

SF: Yes. First of all, we shouldn't assume that any right a state claims for itself, for any particular time, is essential to the concept of the state, because we know that now states no longer claim some of the rights they used to claim for themselves. But also it doesn't look as though it's essential to the very functioning of the state to be able to exclude anyone at any time in any place for any reason. We can think that states could have the grounds for excluding *particular* individuals for *particular* reasons, without also having something like a general right to exclude. If we look at the example of the member states of the European Union, they've committed themselves to some common regulations regarding immigration, and they don't have (at present) the right to exclude nationals of other member states in the same way that they have rights to exclude third-country nationals, for instance. But those member states of the EU haven't stopped being states just because of this current lack of control over those kinds of issues. They remain states. And, moreover, the

EU itself hasn't *become* a state just in virtue of having that kind of control over questions related to immigration.

NW: *Are there other reasons that people give for saying that states have some kind of moral authority to exclude people?*

SF: Yes. We've already talked about arguments emerging from the idea of the state itself. Another kind of argument that people offer is related to democracy. They might say that democratic peoples have a right to decide who gets to come into their state and who may become a member of that state.

NW: *So this might be that you take a vote on it, and you don't want certain kinds of people coming in because you don't like their values—that's just a consequence of living in a democracy.*

SF: Yes, that is one way the argument could go. People might think this is just the sort of thing that democracies get to decide for themselves. And if a state didn't get to decide these kinds of things for itself, then we wouldn't call it a democracy.

NW: *Well, it does seem to follow that if you're committed to accepting the values chosen within a democracy, you take whatever the majority votes (or the majority of the representatives' votes) amount to.*

SF: Well, if we think about the idea of democracy as the 'rule of the people', where the people get to rule themselves, and those who are governed get to govern in some sense, then it looks as though those who are governed ought to have some kinds of rights of participation. Now obviously within recent history we know of states in which certain people have been excluded from participating even though they themselves were 'governed'. And part of the case in favour of including them was a democratic argument—they're governed, so they also ought to have a right to participate. That democratic argument pushes against, for example, excluding people who are subject to the laws in the same ways as other citizens, and in favour of enfranchising women and excluded minority groups. So then we might ask, which people get to make these kinds of decisions about who to include and who to exclude? We already know that democracies can't just decide to exclude certain internal groups, because then the people who are governed aren't the ones who are governing. As such, we need to ask, *who* is governed—who are the people who get to make this decision? When we consider questions to do with immigration, it looks as though some people who are outside the borders of the state and who are not citizens of the state are also in some sense governed by the immigration rules and thus by the immigration decisions. Their lives are deeply affected by these kinds of decisions. The laws are in a sense directed at them. So we might think of them as governed. And we might think that this gives rise to some participatory rights with respect to these kinds of decisions. In other words, what people seem to take for granted when they assume that the democratic people get to decide these things is that we have a clear idea of who the people are, and that 'the people' conforms with 'the citizenry'. Actually, that is questionable, and really quite controversial.

NW: *On the other hand, I think it's quite controversial to think that, for instance, somebody who's living in Latin America who wants to come into Britain is, in a sense, part of the group that should be enfranchised in*

*deciding what happens in terms of immigration laws in Britain. Your
position is moving towards the idea that everybody on Earth has some
kind of interest in how each state that they might want to visit or live in
sets its own criteria for entry.*

SF: Well, there are good arguments in favour of that kind of
position. Let's take another kind of example. Let's assume
that Britain decided to start imposing a tax on French citizens
living in France. Britain is just going to start directing these
kinds of tax laws at them, and is not going to give them any
voice in this. People would respond by saying that this isn't
legitimate. You can't just suddenly assume this kind of control
over people who are not your citizens and who don't live in
your state. And isn't that comparable in some sense to what's
going on in the immigration case? A state, like Britain, is
deciding to direct some of its laws at people who are not its
citizens, namely people who want to come and enter and
settle within its territory.

NW: *But would a democratic decision be sufficient to ground people's
settlement, morally?*

SF: It might not be sufficient, because there's still the
question of whether or not that group of people has the
relevant rights with respect to the space that we're talking
about. So let's say, for example, that we had a group of people
who decided to get together and try to exclude others from a
public park. That looks problematic because they don't have
rights over that particular place. Why should they be allowed
to exclude those people? They might be free to exclude them
from membership of their group, but may they exclude them
from entering, and indeed settling, in that particular place?

85

NW: *We've looked at the idea that there's something about the essence of states that allows them to exclude. We've looked at problems with democratic decision-making as the grounds for excluding people. Are there any other arguments that people use to defend acts of exclusion?*

SF: Yes, there are a few more. Another argument is that, just as individuals have a right to associate or not to associate with other people, so too do states. States also have a right to freedom of association, and they may choose with whom they wish or do not wish to associate.

NW: *Are you suggesting that states are a bit like people, and they can choose who they mix with?*

SF: Or a bit like voluntary associations in some respects, for instance. The Boy Scouts don't have to associate with absolutely anybody who wants to associate with them, and a golf club doesn't have to admit absolutely anyone who wants to join. Maybe we want to draw an analogy here with states. A question that we might want to ask is whether this analogy is appropriate. Now, if you get kicked out of one particular golf club, or you're not allowed to join one particular golf club, there are plenty of others that you can join. And actually, even if you weren't able to become a member of any golf club, maybe your life could still be okay. But it's not the same with states. The world is made up of states and it is far more important to be a member of one of these states. Life can be terrible if you don't have a state that claims you as its member—that is, if you're a stateless person. So the stakes are far higher. Moreover, in relation to freedom of association, it looks as though one of the reasons why we respect the rights of particular associations to decide with whom they wish to associate is because we're respecting the decisions of the members of the group to associate together in the first place. Yet, again, that's not true of states. States aren't voluntary associations. We usually don't get to choose to be members of them. Most of us are just born there, and we have to be members of a given state, and the state claims authority over us. So, we can really pick apart this analogy and ask whether or not it's a suitable one.

NW: *You mentioned that there are other justifications that people use to exclude people from the state.*

SF: Another kind of argument is that states have a right to protect the national cultures within their territories, and the right to exclude serves to protect the national cultures against the threats posed by immigration.

NW: *Well, that doesn't sound unreasonable to me, particularly if you have a small state and huge immigration, there would be a change, certainly, in national culture.*

SF: This raises questions about nationality and national identity. Some people say states have a right to protect the national culture or the national cultures within their territories. But it's quite a tricky issue. For one thing, national cultures aren't set in stone. They're constantly changing, and they have to change in order to survive over time. What is more, it's questionable how far any state has a national culture that stretches from border to border. For instance, many states are multinational states that have a number of these kinds of national cultures. Another question might be, what if the national culture includes exclusionary elements that don't represent many of the members within it? Perhaps cultural minorities, or other historically disadvantaged minorities, might feel alienated from that particular national culture. So what exactly is the particular connection between the state and national culture(s)? It's clear that a lot of people are invested in the national culture(s) of their states, that it's very important to many people to try to maintain those cultures, and that they don't wish them to change, at least not at too fast a pace. Thus they have an interest in seeing those national cultures protected in some way. But, similarly, the individuals who wish to migrate have a significant interest in being able to do so. Why assume that the interests in preserving any particular national culture (or at least protecting that national culture over time) outweigh the interests of those who wish to migrate to the society in question?

NW: *Well, I doubt that most people do a balanced calculation of costs and benefits in that respect. People are much more tribal in their reactions to threats to what they perceive as their cultural identity.*

SF: I think that's right. But we have to look at the interests in play here. So, for instance, people have various interests in maintaining the health and vibrancy of their religious communities. But do we think that gives them a right to claim that states should step in to protect those kinds of communities on their behalf, and indeed exclude people in the name of protecting those kinds of religious communities? What is it about national cultures and national communities, in particular, that supposedly supports this kind of claim? There are lots of things that people think are important. Why is this a special one? Why is this the kind of thing that seems to outweigh the interests of others in entering and settling within the state?

NW: *Those people who argue that we need to preserve our cultural identity and the only way to do that is to exclude some people who want to come into our state—are you saying that those people are misguided in assuming that cultural identity is more important than the interests of the people who want to come in?*

SF: I think you can't just assume that. You'd have to make a case for it. One kind of argument might be that national culture is very important for the kinds of things that liberal democracies do. Maybe it has instrumental value—it helps democracies to flourish, or it fosters the kind of social solidarity necessary for supporting certain programmes of social justice, for instance. But then, we might ask, which kinds of national cultures do that? Maybe some do, maybe others don't. So are we making this argument only with respect to the kinds of national cultures and groups and communities that have those beneficial effects, or are we talking about national cultures in general? Now presumably there are some national cultures which don't have those kinds of effects—perhaps they encourage rugged individualism, or perhaps they're anti-democratic in tone. In other words, we need an argument as to why we should prioritize the interests in promoting a particular kind of national culture over the interests of people who want to come in. We can't just assume that protecting national culture(s) takes priority.

NW: *So, to summarize, it seems to me that you've examined most of the plausible candidates on which people attempt to ground their arguments for excluding people from the state. All of them have got problems. Are you suggesting, then, that most people who argue in this area haven't really thought things through properly, that within liberal democracies there aren't particularly good grounds for exclusion?*

SF: There are plenty of people who have given a lot of thought to this, and who do seek to defend the idea that states have a right to exclude. But as I've tried to show, I think a number of these arguments have significant problems. In public discourse, I think there needs to be a lot more discussion of the assumption that states have a right to exclude. And I think once we subject that assumption to critical scrutiny, it's not nearly as obvious as it might seem.

Further Resources

Kimberley Brownlee and David Jenkins (2019) 'Freedom of Association', *The Stanford Encyclopedia of Philosophy*, ed. Edward N. Zalta: http://plato.stanford.edu/archives/sum2019/entries/freedom-association.

Joseph H. Carens (2013) *The Ethics of Immigration*, Oxford University Press.

Sarah Fine and Lea Ypi, eds. (2016) *Migration in Political Theory: The Ethics of Movement and Membership*, Oxford University Press.

David Miller (2016) *Strangers in Our Midst: The Political Philosophy of Immigration*, Harvard University Press.

Christopher Heath Wellman and Phillip Cole, eds. (2011) *Debating the Ethics of Immigration: Is There a Right to Exclude?*, Oxford University Press.

9

ANNE PHILLIPS
Multiculturalism and Liberalism

David Edmonds: *If one person has a perm, another a crew-cut, a third a bob, and a fourth a mullet, we don't say these people are from different cultures. Individuals may differ in many ways—including hairstyle. But only some differences are treated as cultural differences. The term 'multiculturalism' is made up of two components: 'multi', meaning many, and 'culture'. So what do we mean when we say that in a liberal society, multiple groups of different cultures should be allowed to coexist? Anne Phillips is critical of the concept of 'culture', implying, as it does, that cultures are somehow fixed, homogenous, immutable. The term 'culture', she believes, is a distraction. What's important is that in a democracy all citizens should be treated equally, and free to choose how to live their lives. Like all liberals, though, she has to confront the slippery notion of 'freedom'.*

Nigel Warburton: *Anne Phillips, we're going to talk about multiculturalism and liberalism. What's the connection between the two?*

Anne Phillips: The obvious point of connection is that liberalism, if it means anything, involves a critique of state-imposed conformity. If you're a liberal, then presumably you don't think that everyone should be dragooned into homogeneity, and that seems to imply some recognition of the claims of cultural diversity. My own sense, however, is that there's a problem when we overstress the connection between multiculturalism and liberalism, because that frames multiculturalism as a project of tolerance: as majorities tolerating the strange and potentially deviant behaviour of minorities. I find that a rather problematic understanding of what multiculturalism is.

NW: *So, liberalism, with its emphasis on freedom, wants to allow freedom for people to have their own way of living—it's a kind of 'live and let live' attitude. But at the same time, if you merely tolerate somebody, that implies a power relationship which is almost pejorative about what it is that you tolerate.*

AP: I think that's right. For myself, I would rather frame the case for multiculturalism in terms of notions of democracy and equality. Now, obviously that's compatible with liberalism, but I think it brings out the argument more clearly. If you live in societies of considerable cultural diversity, there is an obligation, deriving from democracy and equality, for the society to ensure that it is not unfairly favouring certain groups. Yet virtually all our political, legal, and social institutions make assumptions about who we are, and that leads to all kinds of bias. It very often leads to a class bias; it almost always leads to a gender bias; often a regional bias; and it would be very odd if there weren't also some cultural bias. So, to me, the basic case for multiculturalism derives from the obligation in a democracy, which supposedly presumes the equality of citizens, to address areas where existing political and legal institutions have built into them some covert advantaging of particular groups within the society.

NW: *So does that mean we should jettison the liberal defence of toleration in respect to multiculturalism? Because a lot of us are persuaded by that. It seems to be a good argument that you don't have to agree with other people, but the best way of living is to allow people to make their own mistakes, make their own choices about their own lives, and not, if at all possible, impose your own views on them from outside.*

AP: Yes. But the important thing in framing multiculturalism in terms of democracy and equality is that this helps remind us that these are things we're claiming for ourselves, as well as claiming for others. One of the biggest difficulties that arises in discourses around multiculturalism is a kind of asymmetry that gets written into them: the way in which the very notion of culture comes to be seen as linked to *minority* culture, as if we don't all have culture, as if we aren't all enormously shaped by cultural influences. We all need toleration, the right to be allowed, within certain limits, to make our own mistakes and get on with our own lives; and some of the problems in the ways in which multiculturalism gets framed is that it is represented as a toleration of the oddities of other people, *other* members of our society. Yet we're all pretty odd, right? We all have our strange practices that we engage in, and we all make terrible mistakes. What I would search for is a way of framing the arguments for, and the understanding of, multiculturalism that cuts through the asymmetry that often distorts it.

NW: *One of the issues that arises for multiculturalism is the sense that sometimes people make bad choices for themselves, and they seem to be making them freely. But if only they knew a bit more, they wouldn't be doing that. I'm thinking of cases where, for instance, somebody might willingly enter into an arranged marriage that from my perspective looks like a bad mistake. What do you think about those sorts of cases?*

AP: Well, again, I would want to stress the asymmetry between what have been falsely represented as very different majority and minority cultural experiences. There are lots of decisions we make in our lives that when you track them back don't really seem to be our decisions, in that they're made in a context in which we have a very limited sense of what the alternatives are and what the options might be. And maybe ten years on we look back and think, 'How on earth could I have willingly chosen to do that?' It was one of the experiences of the early women's movement—I remember very much having this experience myself—that we talked about the process of realizing that we were oppressed, which is quite an odd notion. You'd think that if you're oppressed, you would know you're oppressed, right? But, in fact, there is often a process of realizing that certain kinds of experience or practices that you had previously accepted as a norm were actually pretty oppressive or inegalitarian. That, to me, is something that is part of the human condition. But also something that poses a problem.

NW: *So if you recognize that somebody is making a mistake, and it's going to lead to bad consequences for them, what do you do?*

AP: OK, well, bear in mind the first point that I have stressed, which is that this is something that affects us all, so let's not make the mistake of thinking of it as something that only arises for what we describe as minority cultures. To the extent that I have an answer to the 'So what do we do?' question, I have three quite general criteria. One is that we have to be

94

particularly careful when minors are involved. So when people are underage, we have to be particularly careful about assessing in what sense something counts as their own choice. Secondly, things that cause physical or mental harm are particularly problematic. Both of these—being a minor and experiencing physical or mental harm—would be a basis on which one would want to oppose female genital cutting, for example. And thirdly, I'd want to say that where people are doing something that is premised on people not being equals in some way, there's also a problem with that. But the difficulty with that criterion (and in fact with all of them) is in spelling out what it means. So, if you take minors, at what point does somebody become of the age to take responsibility for their lives? This is something that's endlessly debated. The question of what counts as physical and mental harm is also debatable, as it's not always obvious. And equality, again, is hugely problematic. Think of the woman who chooses to devote her life to being a wife and mother, who subordinates her own wishes about which country she wants to live in to the career choices of her husband, who never puts her own wishes first—do I think that she is in an unequal relationship? Well, yes I do. But I wouldn't want to ban that particular relationship. So my equality condition begins to dissolve almost as soon as we look at particular situations.

NW: *Presumably some cultures actively advocate inequality between the sexes, so it seems to be something like cultural imperialism to insist that everybody has got to be equal since that's how we do it here.*

AP: Yes, well, at one level I'd say all cultures advocate inequality between the sexes, though a lot hangs on your point about 'actively': in some it's more active than others. In fact, the main issue is when people argue that men's and women's roles are complementary and different, and when that edges over into something that is in tension with equality. Nowadays, you don't often find people saying that women are inferior to men, but you do very often find them saying, 'well, the appropriate position for a woman is...' and then it turns out to be somewhere that looks pretty inferior or subordinate. So that's your question—how much power does my equality provision carry in those kinds of contexts? Clearly anything put into law that gives men and women unequal rights and authority is problematic. If we need the witness of three women to add up to the strength of one man, and that is enshrined in law, then that's unacceptable, right? But when we have something more like the kind of inequality that might exist in a relationship between one partner who goes out into the world and earns money, and another who stays at home and is responsible for caring for the children, well, we can describe that as unequal, but it's more problematic to know how to operate in that case.

NW: *So are you're saying that the consequence of this is that if somebody says that that's what they freely have chosen, we just have to take it at face value that it was their genuine choice?*

AP: No, that's not my position at all. If you took that position, you'd end up saying 'so long as people remain in their current situation, that's proof that there's no problem'. That would be completely unacceptable. It would be like saying the woman who stays with an abusive husband isn't being abused. So it's not at all that there's no problem so long as people say they're happy with what they currently do, even when they are living in conditions that I might consider abusive or oppressive. There is a big responsibility on governments to provide options and alternatives and protections and securities. So if we go back to the example you introduced about arranged marriage, I think there's an obligation on societies to ensure that there is a support system in place for young people who are being pressured into unwanted marriages, that they're aware of this, and of people they can turn to; and in the worst possible cases, that they have access to refuges where they can comfortably live to escape from family pressure. All of these things are, I think, obligations. And they make possibilities available to people. So this is an important difference. If, after having had these opportunities or alternatives made available to them, people nonetheless say, 'this is what I've chosen' (meaning they have chosen the marriage being pressed on them by their parents), then at that point you have to say, 'Okay, I hear what you're saying. It's not the choice I would have made, but it's the choice you've made.'

NW: *One alternative to a multicultural society is to enforce some kind of assimilation that gets around all these points of conflict that we get, for instance, with Sikhs who both want to wear turbans and need to obey the law with motorcycle helmets. These sorts of issues can easily be got around by simply imposing a policy of assimilation. If you don't go down that route, how do you resolve those difficult cases?*

AP: We need a contextual answer to that. In your example about Sikhs and crash helmets, there was some discussion about whether the Sikh turban provides physical protection against injury when falling off a motorbike. What I've noticed is that very few Sikhs drive around on motorcycles without helmets. So it seems to me that most Sikhs have made the judgement that it's not safe. In that particular case, there was a political judgement that it was better to make a concession in order to recognize the importance of the Sikh turban, but the expectation was that individuals would make sensible judgements about the safety of their transport.

NW: *Well, that has resolved the motorcycle helmet issue, but I understand that Sikhs are, by their religion, obliged to carry a kirpan— male Sikhs anyway—a little knife everywhere that they go. That creates huge problems in terms of airline security and so on.*

AP: That's a much more difficult one. It's also relevant for schools: it's a huge issue for schools to ensure that children are not carrying knives in school. The example throws up the judgements that have to be made when weighing up the significance of something like a kirpan to people's sense of identity, and the disadvantages they are put to when required to choose between, say, airline travel and their sense of religious identity. That's a huge choice, but maybe the choice that people have to accept. The point about addressing the inequalities and disadvantages that arise out of cultural bias is not that anything then goes. Multiculturalism doesn't mean that whenever anyone makes a cultural claim, we then accept it. But it has to mean that we start a process of assessment. How that assessment works out is going to be very contextual—I don't have an algorithm to resolve that one. What's important is the recognition, on the one side, that political, legal, and social institutions almost always contain some kind of bias, hence the obligation, in terms of democracy and equality, to try and address that; but the recognition, on the other side, that there might be compelling reasons why a particular cultural claim can't be met.

NW: *What do you think about education in this respect? I can see arguments both for and against having schools where people from different groups can educate their children in the way that they wish to. You might say that's a right—a basic human right. But at the same time, if you want a flourishing multicultural society, it seems to me that segregation isn't the way to achieve it.*

AP: One thing that liberalism always stresses is individual rights. And one of the tensions in the liberalism and multiculturalism debate is that multiculturalism comes up with what look like liberal arguments, based on either equality or toleration, for group rights or cultural rights. I think that is part of what is coming out in your example of education. The group says that, as a group, they are entitled to ensure that their children are brought up in particular precepts and ways of understanding the world, maybe even entitled to ensure that their children are protected from contamination by other ways of thinking about the world, and the group claims this as their right as a culture. There's a tension between that claim and the rights of the individual children involved, who might also be said to have rights to engage with, enter into dialogue with, and be exposed to a whole range of other ways of being in their society. I would like a multiculturalism that is more on the side of individual rights than the side of cultural group rights, and I think this is part of what is currently played out in relation to education. The good thing that has happened in the debates around multiculturalism is the modification and development of a classic liberalism that talked only of individual rights, because a lot of what matters to individuals are their group identities, and this is something that needs to be thought about when we're thinking about the rights of the individual. That development rightly expanded our understanding of rights. But I think we need to stop short of the move into then claiming a group right—a right for a group or a cultural group. My view is that, in an important sense, there are no such things as cultures. All the things that we describe as cultures are enormously variegated, contain a huge diversity of voices, and interchange in all kinds of ways with supposedly separate cultures. So attaching rights to entities called 'cultures' seems to me problematic. But that first move, from the classic liberal focus on individual rights to some recognition of the ways in which the group matters for individuals, is an important move.

NW: *Are you saying that our identities are more complex than simply membership of a particular culture? Lots of things that make us what we are are attachments to groups which have nothing to do specifically with culture, for example our gender or sex, or whether we're left-handed or not. As such, it's slightly arbitrary to narrow down one group type, namely the culture.*

AP: I very much agree with that. In a way, I'd like to move away from the talk of culture and back to the notion of the social. All of us are very much shaped by a whole range of social influences; you've mentioned gender, we can add in class, ethnicity, religion, region, country, all sorts of influences that enter into our identity and can be enormously important to the ways in which we see ourselves and the kinds of lives we choose to live. Recognizing the significance of these social influences and social identities is very important, but I don't think it helps to identify some of them as the cultural ones, which then get some special status. What people call culture is actually social. We are back to the point about needing to challenge the asymmetry between the ways in which majorities and minorities are treated. We need to get out of this box of thinking that there are certain people who have a 'cultural' identity—and then the rest of us just have gender identities, or class identities, or any number of other kinds of identity. We all have social influences working on us, and the question in liberal democratic or egalitarian societies is what policies and institutions we need to develop that can recognize this complexity, and make sure that none of us is put at a disadvantage by them in relation to other members of the society.

Further Resources

Tariq Modood (2007) *Multiculturalism*, Polity Press.

David Owen and Anthony Simon Laden, eds. (2007) *Multiculturalism and Political Theory*, Cambridge University Press.

Anne Phillips (2007) *Multiculturalism without Culture*, Princeton University Press.

Anne Phillips (2010) *Gender and Culture*, Polity Press.

Sarah Song (2017) 'Multiculturalism', *The Stanford Encyclopedia of Philosophy*, ed. Edward N. Zalta: http://plato.stanford.edu/archives/spr2017/entries/multiculturalism.

10

JENNIFER SAUL
Implicit Bias

David Edmonds: *Will your judgement about the quality of the interview that follows be shaped by the fact that the interviewee is female? Sadly, even if you think of yourself as a feminist, the evidence is that it might well prejudice you at an unconscious level. Such are the philosophical implications of what's called 'implicit bias'. Is it one explanation for why there were so few women in philosophy? Here's Jennifer Saul.*

Nigel Warburton: *The topic we're going to focus on is implicit bias. What is that?*

Jennifer Saul: That's a difficult question. The way I'm going to be using the term is to refer to a collection of largely unconscious associations that psychologists have shown over the last few decades that pretty much all humans are prone to. These largely unconscious associations affect how we perceive, interact with, and evaluate members of social groups in our societies. I'm especially interested in the ways that they affect our interactions with members of groups that are stigmatized in our societies. Which groups these are will vary from society to society. Exactly what the associations are will vary from society to society. But it seems that all human beings are prone to

102

these (largely) unconscious associations, which are really quite disturbing, and which we *may* be totally unaware of.

NW: *Are you saying that I've got negative feelings, or negative beliefs, about particular groups of people?*

JS: Implicit biases are probably not beliefs. It's a very tricky issue exactly how to characterize them. But, for example, it's been shown that most people living in a society like ours, which is racist in the way that it's structured, will have implicit associations about, say, black people, which are very negative. And this is true even of members of the stigmatized groups; even of people who devote their lives to fighting against these biases. So, one example that's frequently discussed is that of Jesse Jackson, who is a very well-known American civil rights campaigner, who is also African-American. And he tells the story of walking down the street late at night in an unfamiliar city, and realizing that he feels relieved when he hears footsteps behind him and discovers that the person behind him is a white man. And that moment of realization and horror that he has this belief is a moment that he realized he had these implicit biases—the association that was present in him that black people are dangerous, or black men are dangerous, even though he's devoted his whole life to fighting against these associations. So, these biases are something that we can be prone to even if we're members of the groups the biases are against; even if we genuinely deeply reject these biases in a conscious way; even if we devote our lives to fighting them.

NW: *What sort of scientific evidence is there to back this up?*

JS: Over the last several decades there have been hundreds of psychological studies showing these biases exist in various ways, using lots of different methods. The best-known method is the 'implicit association test', and this is best known because anyone can do it online right now. I want to emphasize that it's not the only way that this has been shown, but it is the one that you can try out for yourself. So what the implicit association test asks you to do is to very quickly pair, say, black faces and white faces with good and bad adjectives, or women and men with arts and humanities versus sciences, and what the tests find is that the overwhelming majority of people will have great difficulty, say, pairing black faces with good adjectives, or they are much slower at that and more prone to error than they are at pairing black faces with bad adjectives.

NW: *And how did you get interested in this? It is quite a specialized subject.*

JS: I got interested in this because I was interested in understanding, and doing something about, the very low numbers of women in philosophy. So, in the United States, women in professional philosophy are at only about 17 per cent in comparison to men. The UK is much better in that women are at about 24 per cent—but still this is really quite surprising because most arts and humanities subjects are fairly close to 50 per cent, and so philosophy looks a great deal more like the sciences. In fact, there are some studies showing that philosophy is more overwhelmingly male than even maths.

NW: *And so the suggestion is, then, that there's some kind of implicit bias in the hirers, who are not seeing the virtues of potential women philosophers?*

JS: No, the suggestion is a lot more complex than that, because implicit bias can come into many different sorts of behaviour—either large behaviours or small behaviours. So, yes, one thing is that implicit bias has been shown to have a significant effect on hiring decisions. So if you present exactly the same CV with a female name versus a male name at the top of it, it will be rated as a better CV—more likely to be invited for interview; offered a higher rank; offered a higher salary—if it's a male name rather than a female name. It definitely does come into decisions at that level and those are some very nice, clear, well-confirmed studies. The effect is shown equally strongly for all age groups, so it's not dying out. This bias is widespread, and men and women are both likely to show it. However, that's not the only place where it comes in. It affects the way that we interact with people, as I said. So, both men and women will be more likely to call on men than women in class; more likely to charitably interpret some inchoate comment from a student if it's from a man rather than a woman; they write better letters of reference for men than women; they're more likely to encourage men to continue in a subject than women...So it can come in at all of these different points which cumulatively can have a very large effect.

NW: *This is really bizarre. You're suggesting that philosophy is the worst, or one of the worst, subjects in this respect. But you would think that for philosophers—in terms of reflecting on the nature of belief, and worrying about fairness and justice—that these kinds of prejudice would have come to light, and that we wouldn't be wandering around with such dangerous biases that we're scarcely even aware of.*

JS: Yeah, it's an interesting thing. Philosophers have, at least until recently, been very hostile to the thought that these biases might be creeping in. Part of this is our self-image as the most objective people around. It turns out that even being primed with objectivity makes you more prone to biases, and certainly also reflecting positively on your own objectivity makes you even more prone to biases. But fascinatingly, each professional group has a reason that it wouldn't be prone to biases. So the physicists will say that they're smarter than everybody else. The psychologists will say that they don't need anonymous review because they understand how all of this works. But the philosophers say we're more objective. Everybody's got some reason that implicit bias can't be true of them.

NW: *Now, what is the philosophical interest in this? It's clearly of psychological and sociological interest, but are there philosophical questions that are brought up by recognizing the existence of quite widespread implicit bias?*

JS: There are a lot of philosophical questions raised by this. Some of them are about the nature of these biases—whether they're beliefs, whether they're associations, whether they are some kind of quasi belief. There are also lots of really interesting questions about culpability for biases that are strongly affecting our behaviour in ways that we find abhorrent, where we're not aware of such biases and don't quite know what to do about them. Most recently I have been focusing on some implications for epistemology, because I think it gives rise to something that's akin to a kind of scepticism.

NW: *It's not obvious how you get from implicit bias to scepticism. Could you just take us through that?*

JS: Yeah. I think people have tended to focus much more on the ethical and political consequences of implicit biases and trying to understand them in terms of psychology. But I think there are really important epistemic issues raised by them as well. One thing we know from implicit bias is that we're very likely to be making certain sorts of errors a lot of the time. For example, when we judge the CV with the male name to be the better one, we're making an error because it's the same as the CV with the female name, right? But one of the nicest studies of implicit bias that I find most disturbing is not about gender or race, but about prestige. The psychologists took a group of papers that had been published by top psychology journals and resubmitted them to top psychology journals with fictitious names and fictitious, very unprestigious, university affiliations. Ninety per cent of them were rejected by the journals. Now, they weren't rejected because 'we've published this before', or 'that's plagiarism'—which would've been extremely good reasons to reject the papers—instead they were rejected for 'serious methodological errors'. So, we have psychologists who are experts assessing something that they're experts on—the methodology of their own field—and going badly wrong, either in the first instance when the paper was assessed as publishable or in the second instance when it was assessed as having serious methodological errors. One of those has to be a mistake. This should be tremendously disturbing to us. We know humans make mistakes. That's not a shock. We know we make mistakes if we're trying to do something that we're not very good at, or if we're really drunk. There are lots of circumstances where we expect to make mistakes. But this is making mistakes under what seemed to be pretty ideal conditions. These are experts assessing a subject matter in which they're experts. Presumably not many of them were drunk. They're probably in a good state of mind for being able to assess these things well, and yet, they're still making these errors. Now, let's compare this scepticism about bias to a more traditional 'dreaming scepticism'. The way those traditional sceptical scenarios work is that a possibility is raised (such as the possibility that you are actually dreaming right now as opposed to being awake engaged in whatever activity you think you are doing) which is meant to show us that we might be making errors of a certain sort. So, I might be mistaking a dream for reality, but I'm not actually given a good reason to believe that I am mistaking a dream for reality—all that has happened is that the possibility of the mistake is raised, and without proof against that mistake we may be left in a state of scepticism. And then, taking it to the extreme, that doubt about whether we are actually awake or dreaming is supposed to make me doubt whether I know that there is an external world out there at all. In the case of implicit biases, what we have is very good evidence that we are extremely likely to be making mistakes all the time, as we assess the evidence that's presented to us or the argument presented to us or the person we're interacting with. Because usually when we're getting evidence or an argument presented, it's being presented by a person, and usually we can identify that person's social group—we may be wrong about it but we'll have some belief about what their social group is, and will be affected by that. This shows not just that there's a possibility that we're going wrong, but that we're extremely likely to be going wrong, and we don't know when we're going wrong. So, although this can't lead us to doubt whether there's an external world out there—as it's not that general—what it can lead us to do is not know exactly when these errors might have arisen. And it's stronger than the traditional scepticism in that we've got very good reason to believe we're making these errors.

NW: *How widespread is implicit bias? How widespread are our errors as a result of bias, and how widespread are the biases themselves?*

JS: Well, none of us can really know which of our beliefs may have been affected by implicit bias, because most of our beliefs have been formed on the basis of things that people have said to us. Now sometimes it's because we are accepting their testimony; sometimes it's because we think they've given us a good argument; or they've handed us some solid evidence for a claim. It's not just our beliefs about who to hire; it can be our beliefs about whether climate change is real. It can affect who we decide to believe on the street when we ask for directions.

NW: *But some of these biases are actually rules of thumb, as it were, which could be useful. There might be implicit generalizations which may on occasion be shown to be false but in general will hold.*

JS: The general capacity to make fast associations and act on those is a useful one and we couldn't get by without it. But I don't think the tendency to think that a CV with a male name at the top of it is better than a CV with a female name at the top of it—I don't think that is useful in any way.

NW: *But that's different from looking at a paper that's come from the Harvard faculty, where you know the people who are writing the paper have been through a certain kind of process to get there which is highly competitive, as compared with a minor college, where you can't know for sure whether the people there are at the same academic level.*

JS: Yeah, and if you weren't an expert in the field, that would be all you had to rely on and that would be what you should rely on. But if you're an expert in the field, you shouldn't need that—you should be able to look at the methodology and make a judgement of that methodology.

NW: *So how do we get around this? Do we just end up as the kind of sceptic who says, 'well, I can't take anything on trust'?*

JS: Well, another way that implicit bias scepticism differs from traditional scepticism is that it makes us feel a real demand for action. It's hard not to think 'how do we get around this', or 'how do I get past this'. You don't really feel that way about the dreaming scepticism. You don't really care that much. And the good thing is that there actually are things that you can do about implicit bias scepticism, unlike other kinds of scepticism. If you want to know that you're making judgements on the quality of the work you're presented with, you make sure it's presented to you in an anonymized form so that you're not being affected by the social group. And that's why one wonderful thing about the United Kingdom that I was absolutely shocked by when I came here is the widespread anonymous marking which is totally unheard of in North America. Anonymous marking has been shown to result in higher marks for women. So this is a case where implicit bias has been successfully corrected for. Now, it can be much more difficult to introduce this for other things—you can't totally anonymize the process of hiring a lecturer if you want to know what they're like as a lecturer, as you can't make their voices distort and talk behind a screen! But you can anonymize parts of the process: you can do long listing anonymously, where all you're basing it on is the publications; you can circulate anonymized writing samples as a part of the hiring process and get people's feedback on those samples without them knowing who the samples are from. So there are ways that you can improve your processes by anonymizing them further. But that's not going to affect everything. We need to improve our tendencies because not everything can be anonymized. Now there are ways to improve that, but that's a little trickier. So one of the best things you can do is change the regularities in the world that give rise to this. If you want to stop assuming that women are less good philosophers, then the thing you should do is have more women philosophers around. Counter-stereotypical exemplars who are members of the stereotyped group but who don't fit the stereotypes of the group are tremendously effective in combating implicit bias. Feminist philosophers have sometimes talked about scepticism being a very individualistic philosophical problem that is limited in its capacity to engage with non-individualistic philosophy. But this kind of scepticism seems to require a non-individualistic solution. You have to change the society in order to change these regularities; that's the only way to ensure that we're not affected by these biases. You need to change the processes, but you also need to change who is in which position in society.

NW: *I've always thought of philosophy as a strange combination of arrogance and humility—the arrogance of Socrates to go and question people about their fundamental beliefs, and argue that they're wrong about most of them, or can't consistently defend them, but also the humility to recognize that you don't know all that much and you could be wrong about the things you think you know about.*

JS: Yeah, I think philosophers have both of those tendencies, and I think a bit more humility would be good for the profession.

Further Resources

Michael Brownstein and Jennifer Saul (2016) 'Implicit Bias in the Age of Trump', OUP blog: https://blog.oup.com/2016/04/implicit-bias-racism-trump/.

Michael Brownstein (2019) 'Implicit Bias', *The Stanford Encyclopedia of Philosophy*, ed. Edward N. Zalta: http://plato.stanford.edu/archives/fall2019/entries/implicit-bias.

Jules Holroyd and Jennifer Saul (2019) 'Reform Efforts in Philosophy and Critiques of Implicit Bias Research', *Philosophical Topics*, special issue ed. K. Manne and B. Takaoka.

11

MARTHA C. NUSSBAUM
Disgust

The ideas in this interview are based on Martha C. Nussbaum (2004) *Hiding from Humanity: Disgust, Shame, and the Law*, Princeton University Press. Her ideas on disgust have since developed (references to which are listed under 'Further Resources' at the end of this chapter and 'About the Interviewees' at the end of the book). She is internationally renowned for her work in Ancient Greek and Roman philosophy, feminist philosophy, political philosophy, and philosophy and the arts, and would have been happy to be interviewed on any of these topics for the purposes of this book.

David Edmonds: *Chances are, you find the idea of cannibalism disgusting. Likewise, eating slugs. The concept of disgust may not at first seem to have anything to do with multiculturalism. But often members of one culture feel disgust at the values or practices of members of another. This could be as basic as repugnance of another culture's food: its diet, cooking, or method of animal slaughter. Some people feel a sense of disgust when they see women from a different culture covering their face with a veil. Those from a more conservative culture might, on the contrary, be disgusted by the sight of women exposing their legs, or by homosexuality. Parents might fear that their offspring will be somehow* 'contaminated' by the values and practices of a culture of which they disapprove. How seriously should we take this sense of disgust? Should we rely on it as a foundation for law? Martha C. Nussbaum is an internationally acclaimed philosopher, who's based at the University of Chicago.

Nigel Warburton: *We're going to talk about disgust. That's not obviously a political topic or a philosophical topic. Could you say a little bit about what you mean by disgust and what part it could possibly play in politics?*

Martha C. Nussbaum: Sure. I think we usually think that disgust is a completely visceral reaction where we just want to throw up. But actually, there's some wonderful new psychological research on disgust that shows that it really does have a cognitive content: that what people think they're smelling, tasting, or touching, makes a big difference as to whether they're disgusted or not. People are given the very same smell, in one case they're told it's cheese, in the other case they're told it's human faeces. And of course, in the first case they're not likely to experience disgust, and in the second case they do. So, it's connected with our ideas. The general conclusion of this line of research is that disgust is a reaction to the prospect of contamination by something that's connected with our anxiety about our animality—our bodily, decaying nature. The primary objects of disgust are human waste products, and then, of course, the corpse. That's bad enough because a lot of irrationality can go into that—things that are not really dangerous are found disgusting, and things that are dangerous are often not found so disgusting. But, it doesn't do a lot of social harm.

NW: *You've written that disgust is a dangerous social sentiment, what did you mean by that?*

MCN: The harm comes when—and this happens in every single society—people project that disgust reaction on to some group of people. It seems to be a way that people have of cordoning themselves off yet further from the base parts of their own animality, to create a subgroup to whom they impute these properties: sliminess, ooziness, bad smell... And then they treat those people as people with whom we really can't have contact with. The idea of untouchability in the Indian caste system is a very obvious instance of that: there were the people who dealt with waste products and corpses, and were thus thought to be contaminated. So, you can't eat food served by such a person, nor can you have bodily contact with such a person. I'm afraid that this is very widespread. American racism in the south was propelled by very similar views: people thought that they could not eat at the same lunch counter with an African-American, as they found that prospect disgusting; they could not swim in the same swimming pool; they would not drink from the same drinking fountain... My father who was a very educated lawyer (a partner in a Philadelphia law firm) came from the deep south and he actually believed that if an African-American person had a drink of water from a particular drinking glass, you could not use that same glass afterwards: it was contaminated. This kind of magical thinking is characteristic of what I call 'projective disgust'.

NW: *It sounds like projective disgust may have its origins in quite sound evolutionary development, in that there are things which we need*

to avoid as animals, and we have these instinctive reactions to some of
those. But the problem is that this has been generalized to things which
it's completely irrational to feel that way towards.

MCN: Yes, that seems to be what happens. Now even with
the evolutionary kind of disgust, the problem is that it doesn't
really track the sense of danger. There are lots of dangerous
things, let's say poisonous mushrooms, that we don't find
disgusting, and that's why so many people die from eating
them. On the other hand, there are things that we do find
disgusting that are not at all dangerous. For example, there are
experiments in which a cockroach is sterilized and then people
are asked to eat it. Of course the people know that they'll
come to no harm, and yet no one eats it. In fact, even when
the cockroach is sealed in an indigestible plastic capsule, they
still wouldn't eat it. That's not very harmful, but somehow
people extend the disgust to danger and attach it to a group. A
lot of discrimination against women over many societies has
been fuelled by this idea that women's bodies are disgusting
because they have all these fluids coming out of them that are
connected with birth. In many parts of the world, men often
feel that women, even though desirable, are also at the same
time disgusting. Jews in medieval Europe and some parts of
modern Europe were found to be disgusting, and in Nazi
books for children they were represented as slugs, beetles, and
other disgusting animals. So it's a very ubiquitous part of
social life. And I think in modern America today, the main
group that's found disgusting are gays and lesbians—I would
say particularly gay men. The propaganda that's spread
against them by right-wing groups always involves the idea
that they're really all about faeces and blood. They try to scare

people and to animate this kind of disgust reaction by the way they portray the sex lives of gay men.

NW: *That's really interesting because it portrays both a very heightened imagination (because they haven't witnessed these events) but also a warped sense of what homosexuals might do in private.*

MCN: Yes, that's very well put. There's prurience about it, an obsession with imagining it, but then a complete refusal to imagine these people as human beings pursuing human purposes. They're treated as monsters that are utterly different. And this is all the more remarkable because a lot of the former sodomy laws in the US were actually neutral about the sex of the partners—they ruled out certain acts, not the sex of those engaged in the act. In one of the most famous law cases in modern times, *Bowers v. Hardwick*, the plaintiffs actually introduced a heterosexual couple who said that the law also inhibits their practices because they can't have oral and anal sex under this law. But interestingly the Attorney General's Office in Georgia held that they had to be thrown out of the suit because they didn't have standing to challenge the law, and they were not at risk of being arrested. So it was understood that even though the law was worded neutrally, it was targeted at the practices of gays and lesbians.

NW: *It's interesting as well because the disgust is aimed at something which isn't present, and that's quite different from the disgust that you might have in the presence of putrid food, for example.*

MCN: Yes, that's a very important distinction. John Stuart Mill called it a purely constructive reaction. I think that it's fine to have laws that regulate the unwilling exposure that people have to genuinely disgusting smells and substances. For example, if your neighbour decides to run an open sewer on his property and the smell comes over to your property, you have a cause of action under nuisance law. But that's because it's an actual physical substance and it's hitting you unwillingly. Now in the case of sex between two people in private, there's nothing about their physical act that impinges on your physical reality: it's only your imagination that's involved. They're doing a consensual act in private, and they're not trying to subject you to it.

NW: *Though would this extend to, say, a really powerful cooking smell? If somebody is cooking a strong curry, do you think you should have a right to complain about the smell coming from people of a different culture cooking next door to you?*

MCN: Well this is a very interesting question because it's often bound up, as you suggested, with cultural prejudice. And indeed, I myself, as a defender of animal rights, do experience some degree of disgust at meat smells. But until our society reaches a point where the pain inflicted upon animals is illegal under law, only then could we start to deal with this. I suppose that I think I don't have a right to impose my views on other people by bringing them to court for their cooking meat next door. Now in the cases you describe, which I think are very common in India for example, people will often try to zone out Muslims by saying, 'the smell of beef offends me'. One group is probably really disgusted by the practices of another. But it's through an imaginary transfer where the beef becomes disgusting because of a kind of generalized disgust towards Muslims, and then you just transfer it onto that smell. In reality, the smell of beef and the smell of lamb are not very different. So why is it that they can't stand to smell beef? It's really because of what they think—they think these are Muslims engaging in godless practices. So I don't think that at the end of the day we should allow legal action in those cases, although they move closer to something we might at least consider.

NW: *Does that mean that you want to rule out disgust as relevant to our moral and legal decision-making?*

MCN: Well, there are of course some people in the history of the law (Lord Devlin was the most famous such person, but actually my own University of Chicago colleague Leon Kass, who was head of the President's Commission on Bioethics, also had a similar view) who think that the disgust of an average member of society is all by itself sufficient reason to make a harmless practice illegal. *That's* the position I'm opposed to. I don't think, though, that that means disgust has absolutely no role in law-making, because I do think disgust at primary objects (for example, sewage, human excrement, corpses, and so on) can legitimately be a source of regulation and of nuisance law. But we better make sure that it really is a nuisance of the kind that I'm talking about. That is, sometimes people close down sex clubs saying that they're a health nuisance—well, actually, they're not a nuisance in the sense that I'm talking about because there's nothing more likely to spread HIV than ignorance, and in the sex club they're less ignorant than the average member of society. And furthermore, those clubs usually have signs advertising condom use and so on. So what is it that people think when they think that it's a health nuisance? I think they're disgusted when they think of the sex acts that are committed, even though, of course, it doesn't impinge on their senses in any direct way. So it is another case of purely constructive disgust.

NW: *You mentioned that disgust towards women and women's bodies is very prevalent in the history of the world. One area in terms of dress that some people find disgusting is when women expose their legs, say, in miniskirts—some cultures find that absolutely beyond the pale. Does that mean that we should just ignore those feelings—that sense that somehow there's a religious affront, or that women are immoral because they're sexually provocative and showing parts of their body that should not be displayed?*

MCN: The most difficult area of this subject is what I call 'direct offence'. That is where somebody is in your face inflicting something on you, but it's not a primary object of disgust: it's not a loathsome smell, or some dangerous germs or something, it's just something that you deeply dislike. Now in general, I think we shouldn't allow the law to be dragooned into the service of people's prejudices. But what should the limits be? What about public nudity? I think it's hard to defend laws that ban public nudity. Certainly if the nudity is in a club where you have to consent to the nudity to enter the club, then I think the law has no business interfering at all. But what about nudity on a public beach or a public bus? Well, it's not a very sound argument to say that it should be banned just because so many people find it offensive. But so long as opportunities for nude bathing would be provided somewhere in that society, it's not a particularly harmful thing to regulate. Public masturbation similarly. Now I can't say that I think it's a very good idea. I don't want people to be subjected to that. One could say that children shouldn't be subjected to that, and that's the way we justify laws against it. But I think even if children weren't involved, it's still probably okay to make it illegal. But once again, we should try to think about the people: if it's a homeless person who has no private dwelling place, then the law should not be harsh with that person. So we shouldn't stigmatize persons because they engage in certain behaviours when they may actually have no other choice.

Further Resources

Zoya Hasan, Aziz Huq, Martha C. Nussbaum, and Vidhu Verma, eds. (2018) *The Empire of Disgust: Prejudice, Discrimination, and Policy in India and the U.S.*, Oxford University Press.

Martha C. Nussbaum (2010) *From Disgust to Humanity: Sexual Orientation and Constitutional Law*, Oxford University Press.

Martha C. Nussbaum (2018) *The Monarchy of Fear*, Simon and Schuster.

Martha C. Nussbaum and Saul Levmore (2017) *Aging Thoughtfully*, Oxford University Press.

12

ELISABETH SCHELLEKENS
Disagreement about Taste

David Edmonds: *I think Mozart is a better composer than Beethoven. You disagree. I think Dickens is a better writer than Trollope. You disagree. I think Van Gogh is a better artist than Monet. You disagree. Is one of us right and one of us wrong? Here is Elisabeth Schellekens.*

Nigel Warburton: *The topic we're going to focus on is disagreement about taste. I wonder if you could begin by giving an example of people disagreeing about taste.*

Elisabeth Schellekens: Well, one of the most discussed examples about disagreement in taste is one that Hume outlines in his essay from 1757. In this example, taken from *Don Quixote*, two of Sancho Panza's kinsmen are asked to taste a wine. Both agree the wine would be good were it not compromised, according to the one, by a taste of iron and, according to the other, by a taste of leather. The men are ridiculed by their audience, who think the disagreement merely shows the so-called experts have no idea what they are talking about and that, so to speak, there is no fact of the matter when it comes to such value judgements. But when the end of the barrel is reached, they discover that an iron key with a leather fob has been lying there all along. So both men were right after all. What Hume uses this example to show is that, first of all, there is an analogy between what he calls 'mental taste' and 'bodily taste'. Here we have an example of bodily taste: the kind of objective features that we can detect in our experience, that can explain, and perhaps even justify, our judgements of tastes, and of gustatory taste in the keg case. Now, in the aesthetic case, where we disagree over who is a better composer/writer/artist, Hume says it works in a similar way. There are features that we think, or that seem to us, to be objective features of the object of our appreciation, that we can point to when we try to support our aesthetic judgements.

NW: *So could you give an example of the kind of feature of, say, a painting that might give rise to this bodily sense or bodily taste?*

ES: Well, when we experience artworks, for example, aesthetically we have a sensory impression, we have a perceptual response, and we might want to justify or explain or support our aesthetic judgements. And we do that, as do art critics, of course, by appealing to all sorts of qualities and features in the object that we are experiencing. So some of those features will be fairly uncontroversial, like colour, or shape, or size, or just the way in which certain parts of a painting, for example, relate to one another. And other features will be what we call 'aesthetic qualities' or 'aesthetic features', and they might have to do with the *harmony* of the colours, the *balance* in certain aspects of the composition, and so on.

NW: *So if I'm looking at a Rembrandt self-portrait, I can talk about the brownish colours in the background, let's say. And we all agree which colours are used on that painting, and we can agree about the size of the painting. But when I say that there is exquisite brushwork—where the notion of it being exquisite is an aesthetic judgement—then we disagree, and I don't understand how we can ever get over that disagreement.*

ES: Well, when we come across a case like that, it is worth asking what we really mean by disagreement. Is it really a disagreement in the sense that we actively disagree? For example, 'I think this artwork has this aesthetic value, or this aesthetic quality, and you think it doesn't'. Do we have contradictory opinions here? You think it has something, and I think it doesn't have it. Another question we should ask is how deeply this disagreement runs. Could it be that we're just engaged in a terminological disagreement, that we perhaps mean slightly different things by the words that we use, and perhaps we can reach an agreement once we've clarified those issues? Another thing is, what kind of disagreement is it that we're really having? Is it purely aesthetic disagreement in terms of aesthetic value? Because we have many different kinds of aesthetic judgements—some of which are comparisons. We also have what we call aesthetic *verdicts*, which are more final or general judgements about something's overall aesthetic value. And we have judgements that just ascribe a particular property to an artwork. So we have plenty of different kinds of aesthetic judgements, and we need to get more into the detail of what kind of disagreement we actually have and what's at stake.

NW: *Okay, so I say a certain Rembrandt is a great painting, and you say it's a terrible painting. That's a disagreement at a very general level. How do we resolve that, or how does Hume think we can resolve it, at least?*

ES: Well, I think Hume would say that he would need some kind of assurance that we are really exercising our faculty of taste, as he would call it, so that we're not just engaged in personal preferences, or idiosyncratic inclinations. Hume would want to ensure that this is not a case of 'I tend to prefer this kind of artist or this kind of artwork, and you tend to prefer something else'. He would want to ensure that we're operating this faculty, which he calls 'the faculty of taste', and that we are in the overall position that he wants us to be when we exercise that taste, so that we're free of prejudice, we have training in these matters, we can compare adequately, we have good sense in some other features that he outlines. And after all that, if we are still disagreeing, then we come to what critics do every day, which is to start supporting our judgements by pointing to the features of the artwork. Now, those features can be, as I said, features that are uncontroversially in the object in some sense, or aesthetic qualities of the artwork, but they can also bring in various features about historical context and contexts in general. So then it becomes a kind of 'may the best person win the aesthetic argument' by appealing to features that are, at least in principle, available to all.

NW: *So if I like a particular Rembrandt self-portrait because it reminds me of my grandfather—that's a kind of irrelevant idiosyncrasy about me. If I'm highly prejudiced because I'm Dutch and I love Dutch art, and I think Rembrandt's the greatest because he's Dutch—that's another irrelevancy in this case. If I haven't had much experience in looking at paintings, I've only seen a few Rembrandts but never looked at any other artist's work—again you might question my judgement. Those are the sorts of things which get in the way of making a good aesthetic judgement. Is that right?*

ES: I'd say that for Hume your first example is definitely not a judgement of aesthetic taste. It is, as you said, just a kind of personal preference. The second case is a bit more complicated, because you might not be aware of your own prejudice: you might think that you're in an excellent position to take on this aesthetic perspective that Hume wants us to take, but you are simply unable to, because, for example, your attachment to Holland is too great. So that could be a case of a personal preference, but it could also be a case of a less appropriate, or perhaps even incorrect, judgement of aesthetic taste.

NW: *So what about the third—the fact that I've only looked at paintings by Rembrandt, I've never looked at any other artist's work?*

ES: That raises an interesting question. Hume was very clear, and he outlines these five criteria: the first is good sense; the second is a delicacy of sentiment—a certain kind of refinement in that way; the third is practice in exercising that refinement; the fourth is having no prejudice whatsoever in your aesthetic experience; and the fifth is being able to compare with other artworks, or having that ability of comparison. There are some examples where our aesthetic impression is strengthened, or in some sense, at least, more valuable, if we come to it without this baggage of knowledge or understanding, and are struck by its aesthetic value without any cognitive associations strengthening that experience. So I think that final example you gave is a difficult case for Hume.

NW: *So is Hume saying that what we should do if we're not ideal critics, if we don't have all those qualities, is 'listen to the critics and let them make the judgements'? Or is he saying something else? Is he saying that we should train ourselves to be those kinds of critics if we want to engage with art?*

ES: The idea is that we should aspire to be ideal critics. But Hume is not so exercised about our aesthetic well-being, as it were. Rather, he is concerned about the philosophical problem of trying to reconcile two seemingly opposing or different assumptions that we have about our aesthetic experiences. On the one hand, we seem to disagree about taste all the time and that's just an observable fact. And on the other hand, there seem to be some aesthetic judgements that are just better or more spot on than others.

NW: *So if somebody says to me, look, Sid Vicious is a greater composer than Schubert, they're just wrong?*

ES: Well, I can't speak for what Hume would say about Sid Vicious! But it would be more fair to anyone, who (like Hume) tries to take this problem as a philosophical problem and take it very seriously, to compare two composers that are roughly in the same ballpark, say Beethoven and Hummel. Is the oeuvre of one of those composers better than the other? For Hume, most probably yes.

NW: *Does that mean there's an objective answer? You play a piano concerto by Hummel and you play one by Beethoven. You compare them, and one is better than the other, and it's objective?*

ES: In a sense, yes, because what he's trying to establish is an objective standard of taste. But what do we mean by objective? Well, Hume is a philosopher who wants to encourage us to take our subjective experiences very seriously, in terms of the access they give us to the world and what we can understand about the world through our subjective experiences. And aesthetic and moral judgements are fundamentally subjective for Hume. But he's also trying to establish a standard. You could call it inter-subjective or you could call it objective. But the important thing is that it's not going to be objective in the sense of a law of nature, for example, and it won't just point at entirely objective features of the object of experience. But it is a standard which is applicable and which holds for more than just one person. It holds for all of us, and it holds for ideal critics from across time and across cultures.

NW: *He's got this notion of the test of time—that great works of art have passed the test of time.*

ES: That's right. And when we think about Hume's aesthetic theory, it's very easy to start thinking about these ideal critics who have met these five criteria that he outlines very strictly and so on, as a bourgeois elite of Western culture. And it's easy to forget in all that that the true critics, or the standard of tastes which relies on the sentiments of the true critics, is one that must hold across time, and also to a certain extent across cultures. So they have to stand the test of time—that's to say they have to be able to evoke the sentiments of approbation, sometimes across centuries. And it is a mark of an aesthetically valuable artwork that it does pass this test of time.

NW: *Kant also is very interested in the question about disagreements of taste and how we might reconcile the subjective individual judgement with the sense that, when we make some of these judgements, we are definitely right about them, that it is objectively true that a particular artist is a greater artist than another, a particular work is greater than another, and it's not just a matter of dispute about taste—it's really true.*

ES: Right. So, in a certain respect, Kant addresses the same problem in his aesthetic theory as Hume does in his other standard of taste: namely, how to combine the subjectivity of our aesthetic experience with the objectivity (or the seeming objectivity) of our aesthetic judgements. Aesthetic judgements have a normative force when we are compelled to agree with them: there's a certain kind of 'ought' about them. It's not as simple as the gustatory taste, where it's absolutely fine to say, 'you like apples and I like pears'. Kant specifically mentions that, in the case of beauty, it is not true that every man has his own taste. At the same time, there are no rules for beauty—there are no principles of taste or rule of thumb that we can apply either to make a fantastic artwork or to know when something is beautiful, be it art or not. This attempt to combine the subjectivity of the aesthetic experience with a seeming objectivity of the aesthetic judgement is something that both Kant and Hume are trying very hard to get to grips with. Now, Kant's answer will rely on what he calls a 'sensus communus', or the common sense. That's to say that we're all, pretty much, made up cognitively or psychologically in the same kind of way. And the fact that we all have the same mental abilities (or cognitive faculties, as Kant would call them) makes us equal candidates to experience aesthetic value in a similar way. So, we have this basic common sense in place which helps us understand why, when you say that X is beautiful, and I feel the normative force of that judgement, I am at least in principle capable of seeing, or experiencing, what you're experiencing. Now, it might take some time, it might take some work, and it might take some patience, but you could say that we are all aesthetic agents if we want to be. And so the subjectivity of the experience is also combined with this objectivity, or as I have mentioned before, what we might want to call an inter-subjectivity. The important point being not so much exactly which term we should pick here, perhaps, but the fact that it's valid for other people too.

NW: *Isn't this just hopelessly optimistic about humans, because it assumes that I can really understand art from any culture, that I can understand the motivations and the judgements that people make in another culture? But actually, even the notion of art may be something very different in another culture.*

ES: I think that's right. And of course that's not an issue that troubles Hume and Kant very much, being European men of the eighteenth century! But I think it's a point that's important to us today. We're under much greater pressure to take into account different kinds of art and different kinds of art histories. And it raises a question about whether the relation between art and aesthetic value can be given one unified answer. You know, you might want to say that, if we want to bring in Aboriginal art, cave art, European expressionism, all under one roof, we're expecting too much from our philosophical theories, in that they'll be able to accommodate all those cases perfectly. So where do we go from there? Should there be different explanations of how art relates to aesthetic value? After all, there are plenty of examples of contemporary European art—valuable artworks—that don't particularly have aesthetic value, or don't even aim to have aesthetic value. So I think a twenty-first-century philosopher has to deal with a whole host of questions that Hume and Kant didn't have to worry about.

NW: *I'm really intrigued to know what you think about disagreements about taste. We've talked about what Hume and Kant thought about the issue. What do you think is the solution to the problem that people disagree about taste, but they also usually feel very strongly that they're right in their judgements in particular cases?*

ES: Well, I think it's a phenomenon that we're all familiar with. I think that there is a real onus on us to disentangle the various aspects of an aesthetic disagreement when it does arise. Assuming that we clarify all of that, I think it's incredibly important that we come as far as we can in our discussions and not drop them. There is this common idea that aesthetic disagreement doesn't matter in the same kind of way as moral disagreement might. And of course there are some cases in which you might think, well, lives could be at stake with moral disagreements, yet with aesthetic disagreements there is not so much at stake. But I think that's too simple an answer. Our aesthetic judgements say a lot about who we are and who we want to be. Certainly, when we begin our life as an adult, it's incredibly important to us that we share aesthetic tastes with our friends. It can be difficult to maintain a friendship with someone who has entirely different aesthetic tastes. And I think that we should do well to remind ourselves that the occurrence of disagreement, as such, doesn't tell us anything. What we need to think carefully about is also the issues I mentioned earlier: what kind of disagreement is it; in what way do our set of disagreements tie in with other commitments, such as moral views or moral positions? You might think that someone who shares your aesthetic tastes also shares a life view. And someone who has an entirely different set of aesthetic parameters might well be someone that you don't share some of those other very important attitudes with—it's not always the case, of course, but it might well be the case. So, I think our aesthetic disagreements reveal a lot more than we tend to assume about what's important to us.

NW: *But is there any objective truth in our judgements? Is there the equivalent of Hume's key at the bottom of the keg, somewhere?*

ES: Well, assuming that we are not talking about aesthetic preferences and that this is a bona fide aesthetic judgement, I think that there is a kind of correctness or appropriateness to be had. I think there are features in the object that we appreciate aesthetically, that we can and we should point to in support of our aesthetic judgements. And I think that some qualities, and some features—the way in which they interact and work together in certain artworks, for example—make certain value judgements more appropriate or more true (if you want to use that word) than others. But what do we mean by 'true' and 'objective', and is it the same kind of truth and objectivity of the natural sciences? Such questions are important and are worthy of further exploration.

Further Resources

Jerrold Levinson (2002) 'Hume's Standard of Taste: The Real Problem', *Journal of Aesthetics and Art Criticism*, 60, 227–238.

Mary Mothersill (1997) 'In Defense of Hume and the Causal Theory of Taste', *Journal of Aesthetics and Art Criticism*, 55, 312–317.

James Shelley (2011) 'Hume and the Value of the Beautiful', *British Journal of Aesthetics*, 51, 213–222.

Nick Zangwill (2019) 'Aesthetic Judgment', *The Stanford Encyclopedia of Philosophy*, ed. Edward N. Zalta: http://plato.stanford.edu/archives/spr2019/entries/aesthetic-judgment.

13

EMMA BORG
Language and Context

David Edmonds: *Imagine that I'd said to Nigel after an interview, 'that was the best Philosophy Bites interview we've ever conducted!' Perhaps I was being ironic or sarcastic, but perhaps I meant it literally. If you had more information, you might be able to work out my meaning— say, if you'd heard my tone of voice, or if you'd been sitting in on the interview too. So what is the relationship between meaning and context? We spoke to Emma Borg—to put her into context, she's an expert on the philosophy of language.*

Nigel Warburton: *The topic we're going to focus on is language and context. Now, what's context got to do with language?*

Emma Borg: Let's first think about a question that comes slightly before that—let's think about what it would be to understand a language. How is it that when you learn a language, like French or German, you understand the sentences or the expressions that you are being presented with? One possibility would be that what you've learnt when you're learning a language is something that pairs up the sentences of that language with the meaning in that language. So when someone presents you with a bit of this new language, what you do is you go to your big look-up list and you find the sentence in question and you pair it with a meaning—and that's it, you've got the meaning! That might be one way in which language learning could go. But it seems that after a moment's reflection, that can't be quite right. And it can't be quite right because language looks like it's got this quite surprising feature, namely that we can generate lots and lots—maybe even an indefinite or infinite number—of sentences, within just one natural language. So when you were learning French, you didn't just learn a few sentences—rather, you learned a potentially infinite number of sentences. You learned how to say 'snow is white', but you also learnt how to say 'snow is white and grass is green', or 'snow is white and grass is green and two plus two is not five'—and we could just go on doing that, we could go on generating brand-new sentences. And that seems to show us that you haven't just got a big look-up list, because one thing we know about the mind (or about the brain) is that it's not infinite—you can't have an infinite list of sentences in that way.

NW: *Well, in my case of learning French, I was actually mapping the French onto English, so it was parasitic on my knowledge of English.*

EB: You might think in that case it was parasitic, but let's think about the first language that you learnt. Say you were learning English as your first language—it can't be the case that what you learnt was an infinite set of sentences, because, smart as we all are, we still haven't got infinite minds in that way. And so then we face the question as to what you know and how you understand your language. A suggestion that's been made (and it seems quite appealing) is that what you know are the meanings of some finite number of things (like the meanings of certain words) and you know some strategies or some rules for putting those words together in meaningful ways. So maybe that's what understanding a language consists in—just knowing word meaning and structures.

NW: *By structures, do you mean something like grammar?*

EB: Yeah, something like grammar, something like the structure of a sentence for how bits relate to one another.

NW: *Okay. So you've got this grammar, you've got this vocabulary—where does context come in?*

EB: Well, now we can begin to think about the worry of context. Because that picture I just described doesn't seem to have a place for context. But again, as soon as we start thinking about our language, we can see that there has to be a role for context. For example, when I say, 'I'm happy', I say something different to what you say when you say, 'I'm happy'. In the one case, I say, 'Emma's happy'; in the other case, you say, 'Nigel is happy'. So what's going on in that kind of contextual shift? Or again, if I say, 'Nigel is sitting', it looks like what I'm saying is 'Nigel is sitting at a particular time'. So it looks like in order to get at meaning we've got to have some kind of appeal to the context of utterance—we've got to know things like who's speaking, where they're speaking, when they're speaking, etc. As such, something in our knowledge of language has to capture that context sensitivity.

NW: *Presumably, you have to know even more than that—you have to know if the speaker is playing a game, or if they're joking with a friend, or if they're deadly serious, or being ironic, and so on—there must be quite a lot of contextual things that feed into our interpretation of what a word or a sentence means.*

EB: That's a good point. Someone might think that context sensitivity is quite a limited feature of our language. They might suppose that we need to think about context *only* when we're dealing with words like 'I' and 'this' and 'that' and 'today' and 'tomorrow', and tense markers. And some very smart philosophers, people like David Kaplan and Robert Stalnaker and John Perry, gave us a way of dealing with those kinds of expressions. They said that all you need to know when you're thinking about 'I' or 'this' or 'that' is just a very simple contextual rule which will take you from that expression to the thing it's picking out in the context. So, for 'I', what you need to know is that an utterance of 'I' always refers to the speaker. And then you have to go to context to find out who the speaker is, but it's quite a rule-based kind of activity. But your question just now was picking up on lots of other ways in which context gets in, and that's precisely the way that the debate has gone in recent years. Philosophers, in particular Charles Travis, have raised a number of examples which seem to show that context sensitivity is pervasive in language.

NW: *Before we get onto Travis, I was just thinking about a phrase as simple as 'cat's eyes'—if you're talking about that in relation to your pet, that means one thing, and if you're talking about it as you're driving down the road, its meaning is completely different.*

EB: However, we might genuinely think that 'cat's eyes' has two different dictionary entries—the cat's eyes you find on the road may well be actually recorded in a different way in a good dictionary. So we might think that that expression is genuinely ambiguous. But there are other cases where it's clear that we do get a shift in meaning to do with the expressions that we're putting together. For example, there's a case that gets discussed a lot in the literature about the difference between 'baking a potato' and 'baking a cake'. You do something different when you're baking a potato (in that you're actually cooking the thing), whereas baking a cake means creating it (in that there was no cake before you baked it). But you might think that's not such a weird kind of context sensitivity because it's emerging from the expressions and the way they're put together—it's because in one case we've got a potato and in the other case we've got a cake, and they're different kinds of things, and as such could give rise to a difference of meaning in 'baking' in each case.

NW: *You mentioned Charles Travis's examples that are supposed to demonstrate that context is incredibly important for understanding language. What are they?*

EB: He has this one very famous case, which is probably a good place to start. Imagine this girl called Pia, and Pia has a Japanese maple tree, and as we all know, Japanese maple trees have red leaves. But one morning, Pia looks out of her window and sees her tree and she comes to think that red is the wrong colour for leaves. She thinks leaves should really be green. So she goes out and she meticulously paints every single leaf on her Japanese maple tree in green. And then Travis asks us to consider two different scenarios that Pia might be involved in. In the first scenario, a friend of hers who's an artist rings up and says, 'I'm about to paint a picture, but I need something green to balance out the composition. Have you got anything green I could borrow?'. And Pia says, looking at her painted leaves, 'yes, you can have these, these leaves are green'. And Travis says, in that context, our intuitions are that Pia said something true—speaking to the artist about the painted leaves, it's true to say that they're green. In the second scenario, a botanist friend of Pia's calls up, and she says, 'I'm about to run an experiment on photo-synthesis. Have you got any green leaves that I can have for my experiment?'. And Pia, looking at her painted leaves, says, 'yes, you can have these, these leaves are green'. Travis says our intuitions in this second case are that Pia has no longer said something true. Speaking of the painted leaves to the botanist, it's no longer correct to say of these leaves that they're green. Yet we've got a single sentence—'these leaves are green'—where the circumstances don't change and we're just talking about the same painted leaves, yet in one context we feel something true has been said, and in another context we feel something false has been said. And that shows us that we've got context sensitivity where we didn't think we had it.

NW: *So that's supposed to show that context is everything for language. But does it really show that?*

EB: Well, these kinds of cases have given rise to many different positions in the literature. Some of those positions absolutely endorse Travis's position that such cases show us that context is all-pervasive and we should think about language in a much more Wittgensteinian way. We shouldn't think of getting at meaning as combining stable meanings in certain kinds of repeatable ways; really we should think about language as a tool that we use, and to understand meaning we need to know about the purpose for which that tool is being deployed, and so context is everything. So that's one position—that's Travis's kind of position in the literature. I've adopted a position at the other extreme, where I try and argue that these cases don't show us that context is all-pervasive.

And to get at that kind of position, I think we need to do a couple of things. Namely, we need to think very carefully about each of the cases Travis gives us, because it's not clear that the same thing will be going on in every single case. For instance, there's been quite a lot of work in linguistics about whether colour terms are actually ambiguous, and maybe that's what's coming out in that Pia example. And there might be other things going on in some of the other cases that Travis gives us. But the general motto of my type of position, 'minimalism', is that these sorts of thought experiments aren't the right place to be looking when we're trying to think about literal meaning, because they're just too complicated and too infected by all the different features we bring to bear when we're trying to interpret one another to abstract out literal meaning.

NW: *So minimalism is the position that you can have a literal meaning of a sentence and that meaning is given by the words and their arrangement within a grammatical order, and that the context can be relevant but isn't the determining factor of meaning—is that the right way to describe it?*

EB: Yeah, absolutely. So minimalists are driven by those kinds of concerns we talked about earlier—about learnability and systematicity—and they think that if you haven't got something fixed and stable and unchanging, then you're not going to be able to explain those features of language. And combined with that, they think back to a very influential philosopher in this area—Paul Grice of Oxford—who drew a really clear distinction between sentence meaning and what speakers can say when they produce those sentences. So a famous case from Grice was when he asked us to consider a letter of reference that he is writing for someone. He's writing a letter of reference for one of his students, Jones, and he just writes one sentence: 'Jones has nice handwriting'. And the thought is that if Jones has been applying for a philosophy job and that's the letter of reference Grice writes for him, then the message conveyed to somebody is going to be something like 'Jones is not a good philosopher' or 'Jones shouldn't be given this job'. But Grice says, even if that's right, we're not tempted to think that the sentence 'Jones has nice handwriting' could ever literally mean 'Jones has no philosophical talent'! There's a difference between what a sentence means and what a speaker conveys by it. And what minimalists want to say is that these Travis cases are very nice, but at least some of them are just trading on that old distinction between sentence meaning and speaker meaning.

NW: *Why do you call this minimalism?*

EB: The main reason I call it minimalism is that it adopts a very minimal job description for semantics. So there used to be an assumption, which maybe wasn't always spelt out, that what we wanted from a semantic theory, a theory of literal meaning, was that it captured our intuitions about speech act content—that it would tell us what someone has said when they produce one of these sentences. And a minimalist for me is someone who says that's too rich a job description. A semantic theory couldn't do that at the same time that it was trying to capture facts about learnability and systematicity, because speech act content is affected by a whole range of other things—you need encyclopaedic knowledge, you need to know about socio-economic status, you need to know all kinds of things about the person you're talking to, in order to really get at what message they're trying to get across. Instead, the minimalist says we should think about semantics as just a very limited, constrained kind of activity—it is just trying to get at literal meaning. And then that literal meaning plays a part in working out what someone has said, but it certainly doesn't exhaust it.

NW: *But then what is the role for literal meaning?*

EB: That's a very good question because one of the objections that is made to my position is that I can have the minimal literal meanings, but that they're completely redundant, and there is no reason to want them. However, I think there are a range of ways in which minimal meanings or literal meanings are going to be useful. And I think it's right that minimal meanings don't do all the really nice things that we might have thought semantic content was going to do for us, but they do still have some role to play. This can be demonstrated when thinking about examples of when things go wrong. So sometimes you're having a conversation with somebody and you suddenly realize that you don't really know what they're saying to you, or there's some aspect of the context that you don't know about and it's stopping you from getting the whole meaning. In that case, what can you do? Well, the only thing you *can* do is fall back on the literal meaning. So I can think to myself that I don't really know what Nigel said when he uttered that sentence, and I don't really know what he meant or what he was trying to get across to me, yet I can still know that he said a given sentence with a given literal meaning. Therefore, I can fall back to that kind of content. And if you spend much time with children or philosophers or law-makers, you will find they're very good at accessing that level of content. For example, when I say to my seven-year-old child, 'give some of that cake to your brother', he is very good at passing just the tiniest fragment over. And what that shows is that he is exploiting the literal meaning—he knows full well that's not what I meant, that I meant for him to give some reasonable portion of it to his brother—but he's got a nice grip on what the minimal content was and he's going to exploit it. So minimal contents do have a role to play in that sort of exchange. And if we think about legal exchanges, there are some cases where it's very important that we just get at what someone is committed to by the words that she says rather than the way she says them or the background context. And then the final point where I think minimalism is important is that these different theories about the role of context might tell us something about the nature of the mind as well—they might tell us about the relationship between language understanding and other kinds of cognitive activity that we engage in.

NW: *But what does your understanding of language have to say about the mind?*

EB: My view of language has some quite clear repercussions for what we want to say about the mind. Minimalism claims that when you understand a language, what you understand are the meanings of these primitives—the words—and a way of putting those words together to generate meanings for complexes. But if that's all that's involved in understanding a language, then we could have some quite dedicated part of the mind that is responsible for such understanding. We could have what Jerry Fodor has called a module—a module is supposed to be an encapsulated computational system which doesn't look to everything that you as an individual know, it just looks to a very small subset: a set of rules, and a library of information. And minimalism says that maybe language understanding is like that and so could be underpinned by a dedicated module. And note that this might fit nicely with some cases where things go wrong. We know that in some kinds of cases of impairment, what happens is that your language understanding either gets impaired or preserved, while your general understanding—your pragmatic understanding—is either preserved or lost in a different way. If we think about some cases on the autistic spectrum, namely those with Asperger's Syndrome, patients on the high-functioning autistic spectrum, they have a very well-preserved language ability and they tend to be over-literal—they access the literal meanings of sentences but they're not so good at picking up on the conveyed communicated content. And what the minimalist takes those kinds of cases to show is that maybe this is reflecting a structure of the mind. We could preserve the module that underpins language understanding when there's damage occurring in other areas of the mind.

NW: *Academics are often asked to defend what they do to a wider public. How could you do that when you're just reflecting on the nature of language?*

EB: We do need to justify why we're doing what we're doing, and I think this issue is one that we can definitely find reason for studying. One reason is its inherent interest. These things are activities that we engage in every day—we talk to one another, we get the message, but how does that work? These things are very 'up close and personal' and it would be good to understand what's going on. Another reason that these things matter is that if we think about the impairment cases we were talking about a moment ago, if we're going to be able to design the best kind of interventions for those sorts of difficulties, we need first of all to know what's going on when things go right. If we want to understand what's going on when things go wrong, we need to know how they compare with typical language development. So a good theoretical understanding of language matters for treating those kinds of concerns. And if we think about all the developments that are going on at the moment with brain scans and advances in science, it seems to me that none of those results are going to be fully robust unless we've got a good theoretical model to plug them into. If we want to know why it's useful to understand that this bit of your brain lights up when you're listening to a language and this bit of your brain lights up when you're doing something else, we need to know about the theoretical structures that they plug into. And that's what philosophy delivers for you.

Further Resources

Emma Borg (2004) *Minimal Semantics*, Oxford University Press.

Emma Borg (2007) 'Minimalism versus Contextualism in Semantics', in G. Preyer and G. Peter (eds.) *Context-Sensitivity and Semantic Minimalism: New Essays on Semantics and Pragmatics*, Oxford University Press, 546–571.

Kepa Korta and John Perry (2020) 'Pragmatics', *The Stanford Encyclopedia of Philosophy*, ed. Edward N. Zalta: http://plato.stanford.edu/archives/spr2020/entries/pragmatics.

François Recanati (2004) *Literal Meaning*, Cambridge University Press.

Charles Travis (1997) 'Pragmatics', in B. Hale and C. Wright (eds.) *Companion to the Philosophy of Language*, Blackwell, 87–107.

14

REBECCA ROACHE
Swearing

David Edmonds: *We haven't had to do this before on Philosophy Bites, but this is a warning. If you're offended by swear words, stop reading this right now, for it contains the F-word, the P-word, the A-word, the T-word, the W-word, and several more besides. You know what I mean when I use the phrase 'the F-word'—is that phrase any less offensive than using the full word, you know, 'the f-u-c-k word'? Normally clean-mouthed Rebecca Roache has been thinking about the philosophy of swearing.*

Nigel Warburton: *The topic we're going to talk about is swearing. So I think we need to get clear at the beginning what we mean by swearing.*

Rebecca Roache: Swearing is the use of a certain sort of taboo language. It's generally taken to perform a function where it expresses emotion, rather than being used specifically to denote something—although it can be used to denote too.

NW: *I think you better give some examples.*

RR: Words like 'fuck', 'cunt', 'wank', 'shit', 'arse', 'tits', 'prick'...

NW: *You've given sexual and scatological examples, but there are also words which are considered blasphemous which also fit the category of swearing.*

RR: Yeah, that's right. Words like 'damn' would have been quite forceful to use several decades ago but aren't so much now. Religious terms have more power in certain other languages, such as French and Italian. I'm not so much concerned with religious terms here, as they're not the most forceful swear words to use in English.

NW: *But for some people they are the most forceful—for a deeply religious person to hear a religious swear word may be the worst kind of offensive language around.*

RR: Absolutely. But, at least in English, it's mainly people with religious sentiments who are deeply offended by religious swear words (there are a few exceptions in other languages, where certain religious terms are offensive even to non-religious people). On the other hand, the sorts of words that I mentioned are viewed as offensive by a much wider segment of society.

NW: *There is also this category of really offensive language used for particular groups—whether racial groups, or homosexuals, or people who are different from us who are categorized with a disparaging word. Is that swearing?*

RR: Those sorts of words in the philosophical literature are referred to as slurs. There are various views about how you would distinguish those from the sorts of words that I mentioned. On one view, slurs are offensive because when you use them to refer to another person, you express your contempt and disrespect not only for that person, but for the entire group of people targeted by the slur—and typically the targeted group has historically been oppressed, so by referring to them contemptuously you're participating in their continued oppression. By contrast, if you say, 'Fuck off!' to someone, you express contempt and disrespect only for that person. Philosophically, it's important to separate swearing from slurring because they are offensive for different reasons. Slurring can be oppressive and harmful; swearing is usually not.

NW: *That's really interesting because I'm sure some people will already have taken offence that you reeled off a whole lot of foul language.*

RR: Well, I was *mentioning* the words then rather than *using* them, and that is an important distinction in philosophy. Mentioning a swear word would be referring to the word, rather than using the word to refer to something else. So, if in a newspaper you see a report that Jeremy Clarkson had called somebody a 'cunt' (as once happened in *The Guardian*) where the word appears inside inverted commas, that would be an instance of mentioning a swear word. On the other hand, if you just fucking use swear words in the context of normal conversation (as I'm doing now), then that would be an example of using rather than mentioning. And generally, people are more tolerant of mentioning swear words than of using them. *The Guardian*—which has a policy unlike most British newspapers of printing swear words in full, rather than of blanking any letters out—has editorial guidelines that specify that there's rarely a good reason to *use* swear words rather than merely *mention* them; in other words, according to *The Guardian*, there's almost never a good reason to write a swear word outside of inverted commas.

NW: *You used the words in quite a delicate way there, but if you call somebody a fucking idiot in an aggressive way, that can be utterly humiliating, it can be devastating, especially if it's done in front of the wrong people.*

    RR: That's true: swearing aggressively at someone is worse than swearing non-aggressively at them, and swearing can intensify aggressive behaviour. Even so, you needn't use a swear word in order to upset someone with aggressive behaviour. You can be aggressive to somebody—you can humiliate them, intimidate them, harass them, etc.—without ever swearing at them. And in contrast, you can also be perfectly polite to somebody in certain contexts whilst using swear words.

NW: *But, in my spectrum of words, the swear words are the most powerful ones I have in my armoury and they're the last ones to use before violence. It's like you build up and you build up and if you really want to express absolute anger, aggression, or a really disparaging sentiment, then the swear words are the most effective way to do so.*

    RR: This is one of the interesting things about swearing—it does have this link with emotion. Swearing is often a bit like screaming; like when you stub your toe and yell 'Fuck!'. But this might actually be advantageous. If you're in a situation where you're inclined to be aggressive and you swear at somebody instead of hitting them, then that might actually be a good thing. There are some people who see swearing as advantageous in this way—it's a low-cost form of aggression, where you can express emotion without resorting to violence.

NW: *We've been talking about the emotional power that's often associated with swearing and also that emotion sometimes involves letting off steam—it's not always targeted at somebody else. For example, I can drop a heavy weight on my foot and just swear because that's a release of pressure for me.*

RR: Yeah, in that case swearing would be very cathartic and it would be advantageous for you to be able to swear in that situation. The psychologist Richard Stephens ran a series of experiments showing that people can withstand pain for longer if they are allowed to swear while they're doing it. He asked people to hold their hand in a bucket of iced water for as long as they could, and people who were allowed to swear lasted longer than those who uttered a neutral word. That's quite a good illustration that swearing can be cathartic without being aggressive.

NW: *So we've been talking a bit about what swearing is, but what's philosophically interesting about swearing?*

RR: Well, that's a good question. It's widely viewed as offensive, and there's a question about what we ought to do about that. In a society like ours, there are certain things that are banned merely because they're viewed as offensive. So, you're not allowed to have sex in public, for example, without getting arrested. Something similar seems to hold for swearing. If you swear in the wrong context, you can lose your job, or if you're a broadcaster you can be fined, and there are examples of people being arrested for swearing under the Public Order Act. It's not uncommon for people to be punished for swearing.

NW: *Are you saying there's a philosophical question about where you draw the line, regarding whether there is a good moral argument for outlawing certain kinds of swearing?*

RR: Yeah. Having recognized that swearing is offensive, at least sometimes, there is then a question about how we should respond to it, legally or otherwise. As it happens, it's common for us to respond negatively to it without using the law, just by informal social sanctions (like expressing disapproval) or by penalizing people professionally or financially, and so on. This raises an important philosophical question. If you think about all the sorts of things that people have or ever have found offensive, at one end of the scale you might have something like minor transgressions of etiquette. So, if, for example, you invite me to your house for dinner and I put my feet up on the table you might reasonably think that's offensive, but you don't really censure me or punish me in any way. You might not invite me back for dinner and you might be annoyed at me, but I'm not going to be punished—it's not against the law, and I won't lose my job or anything like that. At the other end of the scale, sometimes we *do* punish people for doing what is viewed as offensive. A few decades ago, in this country, some people found homosexuality offensive, and as a result the liberty of gay people was restricted in certain ways—for example, there was less freedom to portray same-sex relationships than heterosexual relationships in TV shows. We thankfully live in more enlightened times now, and the mainstream view is that while you're free to be offended by homosexuality, your being offended by it is not sufficient reason to restrict the liberty of homosexuals.

NW: *So where does swearing stand in this? Are you saying that we should just be free to swear and if people don't like it, they should just get over it?*

RR: As things stand, culturally, people are penalized for swearing. In order for that to be justifiable, there has to be a plausible story about *why* it's deemed offensive, and why its offensiveness justifies restricting people's freedom to swear.

That story can't just involve the fact that we've been brought up in such a way to view certain words as more offensive than others, because the fact that we've been brought up to view swear words as offensive doesn't justify restricting people's freedom to swear—just as the fact that some people are brought up to view homosexuality as offensive doesn't justify restricting anyone's freedom to express their homosexuality. My view is that swearing is a lot more like putting your feet on somebody's table than homosexuality. We should avoid swearing in contexts where it upsets people, because we should avoid upsetting people without good reason. But I think it's unjustifiable to punish people for swearing, at least in the absence of aggravating factors, such as when someone swears in the course of harassing or intimidating another person.

NW: *Couldn't you see it as more like nudity in public or defecating in public, which are deemed deeply offensive by a lot of people? We're not free to get out various parts of our body in public, and nor should we be free to get out the crude names of those parts of our body or descriptions of actions that we might be prohibited from performing.*

RR: The comparison between swearing and nudity is actually really interesting. Generally, we're more sensible about nudity than we are about swearing. Many people hold the view that swearing is never acceptable; it's common, for example, to hear people claim that swearing is simply unnecessary, with the implication that it's therefore unjustified. On the other hand, we do tend to recognize that nudity is acceptable in some circumstances and unacceptable in other circumstances—nobody would expect you to take a bath fully clothed. In the

UK, the law around public nudity is a lot more nuanced than the law around swearing—in fact, despite people occasionally being arrested for swearing, the law does not explicitly mention swearing at all. The matter is complicated by the fact that people swear a lot more than they go around naked in public. So perhaps our social responses to swearing in a public context are a lot more developed and easier to make sense of than our responses to people being nude in public.

NW: *Are you arguing for a greater toleration of swearing? Is that the philosophical angle you're taking here?*

RR: In one sense, yes. I think it should be better tolerated in the sense that people shouldn't be punished for *merely* swearing, and there shouldn't be draconian social sanctions against it. But on the other hand, I wouldn't want to tell people how to respond to the language they hear. If people don't like swearing, I'm not saying that they have to like it. I'm saying that there is a strong case for tolerating it more than we currently do.

NW: *Is there a special issue about writing down swear words as opposed to uttering them in ordinary conversation? Because sometimes people avoid the precise spelling of a swear word by using asterisks or blanks, so 'f***', or talk about the N-word (I know that's a slur but it's just another similar euphemistic avoidance of putting in the actual word). So is that because it's written down or is there something else going on?*

RR: Obviously, there is this convention whereby you can use asterisks to avoid writing out a swear word in full and then that somehow makes it less offensive. It's interesting to think about how that manages to make the swear word less offensive, given that you intend to communicate the swear word and your audience knows what the word is and that you intend to communicate it. We just have this norm that asterisked swearing is more acceptable than writing out swear words in full. I think that has to do with what we signal to the reader when we use asterisks: using them tells the reader that we recognize that they might find the word offensive, and that we are taking steps to make the word more pleasant for them. In other words, asterisks signal to the reader that their feelings are being considered. That signal is often enough to offset the offensiveness of the asterisked word, even when the reader understands what word is being communicated.

NW: *I must be odd here because I respond more negatively to it because it seems unnecessarily coy, as we know the word and such asterisked usage is like playing 'peekaboo' with the word.*

RR: I completely agree. In contexts where uncensored swearing would be tolerated, censoring it with asterisks achieves little except to signal to the reader, 'Here's a rude word!' There is also some reason to think that using asterisks makes things *worse*. If there is any ambiguity about what word you're using when you put asterisks in there, then your audience has to think really hard about it. They may even think of more offensive words than you would have intended to convey. You mentioned the N-word, and I think that that's an interesting example here. We might think that being able to use the expression 'n*****' (that is, the word with most of its letters replaced by asterisks) actually makes things worse by legitimizing the use of a highly offensive term, and that it would be better if people didn't have any way to refer disrespectfully to Black people at all. We see something similar with asterisked swearing: if it's used too frequently, the asterisks cease to mitigate the word's offensiveness, perhaps because the frequency undermines the message that the writer is being considerate of the reader's feelings about swearing. Censoring swearing with asterisks only works when done infrequently, and in contexts where uncensored swear words are likely to cause significant offence to the audience.

NW: *There could also be a historical explanation—a kind of genealogy—of the asterisk convention: that it came from religious prohibitions on mentioning the word 'God', but also from concerns about libel where certain people's names were given as asterisks when everybody knew the name that was being referred to but the person couldn't say that they were libelled because their name wasn't actually uttered.*

RR: This is a really good point. The linguist Geoffrey Nunberg has compared swear words to magic spells, which must be uttered in full in order to have their effect. And, of course, something similar applies to religious terms, which are viewed as sacred, even when the letters that comprise them are not sacred.

NW: *In Britain in the 1960s there was a big debate about whether D. H. Lawrence's Lady Chatterley's Lover should be censored or not, because it used the words 'fuck' and 'cunt' fairly liberally. But they weren't really being used as swear words. It's an interesting thought that maybe you could use these words as purely descriptive—and so reclaim these Anglo-Saxon words for literary use.*

RR: One of the things that linguists and psychologists view as interesting about swear words is that they are in a lot of ways different from other words—they don't always function in sentences in the way that we expect them to. Take 'Fuck you!', for example. We know that's an insult, but it's not very clear how you would begin to interpret it literally. This doesn't apply to the uses that you're describing there—the way that Lawrence used the words was much more like regular verbs and nouns. The linguist James McCawley distinguished between two different senses of 'fuck'. In one sense, which is the sense used by Lawrence, it behaves like a regular verb; in the other—as in 'Fuck you!'—it doesn't fit neatly into any linguistic category.

NW: *Liberal philosophers often argue that adults should be free in all kinds of ways, but they don't usually feel that about children. They feel that children need certain sorts of restrictions put upon them in order to have graded exposure to reality and become more autonomous agents in the process. So, where do you stand with swearing in children? Do you think children should be free to swear?*

RR: This is a really interesting question, especially as I have young children, so I have to decide a policy on this. We know that children are going to grow up learning to swear, and we just have to work out how it's appropriate for them to learn. What we don't want is for children to grow up swearing in the wrong contexts because they might go around upsetting people. But there are all sorts of ways that children could upset people. For example, if they go around referring to people only by their first names, and then they go to school and call their teachers by their first names, which is inappropriate because it's over-familiar in that context. But our response to that sort of situation is not normally to raise children only to call people 'Sir' and 'Madam', or to refer to them as 'Mr' and 'Mrs'. What we try to do is to teach the children that there are certain contexts where certain types of behaviour are appropriate, and certain contexts where it's inappropriate. I think *that* sort of policy on swearing is probably the most appropriate. If you think it's a really bad thing to expose children to swear words, then a logical consequence of that is to take steps to ensure that they don't learn swear words *at all*—maybe restrict their activity in the playground, and have teachers on hand always to ensure that children use the 'correct' language. But I think that would be a much more sinister approach than actually raising children to know what swear words are, but also to know in what contexts it's appropriate to use them.

Further Resources

Emma Byrne (2017) *Swearing Is Good for You*, Profile Books.

Melissa Mohr (2013) *Holy Sh*t: A Brief History of Swearing*, Oxford University Press.

Quang Phuc Dong, 'English Sentences without Overt Grammatical Subject': http://babel.ucsc.edu/~hank/quangphucdong.pdf.

Rebecca Roache (2016) 'Naughty Words', *Aeon*: http://aeon.co/essays/where-does-swearing-get-its-power-and-how-should-we-use-it.

15

TERESA M. BEJAN
Civility

David Edmonds: *We hope that Philosophy Bites is known for its robust, but civil, discussion. And although on occasion we may offend, we don't set out to offend. But what is it to be civil in discussion? How does civility differ from politeness? In our politically divisive times, do we need more civility or less? Teresa M. Bejan is a well-mannered political theorist at the University of Oxford.*

Nigel Warburton: *The topic we're going to talk about is civility. Maybe you could begin by telling us what you mean by civility.*

Teresa M. Bejan: One of the funny things about popular and philosophic discussions about civility is how very rarely people seem to want to answer that question. But when we talk about civility generally, I think we have in mind a conversational virtue that is meant to govern how people talk to each other, both in the sense of the manner of their speech but also in terms of the substance of what they say.

NW: *So civility is not raising your voice; not insulting people; maybe not going into areas which might be found hugely offensive by people . . .*

TMB: Yes, that's the thought. And implicit in those examples is another important feature of civility—it seems to be a conversational virtue that's important when it comes to disagreement, in particular. Civility is meant to govern how we disagree. And that will include things like the tone of my voice, the volume of my voice, the speed at which I talk, whether or not I allow you to respond, whether or not I'm listening…those kinds of things. So, when we're talking about civility, we're very often worried about *how* people are disagreeing.

NW: *That sounds just like good manners on a personal level—you allow each other a space to communicate and there's a chance to do that without offending the other person.*

TMB: Right. Very often when we think about civility, we link it to other concepts like common courtesy. Often we define civility as a virtue that's akin to politeness. But one of the things I'm interested in is the way that civility deviates from those other concepts and the peculiar features it has.

NW: *What are those features? What are the differences between politeness and civility, because they sound like synonyms to me?*

TMB: One of them has already come up already—it's the fact that civility is pertinent to disagreement in particular. But there are more peculiar features as well. One would be that civility, unlike politeness or deference or respect, seems to have a characteristic minimalism about it—sometimes it even has negative overtones. To be *merely* civil to someone is to be less than polite. It doesn't necessarily communicate respect to them, and in fact it might communicate disrespect or even contempt for them. Finally (and I think that this is one of the really crucial features, and it's a feature that matters historically, too), civility seems to be a standard of behaviour that we expect from people by virtue of them standing in a particular relation to one other—namely, people who engage in a civil disagreement should be members of the same civil society, the same *civitas*, or state. So, the idea is that by virtue of their shared membership in this particular kind of community, they're expected to meet a certain conversational standard.

NW: *So at that point we're getting beyond just a virtue of conversation—we're talking about a kind of interaction that takes place within a particular kind of political setting.*

TMB: Exactly. The idea of civility as being, in some way, a political virtue comes from the very word itself. The root of civility is the Latin *civitas*, and many political theorists and philosophers have been interested to understand modern civility—contemporary civility as a conversational virtue—in terms of these classical origins.

NW: *Maybe you could give us a sketch of the origins, the genealogy of civility, as it were.*

TMB: Well, the story that's often told is that modern civility has its roots in the ancient or classical virtue of *civilitas*, which in Republican Rome was an ideal of public-spiritedness—a kind of civic virtue—and the quality of good citizenship and good governance. And in the 1990s, a lot of political theorists and philosophers became interested in civility as a virtue of good citizenship—of civic-mindedness and public spirit.

NW: *That is a big gap between the Roman era and the 1990s. Was it only from the 1990s that people became interested in the concept of civility and sought its origins?*

TMB: Yes, you might think that the intervening millennia of history could be important in terms of how we use this word!

But the gap is there. In the 1990s and also in the 2000s, theorists were interested in Republicanism and Neo-Republicanism—that is, in understanding modern democracy and representative government as having ancient roots, and looking to the past for certain virtues that could improve them.

NW: *Does it stand in contrast with the liberal tradition which says that people need pretty thick skins, and we can have robust disagreement and offend people, but that's very different from harming them—the kind of John Stuart Mill tradition of free speech?*

TMB: Yes. And thus other theorists who wanted to push that point and argue that the virtue of civility was something else in a liberal society, something low but solid, could point to an alternative history. Many theorists, like the sociologist Edward Shils, pointed instead to civility as the virtue of modern bourgeois society—casting civility as the manners of the marketplace where we bump up against each other. We live together and share a life, but it's often a rough-and-tumble and conflictual kind of life and exchange. Theories of civility in this sense often point to the eighteenth and nineteenth centuries as the crucial time where a modern concept of civility developed. But I argue that civility in the modern sense—in the sense that we touched on at the beginning of our discussion, as a conversational virtue pertinent to disagreement in particular—actually dates earlier. I argue that it's a product of early modern debates about religious toleration that emerged precisely in that time where the boundary between who should be inside and outside the *civitas* was more porous and itself a subject of conflict.

NW: *So who are the sources of this religious civility?*

TMB: The story I would tell actually starts from the opposite side. It starts from trying to offer an account of who the inventors of modern *incivility* really were. Here I think the most crucial figure was Martin Luther himself. You might think of Luther as kicking off the first modern crisis of civility 500 years ago, because in addition to making sophisticated theological arguments against the Catholic Church, he also decided to frame those arguments and to present them in such a way that was deliberately offensive to the social mores of his day. So, for Luther, the idea that evangelism and the 'calling out' of corruption had to be done in an uncivil way was part and parcel of his idea of Protestantism as a *protest* against the status quo.

NW: *Are you suggesting that Protestantism is actually the source of the more honest, in-your-face, telling-it-how-it-is style of debate, that others would see as rude, impertinent, and offensive speech?*

TMB: I think that's exactly right. There is, of course, a risk of exaggerating here. But, I think it is fair to say that you can look to the origins of modern ideas of 'free speech fundamentalism'—especially in the United States—as a kind of in-your-face proselytism, and to the origins of the modern call-out culture as well—the idea that what we need to do is call others out, cry out against injustice whenever we see it, and not care about their hurt feelings.

NW: *I confess to being in the liberal camp here—I can see the virtues of being prepared to state what you believe, not being overly concerned with somebody else's sensibilities when something important is at stake. You*

don't want to go out and offend people, but if they happen to be particularly
sensitive about the issue, then going out of your way not to offend them
could result in a misunderstanding without getting the truth out. So
expressing your own views by compromising to a degree is not satisfactory.
What is the argument for this sort of civil interaction as opposed to the
robust disagreement that is characteristic of the liberal tradition?

TMB: That is an excellent question and it lies at the root of
what I would describe as a strong tradition of civility-
scepticism—the idea that the virtue of civility isn't really a
virtue at all; rather it's a way of trying to silence the speech of
others, a way of trying to suppress ideas that you don't like, or
maybe even to exclude and marginalize those with whom you
disagree or whom you cannot or will not see as members of a
civil or civilized polity. That was the Lutheran position—that
civility in an unjust society isn't a virtue at all. Not only do we
have a duty to tell the truth and not to censor ourselves out of
respect for someone else's feelings, we actually have a duty *to*
offend their sensibilities because those privileged by an unjust
status quo will always be offended when they're presented
with the truth.

NW: *You're making a very good case for incivility at the moment.*
What's the other side of this?

TMB: The other side takes that critical point really seriously.
It observes this dynamic of suppression and exclusion that
seems always to be at work when we're talking about civility,
and more importantly when we're accusing other people of
being uncivil. But then it also says, nevertheless, that if civility
is claiming to regulate or govern our disagreements on the
basis of something shared, then what matters is *what* exactly it

is we're claiming must be shared in order to have a civil disagreement. You might think that we have to have something substantive in common in order to be able to disagree, and that in itself opens the door to an unjust suppression or exclusion. But then you might also think that if we need to share something, then it's really important to define what that shared thing is.

NW: *Perhaps you could give an example to make this clearer.*

TMB: The proponent of civility can come back to the critic and agree that the fears about suppression and exclusion are well founded, but argue that rejecting civility altogether under-reacts to the challenges that disagreements present— particularly disagreements about questions that we think of as being somehow fundamental, maybe questions of religion and politics that go to the heart of how we see the world and each other. Now those kinds of disagreements really are difficult to have. And yet we still need to be able to have them. So when we're talking about civility, we're talking about the qualities a conversationalist needs to have in order to make those really difficult disagreements possible.

NW: *Is this just a pragmatic issue then, in asking what would make a conversation between two people who disagree go well? It is not going to go well if one offends the other, so it's much better that they go out of their way not to offend each other and play by the rules of civility, and thereby have a conversation.*

TMB: That is an intuitive thought—that civility is *inoffensiveness*—yet it very quickly leads to problems. If we define civility with reference to another person's feelings, very quickly the sensitive person would seem to have a kind of veto power over defining what a civil disagreement looks like. This phenomenon occurred historically in this moment after the Reformation, when people became very worried about the uncivil evangelism of Protestants like Luther. There was a lot of talk about the offensiveness of their speech. And very quickly the move was to talk about the offensiveness of the speech of other disliked dissenters, as well. As a result, we have these wonderful handbooks of civil conversation in the seventeenth century talking about how atheists need to be more sensitive to how offensive their discourse is to their Christian neighbours.

NW: *I'm really interested to know how we could adapt this evolving concept of civility and bring it into contemporary debates, because you're an advocate of civility. But so far you haven't really put the best case for it.*

TMB: You're right. Probably what sets me apart most as a theorist of civility and a proponent of civility today is that I started out as a civility-sceptic and a critic of civility. And I remain very sensitive to the ways that calls for more civility and accusations of incivility against one's opponents can be used to suppress, exclude, and silence. But it's also clear to me that critics of civility today are, generally speaking, assuming that their interlocutors are nevertheless going to abide by certain rules of conversational behaviour—that they won't interrupt, that they won't just hurl insults, that they will respond to what is said, and actually *have the disagreement*. This suggests to me that maybe civility isn't a matter of not saying offensive things, or of policing our speech, or of choosing our words really carefully. Maybe civility is something else. Maybe civility is the virtue and the qualities of the speaker and listener that allow us to have those difficult conversations in the first place. And so that's where I started in trying to theorize civility—really thinking about civility as the willingness to stay in the room and continue to engage with even the most deplorable of one's opponents, with the thought that disagreement itself will remain disagreeable, and yet, nevertheless, it's better that we fight our battles with words, rather than swords.

NW: *But I can disagree forcefully with you and maybe offend you in the process without fighting you. There is a distinction still between words and blows.*

TMB: It is a distinction that is being put increasingly under pressure if we think about Austinian accounts of language, and a lot of contemporary theories of hate speech and sexist speech would say that words *are* actions, words *do* wound, and words do the essential work of creating and maintaining social hierarchies and status differences. So, what really interested me in looking to the sixteenth and seventeenth centuries for a theory of what I would call 'mere civility'—as the kind of minimal conversational virtue that makes difficult disagreements possible—was that, in that period, no one would have made the case that robust or offensive disagreement is okay because words don't matter anyway. In early modern Europe, there's a strong sense of the importance of language and the importance of *the word*—including the Word of God, the gospel—as something that must flow freely in society. Thus, if you privilege the power of words in this way, the question becomes: how do you have difficult disagreements in a tolerant society, and allow our words to flow freely, without that society falling apart and collapsing into civil war?

NW: *You introduced this notion of 'mere civility'. Could you just flesh that out a little bit, and tell us what it means?*

TMB: Yes—because mere civility is the virtue that makes robust disagreement and the free flow of words in a tolerant society possible. I define 'mere civility' as a minimal conformity to social norms of respectful behaviour. Specifically, it's the minimum necessary to keep a conversation going. But you can tell from that definition that the particular demands of mere civility in any given conversation will be highly context-dependent and highly audience-dependent. So instead of fixating or focusing on rules of civil conduct—the appropriate way to doff your hat, or the appropriate ceremonial language, or the way that we address or express deference to others—instead we should think about civility as a prudential or practical judgement about what's required in a given conversation with a given conversationalist, so that the conversation can continue. But mere civility has this other element, as well, which is that the merely civil person will also remain committed to telling the truth to her interlocutors. And part of that truth will often be telling them what one really thinks of them and their often execrable views. So one way of thinking about mere civility is as a commitment to both not pulling our punches, but also to not landing them all at once, so that the conversation can continue between combatants.

NW: *I can see that prudentially, as you say, this could be a great virtue to cultivate. But I would suggest it's not a widely distributed virtue at the moment and many people seem psychologically incapable of doing what you're suggesting when it comes to discussing matters that are really important to them.*

TMB: I agree. It would seem today that civility and especially mere civility are in critically short supply. It's also a time in which the critique of civility is increasingly powerful. We see this in the context of American politics today, for example, when activists argue that in the face of gross injustice, civility isn't a virtue at all, it's just a demand for deference from the powerful to an unjust status quo. What worries me, then, as a proponent of civility, is the propensity of some people—in the face of such challenges—to call for civility as an aspirational, elite, and gentlemanly virtue, that says 'oh do but be civil' and 'let's have a civil conversation'. In mistaking civility for more demanding conversational virtues—that is, the more elite and elitist conversational virtues, like politeness, like deference, like respect—we risk crowding out the more low but solid and minimalist ground of mere civility that's necessary for disagreement to be possible in a tolerant society.

NW: *You mentioned your conversion from being a civility-sceptic to being pro civility. How does this change your behaviour?*

TMB: My post-conversion experience has been one of increasing sensitivity to the ways in which incivility and uncivil disagreement have led to a really pernicious process of people retreating into the more agreeable company of the like-minded. One thing I always like to point out to my students is that there's a reason that 'disagreeable' is a synonym for 'unpleasant'. It's much nicer to talk to people whom we can be confident already agree with us. But that's a disaster in a tolerant society. It's a disaster in a democracy. Therefore, my commitment to civility is really, at bottom, a commitment to learning how to tolerate the disagreeableness of disagreement, especially on the issues that I care about most.

Further Resources

Teresa M. Bejan (2017) *Mere Civility: Disagreement and the Limits of Toleration*, Harvard University Press.

Teresa M. Bejan (2018) 'Is Civility a Sham?', *TED Talk*: http://www.ted.com/talks/teresa_bejan_is_civility_a_sham.

Amy Olberding (2019) 'Righteous Incivility', *Aeon*: http://aeon.co/essays/whats-the-difference-between-being-righteous-and-being-rude.

Jonathan Quong (2018) 'Public Reason', *The Stanford Encyclopedia of Philosophy*, ed. Edward N. Zalta: http://plato.stanford.edu/archives/spr2018/entries/public-reason.

Roger Williams (2008) *On Religious Liberty*, ed. J. C. Davis, Harvard, Belknap Press.

16

KATHERINE HAWLEY
Trustworthiness

David Edmonds: *What is it to be trustworthy? Are untrustworthy people necessarily dishonest? Can one be too trustworthy, and why does trustworthiness matter? One philosopher who can be relied upon to address these questions is Katherine Hawley.*

Nigel Warburton: *The topic we're going to talk about is trustworthiness. What is trustworthiness?*

Katherine Hawley: I think trustworthiness can mean different things in different contexts: what you want from a trustworthy spouse may be different from a trustworthy bank or a trustworthy colleague. But what I've focused most on in my work is trustworthiness in relationships with people who you see regularly but they're not your closest friends or family members; for example, people you work with or your neighbours. I partly started thinking about trustworthiness when I had kids and I realized what a big part of your life such relationships are— there's a lot of dependence on the parents of your kids' friends and other adults that you see a lot of, who you have ongoing relationships with, but you're not always close friends with them, yet trustworthiness between you is important.

NW: *So is trustworthiness in this context reliability, where you can almost guarantee that they'll do what they say?*

KH: Yeah, that's right. One thing that's really important, particularly in those kinds of relationships, is people following through on what they've offered to do. So sometimes people can do favours for you, sometimes they can't, and that's okay. And trustworthiness amounts to following through on when someone says they'll do something—they'll be there, they'll pick up your kids, they'll do something for you at work, etc. As such, to be trustworthy is to keep those promises, and not end up letting you down after they've agreed that they'll do something.

NW: *That sounds quite like a psychological trait. Some people are all over the place and they mean well, but they don't get to pick up your kids quite on time because something else distracted them. It doesn't seem obviously philosophical. What's the philosophical issue here?*

KH: This is a topic where philosophy has to work together with psychology, but also actually with sociology and social sciences more generally. One thing I think that's interesting for a philosopher is to point out how often we conflate being an untrustworthy person with being someone who's intentionally dishonest or manipulative or a con artist. But actually, as you're saying, there are people who are basically well intentioned, don't intend to let other people down, and don't mean to manipulate or be difficult. But they take on too much and get over-committed, or they are a bit disorganized and a little bit forgetful. We are all like this from time to time. And I think it's worth remembering that that can be a form of untrustworthiness—that can be just as disruptive for other people's lives and the arrangements that they are making as with the person who is intentionally being dishonest.

NW: *Trustworthiness with children is also more than just showing up on time—it's that the person in loco parentis is actually the kind of person who's going to keep an eye on your kids if something happens, and who is going to be aware of possible dangers to protect your children.*

KH: Yeah, and I think sometimes we can have different expectations of each other in exactly those sorts of situations. So if someone else is looking after my kids, it's fairly obvious that they should stop them falling out of the window or juggling knives in the kitchen—there are some basic things like these that we all know that trustworthiness requires of us. But we might have different opinions about whether it's okay to give them sweets in the middle of the day, or whether to smoke in the house when there are kids around, or whether to let them watch cartoons on TV—different families have different ideas about what's appropriate. And these are the kinds of things that can be a little bit difficult to negotiate. We have to live up to our commitments to fulfil our obligations, but we don't always know what other people think we're supposed to be doing, and that can make things challenging.

NW: *Do you think that underlying all these different kinds of trust-worthiness there's some essential thing—'trustworthiness'—that has particular characteristics? For instance, a trustworthy person is somebody who does what they say they're going to do.*

KH: Broadly speaking, yes. The notion of trustworthiness that I've focused on is about avoiding unfulfilled commit-ments. You put it yourself in terms of doing what we say we're going to do, and that's an important part of it. But I think it's also true that we often end up with commitments without explicitly saying that we're going to do that kind of thing. For example, if I look after your kids, then maybe there is an expectation that now you've got a commitment to look after my kids when I ask you to do so. There are all sorts of reciprocity situations like that. Often we end up with commitments unless we explicitly opt out of them, because silence can indicate consent. And so there is a broader sense of trustworthiness that incorporates avoiding unfulfilled commitments (those commitments being the ones we explicitly speak up for but also a much wider set of commitments that we incur just by engaging with each other in social contexts).

NW: *What's so good about trustworthiness? Is it just a great thing if you happen to have it or is it absolutely essential to being a good person?*

KH: It's not just an attribute that is nice to have. It is something that is crucial to the way that we interact with one another and all the many different social contexts and common projects in which we have to work together. I'm a little bit hesitant about calling trustworthiness a 'virtue' in the sense that virtue ethicists within philosophy have used that word. That's partly because someone's trustworthiness can end up pulling in a different direction from other things we might want to think of as virtues, for example generosity, kindness, or even spontaneity, so there can be tensions between these things. But, nevertheless, it is an ethical matter—being trustworthy and not breaking promises is an ethical matter. And it's not just ethically important, it's also practically important. We need to, at least, be able to give *the impression* of being trustworthy as this is crucial for all sorts of different relationships. If you don't appear to be trustworthy, other people are not going to want to let you get involved in their projects, to work with them, to engage in hobbies together, and so on, and that makes it difficult to get on in life.

NW: *Now, you've just said that you don't want this to be a matter of virtue theory, but Aristotle's discussion of virtue does give a nice framework for talking about character traits because he sees every virtue as lying between two extremes. So we've got trustworthiness in the middle, if it is to be classed as a virtue. I can imagine that on one end of the spectrum you have being completely untrustworthy—it's just random whether or not you fulfil commitments. But what's on the other end of the spectrum? Can you be hyper-trustworthy to the point of being not a good person, as it were?*

KH: I certainly think you can be overly obsessed with your own trustworthiness. There's a kind of 'clean hands' obsession that sometimes people can get into. Imagine the kind of person who is so worried about letting other people down or breaking promises that they're incredibly reluctant to make commitments or promises in the first place—that's someone who, while they may be trustworthy in the sense that they don't break their promises because they have so few promises, they're actually going to be difficult to have a relationship with, a friendship with, to work with. This is the kind of person who says things like: 'I'll try and be there but don't wait for me'; 'I'll text you later'; 'you know I think it's this but I can't be sure, you better check with someone else'. I think it's not that this type of person is hyper-trustworthy, but rather that they are so concerned not to break their promises, not to let people down, not to besmirch their honour, we might say, that they end up being very reluctant to make commitments in the first place or to agree to make definite plans.

NW: *Can trustworthiness come into conflict with other important values, other important traits that we have as moral beings?*

KH: Yes, I think it can. That's one of the things that interests me most in this area—the way in which our concern for trustworthiness, which is important, can push us in different directions to other impulses that we might also have (for example, an impulse to generosity, or to spontaneity, or to kindness to others). Often when people ask us to take things on, they really want us to say yes and agree to a new commitment. But sometimes we know that it's going to be difficult for us to follow through on that commitment, either because it's challenging in its own right, or because we know we've got a lot of other demands on our time. Sometimes the most trustworthy thing to do in that kind of situation is to say no, and as such to be disappointing to the person upfront. Yet that can feel ungenerous. We don't like to say no to people when they're asking us to do things, especially things that might be fun in their own right. But trustworthiness directs us to turn down new commitments when we're not going to be able to reliably fulfil them, whereas often generosity or kindness or spontaneity or helpfulness are directing us towards taking these things on. Now, you might think there's not really a conflict because in the end it's not generous to agree to things and then not be able to follow through on them. So there may be a way of finessing this. But even then, there's an epistemic challenge—a challenge about what we can know in this area. It might be that I'm not really quite sure what I'm going to be able to do. I don't know quite how difficult something is going to be. I don't know how much energy, or how much time, I'm going to have. And trustworthiness is always going to direct me to be cautious there—to leave a margin for error, a safety zone—so I'm offering to do less than I perhaps can do. Then again, generosity might instead point me towards upping what I can offer to do, upping my commitments to help out other people.

NW: *I can imagine somebody who's incredibly generous just giving away all their money very quickly and then not having money to give to somebody they promise to give it to.*

KH: I can imagine similar examples with the resource of time, which I think are really common. Say that we all have a fixed amount of time and we've got our own projects and things that we value and want to be getting on with, but we also have commitments to other people. And if we give all our time away to the people who are standing in front of us making the loudest demands, we can end up being untrustworthy by letting down other people who we may also have commitments to, but who are not quite so good at reminding us about those commitments or extracting our time from us.

NW: *So we've talked so far as if trustworthiness is always a really good thing. But there must be occasions where it's a bad thing. Say, for example, that I'm a torturer, and I tell you that I'm going to show up at 3:30pm. I do, I keep my promise, and I bring all my fiendish equipment with me—I'm completely trustworthy here. But it's not a good thing in this scenario.*

KH: Certainly there are promises and commitments that we make that should not be kept. Keeping promises is not always the most important thing to do. I'm reminded here of the really fascinating work by the social scientist Diego Gambetta, who has done a lot of work writing and thinking about trust and distrust and trustworthiness in the context of organized crime, particularly the Sicilian Mafia. And of course those contexts exactly are ones in which mutual trust is of crucial importance, where they all have to be able to trust each other. And yet what they're all working together to do and trusting one another to do is commit terrible crime. So I would say trustworthiness in that context is not admirable—it's not something that we should be recommending as a model to our children. Nevertheless, these people, these Mafiosi, are trustworthy to one another. And what that tells me is that trustworthiness is, in a sense, not an empty trait, but a formal trait—it's less substantive than some other positive traits. What it tells us to do is, if you've got a commitment, make sure you live up to it. That's what trustworthiness requires. It doesn't tell us *which* commitments to undertake in the first place or what sort of promises to make. One can be trustworthy without having a lot of the other important ethical virtues that are crucial to life.

NW: *Do you have a view about how best to cultivate trustworthiness of a good kind?*

KH: Yes. To some extent I think with young kids it's indoctrination. We have to teach them not to lie, and then a bit later on we have to try and teach them about white lies and when it's sometimes not always best to say things in front of grandma, and that kind of thing. So this is a challenge with children to train them up into trustworthiness. But with adults, if this is something you're thinking about in the first person, then you might ask yourself, how can I become a more trustworthy person? I think self-knowledge is important here—knowing what you can do and what's going to be harder for you. Knowing your strengths but also knowing your limitations is really crucial for knowing what kind of promises you can safely make and which ones are going to stretch you. And that's not to say that we should never take chances or that we should never offer to do things which stretch us. But it can often be useful to set the parameters to explain that this really is a situation in which I'm doing my best but perhaps I'm going to need some support or some more resources to get things done. I think another thing that can help us towards trustworthiness (although it's a bit of a privilege to be able to do this) is to be in a situation in which we can try and be explicit about when we're taking on new commitments and when we're not. That way, we are able to turn things down when we think they're going to be too demanding or push us into a difficult situation. But as I said, that is a privilege—not everyone is able to turn down yet another demand from their boss or yet another request to help out or to do something, even though that might lead them along the line of ending up being untrustworthy. In my work I try to understand how being in challenging or difficult social circumstances can actually make it harder for people to be trustworthy. If it's difficult to turn down commitments because you're at the bottom of the social heap, then that can make it harder for you to be trustworthy.

NW: *Trustworthiness as a concept isn't an abstract concept—it's very much concerned with how we live and what we do. And I imagine that reflecting on it could affect how I behave. Has it affected how you've lived your life recently?*

> KH: I think it has. I think it's made it easier for me to say no to new commitments (which is probably a good thing). It's easy to slip into feeling that saying no to other people is always selfish, that it's always a self-centred matter, and the most social or the most helpful thing is to say yes and to agree to more and more commitments. And I know that men do this as well but I suspect there may be a gendered aspect to this—that women are expected to say yes to things more often. But thinking it through and realizing that sometimes trustworthiness can require us to say no upfront to avoid disappointing people later on has helped me say no, because I can see that saying no to new commitments is actually a more helpful thing in the long run for other people, not just a selfish way of prioritizing my own needs and wants.

Further Resources

Diego Gambetta (2009) *Codes of the Underworld*, Princeton University Press.

Katherine Hawley (2012) *Trust: A Very Short Introduction*, Oxford University Press.

Katherine Hawley (2019) *How to Be Trustworthy*, Oxford University Press.

Carolyn McLeod (2020) 'Trust', *The Stanford Encyclopedia of Philosophy* (Fall 2020 edition), ed. Edward N. Zalta: https://plato.stanford.edu/archives/fall2020/entries/trust.

Onora O'Neill (2002) *A Question of Trust*, Cambridge University Press.

17

ONORA O'NEILL
Medical Consent

David Edmonds: *The United States of America may have the most litigious culture in the world, but Britain is catching up. Nowhere are the implications of this being more deeply felt than in the medical profession. Increasingly, patients are being asked to sign long and complex consent forms before doctors and surgeons will treat or operate on them. Baroness Onora O'Neill, a distinguished philosopher and former head of a Cambridge college, believes this trend has already gone far too far.*

Nigel Warburton: *The topic I want to focus on is consent in the medical area. Consent clearly means different things in different contexts. What is consent in the medical context?*

Onora O'Neill: It has been used in two contexts in medicine: one is in research on human beings, and the other is in medical treatment. Since the 1970s, consent has been taken to be absolutely fundamental for medical treatment, and that's why you have to sign a consent form when you have an operation or when you go to the dentist for a course of treatment. Of course, you don't sign consent forms for every single trivial thing. For example, when you go to your GP for blood tests, you don't sign a particular form permitting the taking of blood.

NW: *But that's presumably implied consent, because if I withdrew my arm, then I'm clearly not giving consent in that situation, and a doctor who continued to take blood would be doing something wrong to me.*

OO'N: Indeed, because they would have to override that implied refusal and in effect coerce you by sticking a needle into you and holding you down and all the rest of it. But usually implied consent is taken nowadays to be insufficient. People want *explicit* consent, and that means documents, signatures, sometimes witnesses to the signatures, record keeping... A lot of the reason that this has become so important is because people are fearful that there may be complaints or even litigation, and if they can demonstrate that everything that was done was something to which the patient gave his or her consent, then it is generally thought that's going to be quite okay. Not merely have we moved from a culture in which people relied heavily on implied consent, towards one in which we require explicit consent, we've also made a parallel move from being satisfied with, what you might call, very general unspecific consent, to demanding highly specific consent. The consent forms get longer and longer and longer.

NW: *In a sense that's actually repeating what happened in terms of international codes with the Nuremberg Code in 1947. In the wake of the horrors of involuntary medical procedures carried out by the Nazis, the Helsinki Code of 1964, as I understand it, actually refined the notion of consent still further. I wonder if you could say a little bit about that?*

OO'N: Yes, that's exactly the sequence with research ethics. It used to just be that you mustn't coerce, deceive, defraud—these are the Nuremberg standards and they are very reasonable standards. But now, if you look not just at the Helsinki Code of 1964, but at the latest edition from 2013, you will discover that they are asking the research subject to understand extremely complicated matters, like the research design, the aim of the research, the financial structures, and so on. I think it's quite questionable whether everybody who is capable of consenting to research can understand all of this detail. Although it's universally agreed that somebody who is a small child, or is senile, or has learning disabilities cannot give informed consent, what consent now amounts to is so complex that many of us who think we are reasonably bright can't really get our minds around the information that the consent procedures require us to get our minds around. That's a real problem.

NW: *If that's so, what safeguards can you put in place for the potential subject of a medical research experiment, apart from informing them in great detail about what may or may not happen as a result of the study?*

OO'N: In a way, it's an illusion to think that the consent procedure does that whole job. In fact, many forms of medical, health, and safety regulation will ensure that the whole process is organized so that the options presented to the research subject or the patient are themselves lawful, do not put anyone at unnecessary risks, and are done by people with the relevant training. It's a bit of an illusion that consent is the thing that makes it all acceptable. Consent is, I would say, necessary, but not sufficient. I believe that we should be more aware of other things that are equally necessary, rather than, as has become the tendency, to think that consent is the only ethically important thing.

NW: *That's really interesting, because it sounds as if the whole notion of consent is being driven by a kind of liberal philosophy underlying it all, perhaps inspired by somebody like John Stuart Mill—you should be free to do what you like and if you consent for certain things to be done to you, then it's not for the law to intervene.*

OO'N: Yet in fact it is not the case that the law doesn't intervene into whatever you consent to. For example, surgery between consenting adults is not lawful. Surgery is only lawful when done by somebody with the appropriate training, professional registration, in appropriate premises, and so on. So we are looking at one small part of the system for ensuring adequate standards in medical treatment when we look at the consent procedure. And my speculation would be that this focus has become so intense in the last thirty years because it is the consent that is seen as limiting the liability of the hospital trust or the professional staff in the event of any complaint.

NW: *Isn't it also possible that the emphasis is on consent because of the patient or subject's fear that their lack of consent might be overruled by somebody who thinks they know better than the patient about what's good for them?*

OO'N: Yes, that is very frequently said by people writing on the subject. Of course, patients have some much more serious fears than those. They have a tremendous fear—legitimate fear—of treatment that is extremely painful, of treatment that is very ineffective, and of not getting treatment. And on the whole, I don't think there's much evidence that people's main fear is that their doctor is going to experiment on them. Consent is useful because it is a sort of 'check point' whereby people have got some view of what's going on, and if they don't have any understanding of what's going on, then they cannot be denied medical treatment (it would be completely wrong to refuse medical treatment to someone who has dementia or learning disabilities, for example). But if you increase the standards to excessive heights then, of course, all of us are going to count as non-competent. I think that consent is useful, but insisting that it be highly specific and achieved by very complex procedures is probably illusory.

NW: *Could you give an example of the sort of thing that a highly intelligent person couldn't understand?*

OO'N: A surprising example is this: for a lot of people who take part in clinical trials of new drugs, where they are assigned to one or other arm of the trial on a *randomized* basis (and they don't know which arm of the trial they're in), if you asked them a month later, 'Why were you in that arm of the trial?', they will say, 'Oh, my doctor thought it was best for me'. That shows that they misunderstood the method of the inquiry. I don't think it necessarily means that they were in any way deceived or coerced—the information was given, but they happened to find the understanding of double-blinds or placebos or randomization difficult. These are fraught moments in people's lives—when you have an illness for which you're hoping there may be a better drug, you may be so keen to try the new drug that you just forget about the design of the trial or don't listen.

NW: *I could see another role for the act of giving consent, or being encouraged to give consent, is to open up a dialogue, because otherwise there's a risk that you'll just be treated by somebody who knows better than you what the right treatment is.*

OO'N: Well, of course, you do on the whole hope that you'll be treated by someone who knows better than you, or otherwise you would simply treat yourself! But you don't want them treating you with disrespect or coercing you. I think the real justification of consent is the classical one—that it is a sign that there has not been coercion, deception, or manipulation. Consent is not an exercise of autonomy. Most of us, when we say, 'Yes, take my appendix out' do not feel that we are exercising our autonomy in a very conspicuous way, but that's what we choose to have done, even if we can't at that moment get our heads around the details.

NW: *From the viewpoint of the vulnerable person making a decision, a long-winded process may be a good thing because it means they don't walk into a procedure without thinking it through.*

OO'N: Much depends on the complexity of the procedure and the risks attached. I don't think any of us wants a long-winded process for things like giving a blood sample or having our temperatures taken. If you're going to have major surgery with a range of more and less favourable outcomes, of course it does have to be a process of communication, and I don't think anyone doubts that. However, it is the attempt to routinize this which leads to extremely long consent forms, even for very routine interventions that patients find pretty burdensome. Yet patients are clever, and one of the things they do is this: when they're getting too long-winded an explanation, they say, 'Doctor, if it was your child, what would you decide?' And the doctor (who is not allowed to advise them because the process has to be non-directive) then will say, 'Well, if it was my child, I'd certainly do this'. Patients are very quick to work out ways in which to get the expert advice that the doctor is, in a way, not allowed to give within the consent process.

NW: *You're a philosopher and obviously your thinking on consent is coming from your philosophical framework. I wonder if you could spell out a bit where your notion of consent comes from?*

OO'N: Consent has been a central notion in political philosophy and in economics for several centuries. The whole social contract tradition, and its modern version called Contractarianism, and more generally liberal political philosophy has the idea that the consent of the governed is what legitimates government. Equally in market economics, it is consensual economic transactions that are legitimate, whereas, by contrast, theft, blackmail, and extortion are not. I come from this with the thought that consent is really best justified as a way in which we, on occasion, will allow other people who have obligations to us to waive that obligation. Let me give a medical example again. If I want my appendix out, I want the person who takes it out not to be taken before the courts for assault because they make a small hole in me. What I am doing here in consenting to it is waiving their obligation not to assault me. And I think that consent generally functions against a background of many other obligations which we selectively waive. The default position is that you can't assault people, you can't make holes in people, you can't poison people, and so on. But we do have reason sometimes to say, 'Yes, you may do this operation, although I know that it is, other things equal, quite bad for me', for example like chemotherapy.

We don't want people who administer chemotherapy to be punished as poisoners.

NW: *What are the implications of your ideas about informed consent for other areas of public policy?*

OO'N: I think one of the things I would say, framing all of this, is that a great deal of public policy is about the provision of public goods. In the medical area, that's public health, for example. In the economic area, it might be things like a stable currency or enforceable contracts. Consent is used all the time, and most of it is implicit consent. For example, you hand over your money and you get your sandwich. For more important transactions the consent becomes more explicit. For example, you take out a mortgage and you sign some pretty complicated documents. But I think we ought to recognize that medical practice spans the whole spectrum from the sandwich case to the mortgage case, and we don't need to take the procedures that are relevant for something like a mortgage case to deal with something like a sandwich case. You don't need to have the same sorts of informed consent that would be relevant to a transplant operation when what you are agreeing to is something relatively minor.

Further Resources

Nir Eyal (2019) 'Informed Consent', *The Stanford Encyclopedia of Philosophy*, ed. Edward N. Zalta: http://plato.stanford.edu/archives/spr2019/entries/informed-consent.

Onora O'Neill (2002) *Autonomy and Trust in Bioethics*, Cambridge University Press.

Neil Manson and Onora O'Neill (2007) *Rethinking Informed Consent in Bioethics*, Cambridge University Press.

18

KATALIN FARKAS
Knowing a Person

Nigel Warburton: *We use the verb 'to know' in many different senses. We know that 3+2=5. We know how to ride a bicycle. We might even talk about knowing someone in the biblical sense. But what is it to know a person? Katalin Farkas, whom I know a bit, explores this question.*

David Edmonds: *The topic we're talking about is what it is to know a person. Before we get into that, perhaps you can just sketch out where this question fits into questions about knowledge generally.*

Katalin Farkas: In the Western philosophical tradition, knowledge of truths has been the paradigmatic example of knowledge. At least ever since the Greeks, ever since Plato, people have been interested in the question of what it means to know something, i.e. what it means when we know how things are, or what it means when we know that something is true. Most analyses of knowledge analyse what it is to know a fact or a proposition or something that is true. But there are people who think that not all knowledge is knowledge of truths. For example, Gilbert Ryle suggested that we have practical knowledge, or knowing 'how', which is different from, and irreducible to, knowing truths. And knowing things or knowing persons is another candidate for a different and irreducible kind of knowledge.

DE: *So let's go through those types. Firstly, knowing a fact would be something like knowing that London is the capital of the United Kingdom.*

KF: Yes, exactly. It would be knowing *that* something is the case: knowing that $2 + 2 = 4$; knowing that London is the capital of the United Kingdom; etc.

DE: *Secondly, knowing how would be something like 'I know how to use this microphone to record an interview'.*

KF: Yes, people often refer to skills as examples of this type of knowledge, like knowing how to ride a bicycle, or knowing how to swim. And the idea there is that you can learn a bunch of facts or truths about riding a bicycle or swimming, and you still won't know how to ride a bike or swim just on the basis of knowing facts about them.

DE: *Thirdly, then, there's knowing things.*

KF: An example of knowing things would be knowing a place—you and I both know London. And knowing people—we have mutual friends so there are people we both know. Knowing a certain kind of feeling—knowing a feeling of sadness, knowing the feeling of joy—these are also examples of knowing things.

DE: *And it's interesting, isn't it, that in some languages (I'm thinking of German) they do have different words for these different types of* knowing. *In German, for example, 'wissen' means to know a fact, and 'kennen' means to know a person or a thing.*

KF: Exactly. In French there is a distinction between 'savoir' and 'connaitre'. In my mother tongue, Hungarian, there is a distinction between 'tudni' and 'ismerni'. And as you said, in German, there is a distinction between 'wissen' and 'kennen'. In all these cases, the second word is used when we are talking about knowledge of *things*, like knowing persons or knowing places.

DE: *It does seem like it's a very natural distinction. Let's talk about what it is to know a person. Do you know me?*

KF: I don't know you—I just met you!

DE: *So, if you were to leave this room right now and somebody asked, 'Do you know David Edmonds?' you would say 'No'?*

KF: Well, after today, I would say 'I met him once', which is an indication that we are perhaps on the way to getting to know each other, or on the way to developing knowledge of each other, but that we are not quite there yet. Obviously, this is going to be a slippery slope. But in the central sense of knowing a person, I think knowing a person presupposes that you met several times and you have developed some kind of relationship with that person.

DE: *Let me suggest a counterexample to that. I have just been researching a character, namely a woman who saved many academic lives, from the 1920s to 1930s for a BBC programme. I've done so much research on her that I feel like I know her. (For your information, the woman was Tess Simpson: http://www.bbc.co.uk/programmes/b08pgm4b.)*

KF: It's one thing to say that you *feel like* you know her, and it's quite another thing that you *actually* know her. Notice why you felt that you had to qualify it: why did you have to say, 'I feel like I know her' rather than 'I do actually know her'? One interesting thing is that you can't know someone who is dead. If you have a friend who passed away, you don't say, 'I know them'; rather you say, 'I knew them'—so you put 'know' in the past tense, and I think that reflects the fact that interpersonal knowledge or knowing persons is a relationship that is created and sustained through meetings and certain kinds of interactions.

DE: *What about fictional characters? If I've read every single one of Agatha Christie's books, can I then say that I know Hercule Poirot—in that I know how he would react in certain situations?*

KF: I do not want to deny that this is how we use the phrase 'knowing someone' in some cases. I think that is true. But there is another sense of knowing someone which is very important, which is reflected in saying things like 'I know a lot of things about David Edmonds, but I don't really know him because we just met'. It is reflected in the fact that when someone passed away you put 'knowing' in the past tense— you say that I knew this person or I used to know someone. If you're talking about an old school friend, then you say, 'I used to know him twenty years ago' because that was the time when you had that kind of relationship. So I think when you 'know' someone like Hercule Poirot, then you know a lot of things about him, but you don't know him in the sense that you know your wife, or you know your mother, or you know your friends, or you know your colleagues.

DE: *What happens if we met every day for the next year, so we fulfilled the main criteria, but I was very bad at reading minds because, say, I was mildly autistic—could I then be said to know you?*

KF: This is a very difficult question because it's difficult to know what goes on exactly in an autistic person's mind. But when people defend the idea that interpersonal knowledge is a symmetrical relationship, they call attention to the fact that most of the time, this relationship consists of reciprocal reactions. As such, I react to you as a person and you react to me as a person. I take you in as someone who is saying things to which I have to respond in some way, and you take me in that way too. Undeniably, some people fall short of that idea. And to that extent they can't get to know me very well. They will know me to some extent. But I think that what we are after when we're talking about interpersonal knowledge is the reciprocal relationship that exists in most cases—this is what we can develop when we face other subjects.

DE: *The inter-subjectivity is interesting because if I know that that door over there is painted black, it doesn't require anything to come back to me from that door, as it were. But you're saying that knowing a person requires these two minds to meet somehow.*

KF: Yes. Maybe I could say here that words (and the meanings we give to certain words) do not matter that much. The question at hand has been 'Is there such a relationship that matters in our life?' People clearly understand it when I talk about knowing a person and what I mean by its being symmetrical. Is that an important relationship? Whenever I put forward the claim to philosophers that knowing a person is a symmetrical relationship, they immediately come up with counterexamples: 'I could say that I know this person even though they don't know me'; 'I know a fictional character'; etc. So, I say, 'okay, fine'. But don't you agree that there is something important happening in our life when we meet people and we develop this relationship with them? That's something that is the basis of other interpersonal relationships so it's very important in our life. And I think it's not unnaturally expressed by saying that 'I know this guy, I know him very well'. Knowing people seems to be a precondition for other kinds of relationships that give the meaning of life, like friendship, love, cooperating with people, or being accomplices. It doesn't make sense to say that you're friends with someone if you don't know them; it doesn't make sense that you're in a loving relationship with someone without knowing them. So it seems that this kind of relationship requires you to take in the other person as a person, and they take you in as another person—that's the basis of all our interpersonal relationships. As such, in a way, the exact use of the English word 'know' is not even that important. The important thing is: is there such a relationship; is that important; does that matter; does it simply consist of knowing a bunch of facts about another person or not?

DE: *And is it linked to predictability, in this sense, that if I know you, I can almost predict how you would respond in certain situations? I understand your dispositions; I know that in this situation you're likely to storm out of the room in a huff; or you're likely to be particularly generous in another situation.*

KF: I think that is a big part of it. That is a consequence of knowing someone. But notice that this is something that you could know about a person you haven't actually met. For example, about the early twentieth-century figure whom you studied—and maybe you read a lot of recollections about them—or your fictional character. You would know all these things about them. Also, all this knowledge could be put in the form of knowledge of facts. If annoyed, X will do this; if happy, X will do this. This is a *consequence* of having the interpersonal relationship, but it doesn't exhaust it.

DE: *So the crucial difference between knowing a person and knowing a fact, at least in some cases, is the inter-subjectivity.*

KF: It is partly the inter-subjectivity. And I also think that it's not an entirely cognitive relationship. Knowledge of truths—the central example of knowledge that has been studied in the Western philosophical tradition—is a kind of cognitive achievement, it's a possession of a true belief. Whereas I think that interpersonal knowledge is partly non-cognitive. That's why your remark about the autistic person was very much to the point, because an autistic person could be very advanced cognitively, but if they have something missing on the social or emotional side, then they will be deficient in interpersonal knowledge. The idea is that this interpersonal knowledge is the basis of other interpersonal relationships (like friendship, love, or camaraderie) and it is partly an emotional-social relationship, rather than a cognitive relationship. I have an analogy that I think illuminates the nature of interpersonal knowledge. It's another sense of knowledge—knowing in the biblical sense. Knowing someone in a biblical sense means having had sex with them. That meaning of knowledge is not entirely unrelated to the central sense of knowledge; it's not just a complete coincidence that we use the same word for 'knowing facts' and 'knowing someone in a biblical sense'. But there is clearly a different meaning. And it refers to a relationship that is interpersonal and inter-subjective. It's not a cognitive achievement (it's some kind of achievement, but not a cognitive achievement). Having sex with someone is clearly not reducible to factual knowledge. You probably gain a lot of factual knowledge if you have sex with someone, but the actual relationship is not *reducible* to factual knowledge. So my view about interpersonal knowledge is that it's analogous to this. It's a relationship between two people that produces factual knowledge, but it's not reducible to factual knowledge, and its nature is different. It's not entirely cognitive.

DE: *This conceptual mapping of different kinds of knowledge and the different categorizations of knowing is fascinating and very compelling, but why should we care?*

KF: Aristotle's *Metaphysics* starts with the sentence: 'All men by nature desire to know'. Hopefully he means all *women* also, who by nature also have a desire to know! Seeking knowledge is a very central enterprise for human beings. Seeking knowledge is an effort to understand the world, to engage with the world. So the question for epistemologists (for people who study the nature of knowledge) is what form this engagement can take. That's why it's very interesting that people say that practical knowledge is different from factual knowledge: because it indicates a fundamentally different kind of engagement with the world which is basic to who we are. And when we're talking about interpersonal knowledge, and how it's distinct from factual knowledge, then we are highlighting another aspect of what human beings are, and how we engage with the world.

Further Resources

Katalin Farkas (2019) 'Objectual Knowledge', in J. Knowles and T. Raleigh (eds.) *New Essays on Acquaintance*, Oxford University Press, 260–276.

Ali Hasan and Richard Fumerton (2020) 'Knowledge by Acquaintance vs. Description', *The Stanford Encyclopedia of Philosophy*, ed. Edward N. Zalta: http://plato.stanford.edu/archives/spr2020/entries/knowledge-acquaindescrip.

Eleonore Stump (2010) *Wandering in Darkness*, Oxford University Press, chapters 3 and 4.

19

JENNIFER NAGEL
Intuitions about Knowledge

David Edmonds: *Do you know that after I finish this cue, Nigel will begin an interview? Or do you just believe it? We go through life drawing what feels like natural distinctions between knowing something and merely, say, suspecting it. I know that Jennifer Nagel is an expert on our intuitions about knowledge.*

Nigel Warburton: *The topic we're going to focus on is intuitions about knowledge. Could you give an example of what an intuition about knowledge is?*

Jennifer Nagel: Right now, I know that you're aware that we're speaking to each other. I know that you're looking at me. And these are things that I'm doing naturally. I'm detecting a state of knowledge in you just by looking at you, just by being aware of which way you're facing. And this is actually a very ordinary part of human social existence. We walk around detecting what other people know, what they think, what they want, and what they believe. We interact as human beings. We're not just seeing each other as moving limbs. We're seeing each other as having mental states, as having these inner conditions that are guiding what we do.

And that's something that's very natural to our existence—
we're not doing any calculating when we see other people as
knowing things. If you look at natural language, the verb 'to
know' and the verb 'to think' are among the most frequently
used verbs in the English language, and that's something that's
true across many languages. In English, 'know' is the eighth
most common verb in the language. There's something
comparable in Mandarin, in Russian, in Welsh, and in all kinds
of other unrelated languages. So we talk all the time about
states of knowing and thinking. And although the philosophical
question 'what is knowledge itself?' is one of the most difficult
questions that there are in philosophy, it's a question that in
practice we're answering all the time—for example, in our
daily conversations, or when we talk about whether people
know that they're about to be fired, or whether somebody
thinks that they're being followed. We are making some kind
of distinction between knowing and thinking all the time, it's
part of our natural intuitive social navigation, and that's
something that I think is philosophically very interesting
to explore.

NW: *I know you're expecting me to ask another question now and
you have an intuition that I'm going to do that, but it's nothing
magical or mystical. The word 'intuition' is sometimes used in a
way which is different from the way philosophers use it, but when
philosophers use it it's talking about a kind of gut reaction, rather
than implying some kind of psychic power that gives me the ability to
detect things.*

JN: Right. It's not a psychic power but it is a fascinating and
mysterious power. There's a word for it in the psychology

literature—it's usually referred to as 'mindreading', which makes you think of something like a circus act. There's something very mysterious about it. How exactly do you tell whether somebody knows that something is true? It looks like that would be some kind of invisible hidden state. We're certainly not consciously calculating what people know. We're doing this on the basis of reading a bunch of cues in the other person's behaviour, even if we're not trying to: we watch what they're looking at; we listen for certain patterns in their speech. You have a feeling that someone knows something or doesn't know something, and there's a lot of interesting psychological work exploring how it is that you can tell what people know and don't know.

NW: *What I just said—that I know that you're expecting me to ask a question—I could contrast that with the thought that you believe I probably will ask a question. There's quite a strong contrast there, between belief and knowledge. That's something that philosophers have been very interested in.*

JN: Yes, they have. And there's some general features of that contrast that philosophers have really attended to over the years. One of the most important characteristics of knowledge, as contrasted with mere belief, is that knowledge has to attach you to a truth. If you *believe* that something's the case, you might or might not be right about that. But if you *know* something's the case, then the thing you know actually has to be so. That's also one of the chief characteristic differences between thinking and knowing—whether you're guaranteed to be latched onto a truth. For example, if I say the two sentences: (1) Jack thinks that he's being followed; (2) Jill knows that she's being followed. The first of those statements is a statement about Jack—it doesn't commit us to the truth of Jack actually being followed. Maybe Jack thinks that he's being followed but it's not really happening. But when I say Jill knows that she's being followed, I'm already communicating to you that it's true that she's actually being followed. So that's one of the key differences between those two verbs.

NW: *There must be something more to knowledge than just the truth of what you come to believe because it matters how you come to believe it, surely.*

JN: Absolutely. As such, it seems like another one of the conditions on knowing is that you should have good evidence for what you believe. So if you're just making a lucky guess, we don't ordinarily credit you as having knowledge. Interestingly, though, it seems that you can have situations in which you have a belief and you've also got good evidence for it and your belief is true, but intuitively you still seem to fall short of knowing. Therefore, knowing seems to be something distinct from having a true justified belief.

NW: *Historically, a lot of people have thought that knowledge was true justified belief. Could you give an example of a true justified belief that isn't genuinely knowledge?*

JN: Here is a great, very simple, example from Bertrand Russell. A man wonders what time it is and glances at a clock. The hands are pointing to three o'clock and he forms a judgement that it's three o'clock. It looks like he's justified, in virtue of looking at a clock that tells the time. And let's say this belief is actually true. But let's add a twist to the story— the clock he's looking at is broken and the hands haven't moved for the last forty-eight hours (that is, since three o'clock a couple of days ago). Do we still want to say that this man who's looking at the broken clock knows that it's three o'clock? Now, this is actually an empirical question. And in some of my experimental work, I've asked people who aren't philosophers, 'Does this man know what time it is?', and the majority answer with a 'No'. Most people don't want to attribute knowledge in that case, even though you've got someone there who has a true justified belief. There's a name for this kind of case in philosophy. These are known as 'Gettier' cases, after Edmond Gettier, who wrote a very influential three-page paper outlining a couple of these cases back in 1963. That paper was taken to refute the classical analysis of knowledge as justified true belief, because you can come up with these funny scenarios in which you've got a true belief, which is held for what looked like good reasons, and yet intuitively the person seems to fall short of having knowledge.

NW: *Was Bertrand Russell with his stopped-clock example the first one to identify this kind of problem?*

JN: Interestingly, Russell didn't advance that case as a case where somebody had a justified true belief that was falling short of knowledge. He was just talking about *true belief* (not justified true belief) being insufficient for knowledge. These cases all have been recognized for a long time in the history of philosophy. You can go back all the way to the eighth century, to the Indo-Tibetan philosopher Dharmottara, who has some great examples. I'll give you one of his cases. It involves a fire that's being built to roast some meat for sacrificial purposes. The fire has just been lit, so it hasn't yet produced any smoke,

but the meat's been placed over the fire and the smell of the
meat has attracted a great cloud of insects. In the distance, a
man looks up and sees the dark cloud on the horizon, and says
to himself, 'There's a fire burning at that spot'. Dharmottara
asks whether the man knows that there's a fire burning at that
place. After all, there he is, relying on what looks to him to be
smoke, and making the very natural, well-reasoned inference
that there is a fire there. And he's right, there is a fire there.
But Dharmottara suggests that this isn't knowledge—the man
doesn't know that this is the case.

NW: *In this example, the man is right that there's a fire, yet it seems he
hasn't discovered that by a particularly reliable method. But why would
the reliability of the method matter if he's got the right answer?*

JN: It matters if what we're trying to do is figure out the
nature of knowledge itself. We're trying to figure out what
our inner checklist might be to ascertain knowledge. On what
grounds are we able to say that intuitively 'this isn't knowledge'? What is it that we are spotting? Philosophers have tried
to advance theories about what exactly it is that we are
spotting. One very popular theory that came out in answer to
Gettier's paper in 1963 (and also, actually, back in the eighth
century) was that what goes wrong in these cases is that they
are relying on a false belief on their way to the truth. In other
words, somehow attaining knowledge is like crossing a
wooden bridge, and if there's one rotten plank on the way
over, then you're not going to make it. So you might think we
could just repair that classical analysis of knowledge by adding
this in: instead of saying knowledge is justified true belief, we
should say knowledge is justified true belief that has been
arrived at without relying on any false belief along the way.

NW: *So the idea is that, if you reveal to the guy in Dharmottara's example that he's looking at a cloud of insects rather than smoke, he will realize that he's got a rotten plank on his way to making that judgement, and reject it as actual knowledge. And furthermore, what he really wants is a bridge to knowledge which has got intact planks all the way through. As such, when he sees something that looks like smoke, he wants it really to be smoke, otherwise it won't provide a way to knowledge.*

JN: That's right—so the idea is, if you can banish false beliefs from your path to knowledge, then you'll be golden. It's a simple answer, but it turns out actually that it is not quite right. Dharmottara himself came up with another type of example to show that you can reach a judgement without relying on any false judgement along the way, and you still have something that feels intuitively like it's not quite knowledge.

NW: *What was that example?*

JN: It involves somebody who's making a judgement perceptually. Instead of thinking on the basis of a signal (like a cloud of smoke) that something else is true (like there being a fire burning over there), it's somebody who's just making a single judgement all at once. The story goes like this. There is a thirsty desert traveller who seems to see shimmering water ahead of him on the horizon—a beautiful oasis. And of course he's hallucinating, since he has been travelling in the desert and is so thirsty. But he goes running down the hill towards where he thinks there is water. And interestingly, coincidentally, it turns out that when he gets there, there *is* water there, hidden under a rock. Dharmottara's question then is, as the desert traveller stood at the hilltop looking down and thinking that there's water down there, did he know that there was water at that spot? And again, it seems like he didn't know this, even though his judgement was just an automatic perceptual judgement, not an inference from anything false, and what he was judging was actually true.

NW: *So what conclusions are we supposed to draw from these examples? You've given us cases of unreliable ways of learning things, and reliable ways of learning things which have got a flaw in the system still. What's the philosophical impact of these?*

JN: The philosophical impact is actually very difficult to trace. Philosophers really hurled themselves at those difficulties throughout the last half-century, trying to come up with more and more elaborate analyses of knowledge. There's actually some pessimism now that we're ever going to get a satisfactory recipe for constructing knowledge out of true belief plus other factors. Some philosophers, most notably Timothy Williamson, have argued that that project of coming up with an analysis of knowledge as true belief plus other factors might be a bad project. It might be that actually knowledge is the more fundamental primitive term, and belief is something that's a derivative notion. As such, you wouldn't be able to define knowledge in terms of belief plus other factors. I'm actually quite sympathetic to that idea. I'm sympathetic in part for reasons that come out of my understanding of our natural psychological 'mindreading' capacity.

NW: *That's really interesting. It sounds as if what philosophers have been trying to do is to take widespread intuitions about knowledge and then create some kind of algorithm that will match that, so that we can work out what's under the hood—as it were—what the machinery is that gives us these gut feelings about whether a case is genuine knowledge or not.*

JN: That's right. I think that's something that a lot of philosophers have tried to do. We're now in a position where we can be a bit more self-conscious about that project as we come to understand more about that underlying machinery. One of the things we've been able to discover is that the machinery has some natural limitations and some built-in defects. And the more you understand about those, the more accurately you can then calculate your story about the underlying nature of knowledge. For example, we have a natural way of detecting heat and cold. But it was known for a long time that that natural system can't be straightforwardly (and in a very simple way) reporting objective states of affairs outside of you. If you immerse one hand in a bucket of cold water and one hand in a bucket of hot water for a while, and then bring them together and dip both hands into a basin of warm water, your two hands will report to you contradictory things about what's going on. We actually have something similar with states of knowledge. If you describe a scenario in one way, then describe the same scenario in a slightly different way, you can provoke conflicting intuitions about whether the person you've just described does or doesn't have knowledge. In other words, you can discover contradictions and paradoxes in your natural intuitions about knowledge.

NW: *Is there a simple example of that?*

JN: Sure. Let's go back to Russell's stopped-clock example. Here's a simpler version of that story where there's no funny business going on: a guy looks at a working clock, and reads the hands accurately and makes a judgement that it is three o'clock. Do we say that this person knows what time it is? Actually, intuitively, we do. Given this simple version of the story, overwhelmingly people say the guy knows what time it is. But I can tell this story in a slightly different way, by just adding a fact that we all knew all along anyway, which gets most respondents to say that the person doesn't have knowledge of what time it is. So here's how I do it. I just add the sentence: 'although this clock is working, sometimes clocks are broken, and John hasn't looked at the clock for long enough to tell whether or not this might be the case'. Most people then deny knowledge in this version. The interesting question is whether you can tell a story about knowledge—a consistent story about knowledge—which takes onboard both what people say about the ordinary unelaborated scenario, and what people want to say naturally about that same scenario with this moment of doubt inserted from the perspective of the narrator. And that actually turns out to be a very hard thing to do.

NW: *This is all fascinating, but does it really answer the question 'What is knowledg?'?*

JN: It takes quite a bit of work to answer that question. If you go back to the temperature from your hands analogy, we did actually get to a place where we could articulate something objective that's out there: molecular kinetic energy, something that our natural thermoreceptors do track, although they don't track it perfectly. We were only able to get to that place by discovering a lot about the molecular structure of the world and about our own thermoreceptors. And I think we're just starting to go down that path as far as knowledge is concerned, too. If you think about that example of the clock which might or might not be broken, you could try to develop a really complicated theory of knowledge or of language about knowledge to try to adapt to that. Some people have advanced a theory called 'Contextualism' where the relationship that's picked out by the verb 'to know' actually changes in different conversational contexts. So if I start mentioning possibilities of error, suddenly the verb 'to know' means something much stronger and much fancier than what it means in an ordinary conversation down at the bus stop about whether you know if the bus is coming in five minutes or not. Contextualism as a linguistic theory about the verb 'to know' is actually really complicated and really subtle. But there are other ways to go. You could stick to a plain, old-fashioned, invariantist theory of knowledge, where knowledge actually always picks out the same relationship (in that it does not vary). And you could say that maybe our perception of this relationship got a bit twisted or a bit skewed when I started mentioning possibilities of error gratuitously in that clock case. If I stipulate that the clock's not broken, but I start mentioning possibilities of error, what I'm doing is getting you to start thinking about your judgement about the time in a different way. And interestingly, when you're evaluating what someone else thinks, if you've got a more elaborate way of thinking about the problem than they do, you'll be inclined to misread *their* way of thinking about the problem. This is a known bias of our mindreading system—it's called the 'egocentric bias'. It's possible that our natural mindreading equipment starts misfiring when we mention these possibilities of error, in just the same way that your natural temperature-detecting equipment can misfire if you immerse your hands in both hot and cold water before bringing them together in the warm pool.

Further Resources

Edmund L. Gettier (1963) 'Is Justified True Belief Knowledge?', *Analysis*, 23:6, 121–123.

Jonathan Jenkins Ichikawa and Matthias Steup (2018) 'The Analysis of Knowledge', *The Stanford Encyclopedia of Philosophy*, ed. Edward N. Zalta: http://plato.stanford.edu/archives/sum2018/entries/knowledge-analysis.

Jennifer Nagel (2014) *Knowledge: A Very Short Introduction*, Oxford University Press.

Stephen H. Phillips (2013) *Epistemology in Classical India*, Routledge.

Stephen H. Phillips (2019) 'Epistemology in Classical Indian Philosophy', *The Stanford Encyclopedia of Philosophy*, ed. Edward N. Zalta: http://plato.stanford.edu/archives/spr2019/entries/epistemology-india/.

20

SUSAN JAMES
Michel Foucault and Knowledge

David Edmonds: *Here's a philosophical quiz question: what do sex, power, punishment, and madness have in common? Answer: they're all topics of books written by the prolific twentieth-century French philosopher, Michel Foucault. Susan James teaches at Birkbeck College and is fascinated by Foucault. A theme that runs throughout Foucault's work, she says, is his preoccupation with what counts as knowledge.*

Nigel Warburton: *The topic we're going to focus on is Foucault and knowledge. Just before we get on to knowledge, could you say something about who Foucault was?*

Susan James: Foucault was a French philosopher, born in Poitiers in the 1920s. He died at the age of fifty-eight in 1984, so it wasn't a very long life. He was educated in Paris and then subsequently had an interesting career—some of it being a regular academic in France, and some of it being a cultural diplomat in Sweden and Poland. He lived for a bit in Tunisia. But when he came back to France he worked at the University of Clermont-Ferrand. He then set up the Department of Philosophy at the University of Vincennes in the late 1960s where he organized an amazing and revolutionary department of some of the greatest young philosophers of his time. And in 1970 or so, in his mid-forties, he became a Professor at the Collège de France. This was a pretty grand thing to become in French cultural life. And that's where he stayed, giving a series of public lectures each year (as professors there have to do), and at the same time, during the 1970s, becoming an international superstar.

NW: *His work covers quite a wide range, but are there common themes that emerge from it?*

SJ: On the face of it, his work looks incredibly diverse and not about what you would usually think of as philosophical problems. His first book is about the history of madness. He also wrote books about the history of psychology, the history of prisons and systems of punishment, and a three-volume history of sexuality. So you might wonder, what on earth is going on here? And in a way it's a good question. Foucault was working this out himself and no doubt he wasn't completely clear where he was heading. But when he was asked about this trajectory, he sometimes said that there is one set of issues— one question—that concerned him: the relationship between the subject and truth. I think the key issue running through his work is fundamentally something about what it takes for us to be able to function as people who are able to be knowers—who are able to tell the truth and know we're doing that—and who are also able to be the objects of other people's knowledge.

NW: *This talk of subjects and objects is interesting, but quite alien to ordinary conversation. Why does he use the term 'subject'?*

SJ: I think it's a matter of historical inheritance. Foucault grew up, after all, during the post-war period in France. The philosophy of the subject, something like existentialism for example, was all the rage.

NW: *Sartre's existentialism, for example, is often criticized for being almost ahistorical, as if the subject just exists and always has existed through time. But for Foucault, everything turns on when you happen to be alive.*

SJ: Yes, that's absolutely right. I think he sees himself as resisting existentialism on that score, and also resisting Marxism, conceived as a theory that posits the idea of a truly human being who will emerge once the veils of ideology are torn away. Foucault came to feel that the way to approach the questions he's interested in is genealogical, and his debt to Nietzsche is enormous. Genealogy offers him an approach to understanding the subject that's attractive in several different ways. First, genealogy tries to unmask and discredit the idea of an essence or an origin, so that there is no essential subject. There is just the history of subjecthood—being a subject of knowledge and being the object of knowledge. With that comes a certain instability that interests Foucault very much, because for him, as for Nietzsche, it's vital that these things change, and you have to understand *how* they change. That's why you're right to say that the story depends on when you live and where you are. But genealogy is also a form of critique. It shows you that subjectivity is a historical phenomenon, and that our own subjectivity is contingent. It can change. And at least in the latter part of his career, Foucault views this as a liberating insight.

NW: *The story of genealogy is to go back into the past and see that people do things differently in certain areas. So for Foucault, that means talking, for example, about how madness was treated or how punishment was meted out. This is not the genealogy of looking at genetics, but of looking at how different practices evolved.*

SJ: Yes. And Foucault says that one of the things he likes about genealogy is that it's concerned with the details. You have to look in all sorts of odd places for the insights that you're going to pull out. Things that nobody thinks are important may turn out to be significant. Foucault therefore uses an enormously wide range of sources—archival materials, paintings, memoirs, and histories of this and that. He also draws on philosophical texts, but it's important that they're just one kind of source among others and are not in any way privileged. His idea is to hit upon strange and unexpected moments of change that reveal the contingency of our own subjectivity.

NW: *Perhaps we could have an example of that.*

SJ: In his first book, called *Madness and Civilization*, we get the beginnings of this approach. He's interested in the way that madness is understood as the dark side of reason and delineates three stages in the way that reason and madness are contrasted. One is the idea that madness is a form of truth—a form of insight—as in the prophet or the seer. The next is that people who are mad are lumped together with people who are criminal. They're just excluded and put outside civil and political life. Then in the eighteenth century we see the beginning of the idea that criminality and madness are *not* the same—that the mad have a particular problem that is a *medical* problem—and this is the beginning of treating madness as a disease to be cured rather than just condemned. There isn't any essence of madness. The way we understand it changes over time.

NW: *And that strategy of looking at how practices evolve carried on through his book* Discipline and Punish *as well.*

SJ: Yes, very much so. In *Discipline and Punish* a more fully worked-out genealogical approach is applied to the history of punishment. The book begins with an incredibly dramatic incident of the judicial execution of a French regicide called Damiens, and a very detailed discussion of the unspeakable tortures that are visited on his body. Aside from Foucault's great eye for a literary coup, this is meant to serve as a point of contrast to the penal processes he goes on to discuss, which mainly emerged in the eighteenth century. Again, Foucault's point is that forms of punishment change, and that the way they change reflects a changing knowledge of the subject. People come to be imprisoned rather than killed. But imprisonment also comes to be an incredibly complicated and detailed regime where every moment of the prisoner's life is measured, observed, and organized. The model for this regime is Bentham's idea of the Panopticon, where the prisoner is constantly under observation, and is punished if they don't stick to their regime, for instance by making their bed at exactly the right moment in the day. The aim of the process is to get prisoners to internalize these demands, so that whether or not they're being observed (and they don't know when or whether they're being observed), they conform to the regime. They become subjects who impose a certain order on themselves. Foucault does something with this idea which (like most things he does!) is very original. He thinks of the Panopticon not just as a model for a prison, but as a general model for a range of institutions that begin to proliferate around this time. They all instil what he comes to call 'discipline'. So he studies not just prisons, but also military academies, schools, factories, and so on—and he finds that all of them develop regimes organized around observation.

NW: *It strikes me that he's got this fantastic eye for particular details that are fascinating in themselves, and then looking to such detail becomes symbolic of a whole way of thinking about things.*

SJ: Yes. But Panopticism, as it's sometimes called, is not just a symbol. Foucault uses it to characterize what he sees as a general phenomenon—a set of practices for forming subjects. He also emphasizes that these are practices which work on the body as well as the mind. They make people who know certain things. For example, a prisoner knows how to be a docile law-abiding person, the factory worker knows how to work on a production line, and so forth. But they also make bodies. For example, you can recognize a soldier by his bearing. Somebody who has been properly educated knows how to write in a particular way—they know how to sit properly in order to write and so on. It's also vital to Foucault's story that the emergence of the kind of discipline we've been discussing is tied to the development of social sciences—to forms of knowledge like criminology, psychology, and educational theory. These forms of knowledge underpin and are expressed in disciplines that make certain kinds of people. So all the detail is in the name of a big philosophical project, about the way that we become subjects who know certain things and who are also known about in certain ways.

NW: *Is there a place for freedom in all of this? It sounds as if the movement that he's describing through history is one of greater control over objects. Subjects become objects almost, to be moved around by people who may not even realize they're part of a system.*

SJ: I think the answer to that is complicated, and Foucault makes it complicated partly by the way that he describes the phenomenon he's talking about. He describes disciplinary practices and the social scientific disciplines with which they're entangled as forms of power. He wants to draw attention to the fact that power (as he understands it) is not something you possess and exercise over me, but rather something that's spread through all these practices such that they partly determine what I can do and what you can do. So it can sound pretty scary and Orwellian. To add to this, there's a very pessimistic chapter at the end of *Discipline and Punish*, where Foucault seems to say that this kind of power is accumulating, and the more social scientific knowledge advances, the more of it there will be. But then, we're bound to wonder, what happens to freedom? Some of Foucault's critics raised that question, and argued that he had destroyed the individual—that there is no individual freedom in his model. Foucault didn't exactly concede this objection; he always said later that the way he thought about power had been completely misunderstood. Power as he understood it is trying to modify somebody else's behaviour—trying to get somebody to do something. And while power in this sense is ubiquitous, one shouldn't think of it as always bad. On the contrary, Foucault says, it can be productive. Surely there's nothing wrong with the fact that there are power relationships between lovers, or that there is a very productive form of power in schools where people teach other people things they really need to know. So power isn't always bad. Power is just a condition of our lives. The question is, rather, how it circulates and how it's distributed. This is what really interests Foucault. He wants to draw a contrast between situations of domination where the circulation has got stuck, and situations in which it's more evenly distributed, or where it's reversible.

NW: *But on some readings, Foucault does present histories of how society operates almost like a machine, and the subject becomes a cog in the machine. To resist power, then, we would presumably need some kind of conscious freedom, and not just the illusion of freedom.*

SJ: Absolutely. And I think it's in recognition of that point that Foucault's work takes a somewhat different turn in what turned out to be the last phase of his life. He wants to try to show how one can produce a genealogy of the subject that, instead of focusing on social practices that seem to form us from the outside, focuses on social practices through which we come to be able to function as individuals who are free in the sense that they can monitor their own knowledge and take responsibility for what they know and do. Foucault obviously doesn't want to say that there's some kind of free *self* which stands outside of this historical genealogical process. So he's going to take the same genealogical approach as before to the history of the inner aspect of the self. Take the question of what it is to be able to act freely. Not anything you do will count as acting freely—some of your actions may be discredited as mere madness. (Indeed, we've got lots of ways of excluding types of behaviours we don't approve of.)

Foucault's general point is that we have to learn to be the kind of subjects who are capable of acting freely, as this capacity is understood. For example, you have to learn to control yourself, so that you become somebody who isn't just a wanton, and isn't just crazy. Perhaps one of the most interesting parts of Foucault's intellectual odyssey are his explorations of the historical practices through which people have cultivated the capacity to act freely; and here Ancient Greece offers an interesting case study. Foucault describes a case discussed by Seneca, where Seneca says, 'when I go to bed at night, and when my wife has finally shut up, I think over my day and ask myself whether I lived well and whether I did what I ought to do'. Greek literature is full of examples like this. Think of Marcus Aurelius in his *Meditations*—it's all about exercising self-discipline. Foucault takes that as a cultural example of the way that social practices are necessary for us to come to be the sort of people who can act freely, and who can also be knowers, in the sense that we can be trusted to tell the truth and can take responsibility for ourselves as truth tellers.

NW: *But this does sound like a kind of cultural historical relativism where what you know is not objective; it's always relative to your personal circumstances, historically and culturally.*

SJ: Well, yes and no. I think Foucault is not terribly interested in questions like 'Were the ethical beliefs held by the Greeks right?' or 'Was Freud right about hysteria?' Of course, he thinks you can ask these questions. But the question he wants to ask is always 'what does it take for ethics or Freud's analysis of hysteria to count as knowledge?'

NW: *So it's a kind of sociology of knowledge, a kind of description rather than an evaluative judgement of whether the kind of knowledge that people are acquiring within this framework is good or bad?*

SJ: Again, this is complicated. Foucault says that the point of a genealogy is to initiate a sort of critique. It's not exactly a critique that tells us whether things are right or wrong. It's a critique which shows that the standards of truth, or of right and wrong, that we rely on are contingent. That being so, we shouldn't be too glib and too confident that we understand the truth, or that our normative standards are the right ones.

NW: *Foucault died in 1985—very young, as you've mentioned. Has he just been sidelined as an interesting quirk in the history of French philosophy, or is he somebody whose impact is still felt?*

SJ: I think his influence has been enormous and is very much present, though not always acknowledged. For one thing, there's been a big genealogical turn in contemporary philosophy, and Foucault's work is largely responsible for this. At the same time, his ideas have also shaped other debates within political philosophy—about liberty, about the status of political agreement and disagreement, and so on. Perhaps most consequential is his analysis of power. One sees its influence, for example, in the huge debate he had with Habermas, where Foucault criticized what he saw as Habermas's utopian idea of a form of communication beyond power. In addition, his revolutionary take on knowledge is reflected in the ever-increasing interest in the social dimensions of epistemology. Foucault's genealogical approach has also been enormously helpful within feminist philosophy. He has been criticized by some writers for not saying anything much about gender relations; and some critics have argued that his view locks women into practices where they are dominated by men. But as I've tried to explain, I think this last criticism is misplaced. It seems to me that thinking genealogically about gender has had a liberating effect, and that this owes a great deal to Foucault.

Further Resources

Michel Foucault (1977) *Discipline and Punish: The Birth of the Prison*, translated by A. Sheridan, Penguin.

Michel Foucault (1986) *The History of Sexuality*, vol. 3: *The Care of the Self*, translated by R. Hurley, Penguin.

Michel Foucault (1994) 'The Subject and Power', translated by L. Sawyer, in J. Faubion (ed.) *Power: Essential Works of Foucault*, vol. 3, 326–348, Penguin.

Ian Hacking (2002) 'Making Up People', in his *Historical Ontology*, Harvard University Press.

Colin Koopman (2017) 'The Power Thinker', *Aeon*: http://aeon.co/essays/why-foucaults-work-on-power-is-more-important-than-ever.

21

KATE KIRKPATRICK
The Life and Work of Simone de Beauvoir

David Edmonds: *The best-known book of the French philosopher Simone de Beauvoir is* The Second Sex, *published in 1949. Beauvoir was an existentialist and a feminist. She had a long relationship with another philosopher, Jean-Paul Sartre. That relationship is relevant for how her work has been read. There is a famous line in* The Second Sex: *'One is not born but rather becomes a woman'. But is that the correct translation? Kate Kirkpatrick has written a biography of Beauvoir and believes a study of her life can help us interpret her philosophy.*

Nigel Warburton: *The topic we're going to talk about is the life and work of Simone de Beauvoir. Now, you've written a biography of Simone de Beauvoir—but you're a philosopher. Why would you be interested in writing about her life rather than just looking at her ideas?*

Kate Kirkpatrick: I started off by being interested in the ideas, and then I discovered that, in fact, significant aspects of her life—neglected by a lot of philosophers in both the English-speaking and French-speaking scholarship—have led me to understand the ideas differently.

NW: *Simone de Beauvoir is very famous as an existentialist thinker, and as a great feminist thinker with her book* The Second Sex *particularly. What sort of ways was she misunderstood? Since she left huge numbers of letters and an autobiography, she's somebody who is very widely written about in her lifetime and afterwards.*

KK: Well, the word 'existentialism' plays a significant role here, because it was coined in the 1940s by Gabriel Marcel to refer to Sartre's philosophy, and it was applied quite quickly thereafter to Beauvoir's novels, when in fact she denied that some of her novels were existentialist (especially *The Blood of Others* which came out just after the end of the Second World War). There are several cases in Beauvoir's life where she's been accused of popularizing Sartre's ideas, or of not being critical of Sartre. When she died, *Le Figaro*'s obituary headline said that her work was more popularization than creation. Another claimed that she was as imaginationless as an inkwell. And you frequently find the verb 'applied' being used, claiming that Beauvoir applied Sartre's ideas, even in *The Second Sex*. Yet actually there are a lot of reasons to think that is not the case.

NW: *As you say, there is a view of Simone de Beauvoir's work that claims that essentially what she was doing was taking Sartre's existential philosophy and applying it in other areas—particularly in relation to the ways that women become who they are within a culture which has certain expectations of them and roles that they're expected to play. But your research suggests that that is a complete caricature.*

KK: Yes. The research goes much further back than the 1940s, when Sartre and Beauvoir both became famous intellectuals in France. In fact, there are some significant publications that have come out over the past decade and a half in France which have challenged the traditional narrative about the relationship of Beauvoir and Sartre—one of the most significant from the point of view of their philosophical relationship is her student diaries which were published in 2008. Reading those diaries shows that, before Beauvoir met Sartre, she was already interested in the question of what it means to become a 'self'. She was reading philosophers who are well known in the English-speaking world, including Nietzsche, who famously said we should become who we are. But she was also reading less well-known French philosophers like Maurice Blondel, who said that the substance of man is his action and that any individual is what he makes of himself. This is an almost verbatim anticipation of what Sartre became famous for saying in *Existentialism Is a Humanism*. It is well known that Jean-Jacques Rousseau claimed that man is born free but is everywhere in chains, whereas Alfred Fouillée (who is a philosopher who worked on freedom and determinism) disagreed and said that one is not born free, but rather becomes free. So in French, Fouillée wrote 'on ne nait pas libre, on le devient'—and that is exactly the formulation of the sentence that Beauvoir became famous for in *The Second Sex* when she wrote 'one is not born, but rather becomes, a woman'. I think when we read the literary allusions that she is making in *The Second Sex*, we see that it's not an 'existentialist' question in the narrow sense of the word. The questions that Beauvoir was asking were the same questions she asked in the 1920s before she met Sartre: 'how do I become a self?'; 'who will I be? Is it something that exists before I act, or do my actions make me who I am?'. Then, when we get to *The*

Second Sex, the question is: 'why is it that men are encouraged to have projects outside of love—to have vocations that aren't restricted by biology—and how can we encourage women to see freedom and becoming themselves as a project?'

NW: *That's fascinating. So what is often taken to be Sartrean actually has its roots (as these early journals suggest) in Beauvoir's childhood—she must have been very young when she was writing these diaries because she met Sartre when she was quite young, didn't she?*

KK: Yes. She met Sartre when she was twenty-one, but already before meeting Sartre she was writing novels or beginnings of novels—one is called 'An Attempted Existence'. There is another where she says that she wants to chart the discovery of a woman that she is free to choose herself. So before she even meets Sartre she is thinking, 'why is it that men are enjoined to become themselves—to develop projects for their lives—and the same injunctions don't seem to be communicated to women?'

NW: *Does knowing that Simone de Beauvoir was probably conscious of the Fouillée formulation of that phrase when she wrote this line about becoming a woman affect how you interpret it?*

KK: It does affect how I interpret it, because I think it fits into her project of wanting women to become free, to become themselves, and to set projects for their lives that aren't constrained by the mythology of being a woman that she rejects in *The Second Sex*. However, that line has had an entire book dedicated to it. It's a much-contested line. It's translated in different ways in the two English translations of *The Second Sex*. One of them included the indefinite article and says, 'one is not born but rather becomes *a* woman', which emphasizes the particularity of individual women. The other, more recent, translation does *not* include the indefinite article and says, 'one is not born but rather becomes woman', as though one's becoming places one in a certain category. Personally, I prefer the former translation because it emphasizes the particularity of individual existences and the particularity of individual women being able to pursue their own projects for their lives. There are reasons for and against each translation, but Beauvoir's own behaviour shows how much she valued individual women and how much she wanted to support them in becoming who they were.

NW: *What do you mean, 'by her own behaviour'?*

KK: It's not widely known that after the 1950s (especially when she began to publish her autobiography) she corresponded with her readers in extraordinary volume. She set aside an hour per day to write to readers. There are around 20,000 letters at the Bibliothèque Nationale from her readers. In many cases women would write to her saying, 'I felt so alone, I felt like no one had ever felt like this, being dissatisfied with the things that I was supposed to find fulfilling'. There were people who felt unfulfilled by being housewives and mothers, and there were aspiring writers. In some cases she had correspondences that lasted up to ten years. Sometimes she would meet those who wrote to her, she would read their literary works, and in some cases she would promote their careers. She thought that particular women needed to be able to make choices about what their projects were for their lives. As such, to the extent that she emphasized particularity, I think the 'a' is a good thing in that much-contested sentence.

NW: *Do you think that knowing about the original philosophical source for this pattern of the quotation—the rhythms of the sentence, and so on—and also knowing about Simone de Beauvoir's assiduous letter-responding to particular people affect how you understand that line?*

KK: It does, because it helps me understand what her project was in writing *The Second Sex*. She situated it in a long historical discussion about what it means to be free, and she was in fact dismissing Sartre's definition of freedom as he gave it in *Being and Nothingness*. But her independence of thought, before and after meeting Sartre, has been under-recognized.

NW: *So that's part of your project in writing a biography, as I understand it—to give her her appropriate place and acknowledge that she wasn't simply a mouthpiece for Sartre. That's a very common view of her philosophy—that when she's writing novels she's doing one thing, but when she's doing philosophy she's really just part of 'Team Sartre'.*

KK: Yes, it's a view that has been unfortunately promulgated even by feminist philosophers. She's been accused of being Sartre's disciple, and of being content to play this role, even though in many places she explicitly rejects it. She was critical of Sartre's philosophy in person and in public, at the very least from 1944 onwards. In 1943, Sartre's *Being and Nothingness* was published which advanced the Sartrean account of freedom that was sometimes called 'radical freedom'. He said that we're condemned to be free because we can't avoid our own freedom, but that freedom is a process of being alienated from ourselves and from others. Beauvoir agreed that human beings are free in a metaphysical sense. But she thought that Sartre needed to keep a distinction closer to what Descartes had between freedom and power. We can recognize that all humans are free metaphysically, but not all humans have the same power to exercise their freedom. And so in the 1930s, she had articulated this objection in conversation using the example of a harem. What good is it to be free if you're kept in some man's harem? And then in 1943 she was invited to write her objections to Sartre's view of freedom, and she did this in the essay that was published in 1944, called 'Pyrrhus and Cineas'.

NW: *So, what you're saying is that Simone de Beauvoir was actively criticizing Sartre, not buying into this radical freedom—the freedom that many people felt and still feel goes far too far. Radical freedom seems at times to imply that you can will yourself into anything—that if you want to get away from depression by the power of thought, you can just do it.*

KK: Yes. So she explicitly rejects Sartre's view of freedom, and moreover her criticism was that existentialism did not contain an ethics. In a 1945 radio interview she said that what she was setting out to do in 'Pyrrhus and Cineas' was to provide the ethics of existentialism.

NW: *And was that something different from Sartre's approach?*

KK: At that point Sartre didn't have an ethics. By the time he starts to write things that look ethical in *Existentialism Is a Humanism*, Beauvoir has already published 'Pyrrhus and Cineas', and he's started to adopt certain aspects of her view. To give one example, the idea that existentialism is a humanism: Sartre was on the record, prior to this point, for saying that humanism is shit!

NW: *You're suggesting that by doing biographical research, by looking at what Simone de Beauvoir wrote and said, you can see that the direction of influence was often from Simone de Beauvoir to Jean-Paul Sartre, and not always the other direction.*

KK: Yes. I think it's difficult to say that there is a clearly identifiable direction of influence in all cases. Their contemporaries wrote about them in the 1930s, that their relationship was one of constant conversation. My project hasn't been to show that Sartre stole Beauvoir's ideas—other academics have written books making those sorts of claims and I think they go too far. But there was a rich philosophical friendship here that generated intense disagreements, and the intense disagreements haven't been recognized because Beauvoir's originality has been overlooked.

NW: *And why do you think her originality has been overlooked?*

KK: Partly because 'Pyrrhus and Cineas' wasn't translated into English until 2004. There's a kind of ahistorical way of doing philosophy which sometimes involves neglecting the texts in their original languages. I think it's partly because she claimed herself that (and this is a very controversial and bothersome claim to many feminist philosophers) she was not a philosopher, whereas Sartre was. But when she said that, she was, I think, actually being critical of Sartre. This is because one of the distinctions she makes in other places about different types of philosophers is that some are 'systems' philosophers and some are 'subjectivity' philosophers. To the extent that someone emphasizes a philosophical system—someone like Spinoza or Leibniz—would never write a novel, for example. But to the extent that someone is interested in the subjectivity of an individual person trying to become free and discover what their projects are for their own life, they tend to consider writing in a wider variety of literary forms. She placed herself in the latter category. She doesn't want to be a philosopher whose work isn't relevant to life. She wants philosophy to be something that's lived. And she thinks that literature can facilitate that in some cases better than philosophy (in the systematic sense) can.

NW: *That's interesting because that suggests that when we read a simple translation saying, 'I'm not a philosopher', we get it wrong because we don't understand the context in which she said that—the wider context being that she had these different conceptions of different styles of thinkers.*

KK: Yes, and I think this is partly something that gets lost in translation between the French philosophical context and the Anglo-American context of philosophy today. A philosopher in France, like Pascal, can write in multiple literary forms. Voltaire writes satire of other philosophers, including Pascal. And so there are multiple forms or genres of philosophical writing in France that are recognized as philosophical. Whereas in the world of English-speaking philosophy today, the constraints tend to be a bit narrower.

NW: *Some hardline philosophers will say that it's all very well to write biographies, as it's kind of interesting gossip, but it doesn't really relate to philosophy. They might ask why we would want to know about their life, when what we want is to engage with the arguments and the ideas. What would you say to them?*

KK: I think that case might be easier to defend with some philosophers rather than others. Take the example of Immanuel Kant. I'm not sure what it benefits us to know his walking habits in Königsberg. In the case of Beauvoir, however, her life has been politicized and her philosophy has been dismissed (or even unrecognized) to the extent of not being seen as worth translating for several decades. So I think in her case, the very way her life has been politicized raises philosophical questions.

Further Resources

Simone de Beauvoir (2004) *Philosophical Writings*, ed. M. A. Simons with M. Timmerman and M. B. Mader, University of Illinois Press.

Debra Bergoffen and Megan Burke (2020) 'Simone de Beauvoir', *The Stanford Encyclopedia of Philosophy*, ed. Edward N. Zalta: http:// plato.stanford.edu/archives/sum2020/entries/beauvoir.

Laura Hengehold and Nancy Bauer, eds. (2017) *A Companion to Simone de Beauvoir*, Wiley Blackwell.

Kate Kirkpatrick (2019) *Becoming Beauvoir: A Life*, Bloomsbury.

Margaret A. Simons, ed. (2006) *The Philosophy of Simone de Beauvoir: Critical Essays*, University of Indiana Press.

22

KATHERINE J. MORRIS
Merleau-Ponty on the Body

David Edmonds: *Jean-Paul Sartre, Simone de Beauvoir, Michel Foucault, and Albert Camus achieved celebrity well beyond France and well beyond philosophy. They had a friend, Maurice Merleau-Ponty, who was much less famous. A leading exponent of phenomenology (the study of how things appear to us, the way we are in the world, and how we experience it), Merleau-Ponty argued that knowledge comes through the body. Katherine J. Morris believes Merleau-Ponty deserves wider recognition.*

Nigel Warburton: *The topic we're going to focus on is Merleau-Ponty and the body. Just to begin, who was Merleau-Ponty?*

Katherine J. Morris: Merleau-Ponty was a twentieth-century French philosopher, a friend and colleague of Jean-Paul Sartre and Simone de Beauvoir, and he lectured partly in philosophy. One of the things that's interesting about him was that he engaged very much with the human sciences, such as anthropology, sociology, and especially psychology. He held the chair in Child Psychology and Pedagogy, which he took over from Piaget, and he died terribly young, in his early fifties.

NW: *Merleau-Ponty was a phenomenologist—that is a difficult word to say, but what does it mean?*

KJM: Phenomenology is a very broad way of doing philosophy, devised by Edmund Husserl, and taken up in various forms by people like Martin Heidegger and Jean-Paul Sartre, then Merleau-Ponty and various others since then. Its basic approach is to first of all describe the world of human experience—to describe the world *as experienced*. And the further stage is to try to work out the essential structures of human experience. I suppose you could say that it's a little bit similar in some ways to what Kant was doing when he described the structures of the experienced world as space, time, and causality. One thing that the phenomenologists add to those basic structures (apart from elaborating them in wonderful detail) was the body (about which Kant said nothing), but also seeing others as an essential structure of human experience.

NW: *So this emphasis on describing lived conscious experience led Merleau-Ponty to focus quite heavily on the body. What was his general approach there?*

KJM: I think it might be helpful to give a distinction which you can make in German but you can't make in English between *Leib* and *Körper*. *Leib* is often translated as 'the lived body', whereas a *Körper* is the 'body-thing'. When most of us hear the word 'body', we tend to think of the body-thing—that is, an anatomical physiological object. And that's very much *not* what he means when he talks about the body. He means *Leib*—a lived body. Merleau-Ponty famously says that 'my body is my point of view on the world, not just another object in the world'. The so-called existential phenomenologists—Sartre and Merleau-Ponty—were drawing very much both on

Heidegger and Husserl, but what they took from Heidegger in particular was his basic idea that human beings are 'being-in-the-world'. The idea is that we would not be human beings unless we were in the world, and the world would not be the world that it is—the lived world, the life world, the *Lebenswelt*—unless it were a human world. And even if Heidegger never quite noticed that in order to be in the world you must be embodied, Sartre and Merleau-Ponty certainly did.

NW: *There is a tradition of talking about our experience of the world through the senses and putting together a picture of the world via those senses. This is very much a Humean and Lockean empiricist position that Merleau-Ponty didn't have much time for. Is that right?*

KJM: Certainly, I think one of his main targets was empiricism. And one thing that you notice about empiricism is that, as soon as you try to make it concrete, it's bound to treat the body as a mere object—as a kind of relay station for sensations and nothing more. But one very characteristic feature of empiricism (partly because it thinks of the body that way) is that it thinks of perception as consisting of separate sensations coming from each individual sense. For example, when I say, 'I see a lemon', what I am strictly speaking seeing is a bunch of different sensations: I'm seeing yellow sensations via my eyes; I'm feeling tactile cool sensations via my hands; I'm tasting sour sensations through my tongue, etc. That seems to Merleau-Ponty to be a misdescription of how we actually experience the world. What we perceive are *lemons* which are whole, and we don't really distinguish these separate sensory inputs. For Merleau-Ponty, it's really important that it's the body which unifies those separate sensations.

NW: *Just to be clear, when you say that Merleau-Ponty is anti-empiricist, it's not that he's anti all empirical research—he's not anti the idea that we do science and study how people actually behave?*

KJM: Indeed not, no. What he is anti is what is sometimes called 'scientism'. Scientism is rather similar to what Anglo-American philosophers call 'naturalism': first, the idea that the methods of the natural sciences are the only methods for achieving knowledge; and secondly, the idea that what the natural sciences say there is exhausts the nature of reality (so-called ontological scientism or ontological naturalism). But if one can do science without scientism, then Merleau-Ponty is all for it. He really engages with the sciences—most prominently psychology—in all of his works.

NW: *One feature of our body is that we do things repeatedly—we get into habits. I know that for Merleau-Ponty, the study of habit was quite revealing about humanity and our position in the world.*

KJM: It's really interesting that very few philosophers have actually looked closely at habits. Let's be clear that by 'habit' Merleau-Ponty doesn't just mean *bad* habits, like smoking cigarettes or biting your nails. A better term might be something like 'motor skill', like being able to drive a car or being able to type. I think there are a number of reasons for his interest in this topic. One is that, as he says, the acquisition of a habit is really difficult for either empiricists or intellectualists to explain. For an empiricist, a habit or a motor skill can really be nothing but a concatenation of atomic reflexes. And Merleau-Ponty argues very persuasively that that's precisely not what such things are. If I'm a pianist, I can play a piano sonata with very little new practice on a piano that is bigger or smaller than the one I'm used to. Even if I'm used to driving with a right-hand-drive car, I can, without having to learn over again from scratch, pick up the habit of driving a left-hand-drive car. We really can't make sense of habits as the empiricist would suggest as a kind of concatenation of reflexes. But likewise, the intellectualist really would be troubled by habits, because when we're actually acquiring a habit, for example learning how to drive a car, our minds have to be going all the time—we have to be thinking about it. I remember, because I relearned how to drive a car when I came to the UK many years ago, that I really did have to learn from scratch. When learning to drive, you may be thinking, 'oh my goodness, there are so many things I have to think about all at once—I have to think about pressing on the gear shift and pushing it forward and pressing on the clutch and looking in my mirror all at once', and you're almost paralysed with all the things you have to think about. Once you learn how to drive, though, your body does your thinking for you, so to speak. You no longer have to think about it at all. And of course the intellectualist is going to say, 'oh, that's because all the thinking has now become unconscious'. Intellectualists, rationalists, and transcendental idealists like Kant imagine that it's all got to be done by the mind or by thought. But it is not conscious thought that goes into my just being able to do it, as it were, automatically, so it must be unconscious thought. For Merleau-Ponty, it's the body doing your work for you, as it's relieving you of the necessity of having to think about what you're doing.

NW: *You've mentioned that Merleau-Ponty is an existential phenomenologist, that he's allied with Sartre and Beauvoir in that respect.*

Does that mean that he thought that we are fundamentally free, and unconstrained in our choices with what we do with our bodies?

KJM: I think the notion of habit is really important to him here. Habits, as he understands them, are both constraining and liberating. If we didn't have the motor habit of being able to speak or being able to read, then we couldn't speak or read. So these motor skills are clearly liberating. The whole process of socialization is a process of the acquisition of motor habits. We could not do anything unless our body had this wonderful ability to acquire habits. But at the same time, they can be constraining. In fact, when Merleau-Ponty is arguing against Sartre's rather radical version of freedom, he points out that if I've been going about in the same way for the past thirty years (he uses an example that Sartre uses of having an inferiority complex, which may not sound like a motor habit, but it does involve motor habits—the way you walk, the way you speak, the way you interact with others), then it's really difficult to change. And that's something that Sartre really never recognizes—he recognizes it's difficult but he doesn't see why. Merleau-Ponty has this notion of 'sedimentation': the way in which your past practising of a skill on the one hand, and the past ways of behaving on the other hand, become sedimented in the body. As much as it's hard for a river to move in different directions, it becomes harder, though not impossible, for you to start moving in different directions if you've always been doing something in a particular kind of way.

NW: *We talked about relations with lemons and with cars, but the body in its relation to other people seems fundamental for us.*

KJM: It seems to me that Merleau-Ponty sees a role for the body in our relations with others that even really brilliant philosophers like Sartre didn't quite see. In the tradition of Anglo-American philosophy, there's a so-called problem of other minds, where the idea is somehow that what I encounter when I encounter another person is just this body (or this *Körper*, this body-thing, this physical object moving about), but then there seems to be a real issue about whether that body hides a consciousness or a mind. Sartre made some really important moves against this simply by pointing out that what we encounter when we encounter another person isn't a mere physical object moving about: we don't see, for example, a clenched fist and a face turning red. What we see is a man in a certain situation, perhaps a little urchin has just stolen his wallet and his face turns red and he clenches his fist. And if we see the body of the other *holistically* in a situation, then there's no issue about whether we can see his anger. That seems to me to be a really important move that Sartre makes. But Merleau-Ponty makes a really interesting further move, because he wants to say that we actually understand others *with our bodies*. He starts out this discussion with the example of an infant, who, when I take one of his fingers playfully and pretend to bite it, opens his own mouth. Surely the infant is not arguing from analogy by thinking, 'when the other person opens his mouth he intends to bite, and when I do that I intend to bite, so I'm going to play the game and pretend to bite'. Of course not, that would be ridiculous for an infant to do that! Rather, the infant's body contains within it a body schema, which is what Merleau-Ponty calls a system of equivalence, such that the look of your mouth when it opens and the feel of its mouth when it opens are equivalent. There is no issue about making any inferences. When you open your mouth, it's as if it feels your intention in its own body. Now, he does say that at a very early stage, an infant doesn't fully distinguish itself from its caregiver, so it's not even an individual. So there can't be this gap between the infant and its caregiver. But he also crucially says that we *do* become individuals and we gradually separate from our mother, but we retain something of that bodily reciprocity. As such, even now, especially with somebody with whom I share a class and a culture and so on, I retain that immediate bodily understanding, so when I reach for my glass, for example, it doesn't even occur to you to wonder what I am doing. Your body immediately recognizes my intention in my gesture.

NW: *This is all fascinating and it seems to me that the idea of the body understanding other people and the world is important. Yet, it's odd that it features so little in recent philosophy. It seems that Merleau-Ponty's work on this has been eclipsed by people like Sartre and Heidegger, and other philosophers of mind who've emphasized the cerebral.*

KJM: I find it puzzling, though I also think it's probably explicable. But first of all, I don't think Sartre and Heidegger figure that much yet in mainstream Anglo-American philosophy. They perhaps figure a little bit more than Merleau-Ponty simply because they were better self-publicists than he was. Furthermore, Merleau-Ponty was in opposition to what I called 'scientism' or what Anglo-American philosophers call 'naturalism', and the trouble is that it seems to me that a great deal of at least Anglo-American philosophy very much adheres to naturalism.

NW: *Has Merleau-Ponty had an influence beyond philosophy?*

KJM: It is interesting that you should ask that. I think he's been hugely influential outside of philosophy, in other disciplines.

Certainly one discipline in which he's been very influential is in anthropology, and more specifically, in medical anthropology, where on the one hand you've got biological understandings of diseases and on the other hand you've got cultural and social understandings of diseases. I suppose that the notion of the body as a thing—a *Körper*—goes very nicely with the biological understanding of disease. But for an understanding of disease from a cultural or social perspective, a Merleau-Pontian understanding makes a good deal more sense. He's also been very influential in sociology, and more recently in theology. He's also certainly been very influential in literary studies, and feminist studies have picked up a lot on Merleau-Ponty. I've even heard of Merleau-Pontian geographers. So his influence is all over the place. It's just philosophy, or at least Anglo-American philosophy, that tends not to have recognized him yet.

Further resources

Thomas J. Csordas (2002). *Body/Meaning/Healing*. Palgrave Macmillan.

Kathleen Lennon (2019) 'Feminist Perspectives on the Body', *The Stanford Encyclopedia of Philosophy*, ed. Edward N. Zalta: http://plato.stanford.edu/archives/fall2019/entries/feminist-body.

Maurice Merleau-Ponty (2002) *The Phenomenology of Perception*, translated by C. Smith, Routledge Classics.

Maurice Merleau-Ponty (2008) *The World of Perception*, translated by O. Davis, Routledge Classics.

Katherine J. Morris (2012) *Starting with Merleau-Ponty*, Bloomsbury.

Iris Marion Young (1990) *Throwing Like a Girl and Other Essays in Feminist Philosophy and Social Theory*, Indiana University Press.

23

ALISON GOPNIK
Hume and Buddhism

David Edmonds: *The Buddha was born in around the fifth century* BCE, *probably in modern-day Nepal. David Hume was born in the eighteenth century in Scotland. By all accounts, both were corpulent chaps. But what, if anything, do their philosophies have in common? And is it possible that Hume was influenced by Buddhism? Alison Gopnik, a renowned psychologist and philosopher, has been investigating a possible link.*

Nigel Warburton: *The topic we're focusing on is Hume and Buddhism. What's the connection between these two? Because apart from their physique, it's not obvious.*

Alison Gopnik: When you look at a lot of Hume's philosophical ideas, they're strikingly similar to some of the ideas that are in the Buddhist tradition. I got interested in this particularly because of Hume's ideas about the self. Hume has a radically new idea about the self—quite different from the ideas that people had before. So, someone like Descartes thinks that it's obvious that you have a self—you look into your head and there it is; it exists, and it continues over time. In fact, Descartes thinks that the only thing that you know for sure is that you have a self. But Hume does something really surprising, which is to say that when you look inside your head, you see thoughts and ideas and beliefs in combination, not anything that's *you*, the self behind all of them. And that debate is very relevant to contemporary debates in psychology—one of the big discoveries in psychology in the past twenty years or so has been that it looks as if there's not much evidence that we do empirically have a single continuous self. The work that I've done in developmental psychology, in particular looking at children, suggests that we invent the idea of a continuous self rather than discover it.

NW: *That's really interesting. So you're saying that children become storytellers of their own lives, as it were?*

AG: Exactly. There's quite a bit of evidence that autobiographical memory (which is the most central thing that we think of as evidence for ourselves) is actually something that's developed and constructed—it isn't there to begin with. Now, it turns out that if you look at the Buddhist tradition, specifically to one of the central texts in Buddhism called 'Nāgasena's questions', you will see that it makes exactly the same argument—almost word for word—that Hume makes about the lack of existence of a self.

NW: *So Hume's got this really nice analogy of introspection to viewing something like a theatre stage with characters going across it. But introspection gives him no sense of a self that is there all the time.*

AG: The analogy in the Buddhist tradition (which is also a wonderful analogy) comes in this dialogue between the great sage Nāgasena and the King. The King says, 'Nāgasena, you're crazy, you can't believe that there's no self—look, who am I talking to?' And Nāgasena says, 'Well, your majesty, first tell me: how did you get to the palace?' And he says, 'I came in a chariot'. And Nāgasena says, 'But what is that chariot—is there something about the chariot that goes beyond just the reins and the wheels and the body of the chariot?' And the King says, 'No, of course there's no extra thing, the chariot is just the combination of all those things'. And Nāgasena says, 'That's just the same as with the self—there's no Nāgasena aside from my thoughts and beliefs and other parts of my experience'. This is exactly the same argument that Hume is making.

NW: *That's an interesting story, and it is interesting to see the parallels between the Buddhist sense of the self and David Hume's. But that's just a parallel. How could we ever know whether there's any causal influence there? Some people have speculated that Hume may have been influenced by Buddhism, but it seems like you are now telling a particular story.*

AG: Well, in fact, for most of history, people would have thought that there couldn't possibly have been any connection. And when I first read these two passages, I thought there couldn't be any connection. This is because Hume was writing in the 1730s, and at that point almost no one knew anything about Buddhism in Europe—Buddhism hadn't really been discovered in Europe. And what's more, if you look at the official history of Hume, people say that he was writing the *Treatise of Human Nature* in an obscure town in France, very far away from everything—'rusticating' is the word that his biographer uses. However, when you actually look carefully, there *was* someone who knew about Buddhist philosophy in great detail in the 1720s—Ippolito Desideri. He was a Jesuit missionary who had travelled all the way to Tibet from Rome just in order to convert the Tibetans. But when he actually got to Tibet, the Tibetans said they were happy to be converted, but first he must make sure that he understood what the Tibetans' religion was like, and prove that his religion was superior. So he spent five years in the monasteries in Tibet studying the Tibetan philosophical and religious tradition. He learned Tibetan, he translated the great philosopher Tsongkhapa's books into Latin, and translated Latin books into Tibetan. And he wrote a book himself, which to this day is one of the very best accounts of Tibetan philosophy. The only trouble was, at the time, because it was a book about Tibetan philosophy, it was squelched by the church and it mouldered in the Vatican unread as a manuscript until the twentieth century. So someone *did* know about Buddhist philosophy.

NW: *But how could Hume possibly have known about all of this?*

AG: Well, Desideri came back to Rome in 1727. In fact, he was kicked out of Tibet by the religious authorities. It turns out that he came back through a town in France called La Flèche, which just happened to be where, eight years later, Hume was writing the *Treatise*. And what's more, it turns out that the reason he came through La Flèche was because, in this tiny little rustic town where Hume was sitting and thinking 'by himself', there just happened to be one of the largest Jesuit centres of learning in all of Europe—the Royal Collège at La Flèche. And that had actually been Descartes' university. It was not an obscure place at all, it was a place where there was a great deal of intellectual activity and thought. So, Hume wasn't sitting there being isolated. Hume was right in the midst of this college of Jesuits—a college that Desideri had actually visited.

NW: *Presumably, too, Hume would not have travelled with an entire library—he'd have to have access to books as a thinker and a writer.*

AG: Exactly. In his letters, he states that the college at La Flèche had 40,000 books, which meant it was an enormous library at the time. It was actually a better library than he would have been able to find in most of England at that point. Also in his letters, he explicitly says, 'I'm here in La Flèche, it's much better to have a good library than it is to have university teachers, it's great to be here, there are people to talk to, there's this college of Jesuits . . .'. And much later in his letter about miracles he actually says, 'this idea came to me as I was walking in the College of La Flèche with a Jesuit of some parts and learning'. So then the great question for me was, who was this Jesuit of some parts and learning? Who could he be?

NW: *Presumably you couldn't ever actually discover that. I mean, it's just a conversation in La Flèche hundreds of years ago. How could you possibly work that out?*

AG: It was surprising to me that no one had actually tried to figure this out. Thankfully, though, the Jesuits kept extremely good records of everybody in all the colleges. So what I did was I actually went to the Jesuit archives in Rome (which was a great adventure). And it turns out that in the Jesuit archives it actually lists the names and information about everybody who was in any of the Jesuit colleges. And when Desideri had written about his trip to La Flèche, he said, 'I spent a lot of time talking to Father Dolu'. And when you looked in the Jesuit archives, sure enough, there's someone named Charles François Dolu, who was there throughout the time that Hume was there, and was also there at the time that Desideri was there. And Dolu turns out to be this fascinating character. He knew all about science. He'd actually been involved in the expedition from France to Siam in the 1680s. He'd taken telescopes, and he'd actually done astronomical observations in Siam. And Siam was a Buddhist country. So he had also lived right next door to a Buddhist monastery, and many of the Jesuits had gone back and forth between the two places. Rather than thinking of Hume as being off in this obscure place, he was right in the centre of the one place in Europe in the 1720s where people knew about Buddhist philosophy.

NW: *This is circumstantial evidence. Do you think it's strong enough to suggest that Hume was really influenced by Buddhism?*

AG: We don't know. For me, the clincher is that we have one wonderful description of Charles François Dolu. And it describes Dolu as being an incredibly charming man who understands wit better than any man of the world does. And from everything we know about Hume, if Hume had found someone who was funny and interesting and knew about science and had travelled all around the world, it seems clear that Hume would have really enjoyed talking with him. That's what Hume was like—Hume was witty and knowledgeable and loved talking to other people who were witty and knowledgeable. It's at least interesting that ideas about atheism, ideas about anti-foundationalism, particularly these ideas about the self were ideas that Hume very likely would at least have heard of.

NW: *Are there any other aspects of Buddhism that have parallels with Hume's philosophy?*

AG: Yes, Hume was very interested to begin with in the idea of atheism. He wrote a lot about it, even before he wrote the

Treatise, and he thought a lot about whether it was possible to actually have a civilization without God. And one of the things that was very striking to everybody who found out about Buddhism was that here was this highly evolved civilization in which explicitly there was no sense of a foundational God (there were gods, but these were kind of mythological gods, more like spirits than a single central God). The Buddhist position was in other ways also like Hume's. Buddhists argued against the idea of any kind of foundationalism. So sunyata (which is the doctrine of emptiness) is the doctrine that there isn't anything beyond experience, that experience is all there is. There isn't even, as Descartes had said, the self that was behind experience. A way of thinking about Hume's moment in history is that scepticism had become increasingly articulated, and you could start out being sceptical about the specific ridiculous miracles of religion, then you'd be sceptical about God, then you'd start being sceptical about whether there's any independent reality (which is the route that Descartes discussed), then, well, at least you have the self, but you can be sceptical about that too! And the question is what happens when you take that sceptical route? And exactly what happened in the Buddhist tradition was that Buddhists take that sceptical route, and then at the end of it say that it doesn't matter—actually everything's fine. Even if there isn't a God, even if there isn't a foundational external reality, even if there isn't a self—our experience, our everyday lives, the richness of our experience, is all just the same. And that's exactly the route that Hume takes (I think independently, rather than because of Buddhism). But it's a very similar intellectual trajectory. There's this wonderful moment in the *Treatise* where Hume reports that he had an early life crisis, which we know that he actually *did* have. He has this kind of nervous breakdown from starting with being sceptical about God, to being sceptical about reality, to being sceptical about the self, such that everything's fallen apart and there's nothing anyone can do about it. And there's this wonderful moment where Hume asks us to wait a minute—actually everything's exactly the same. And that positive feeling is the feeling that comes in Buddhism as well.

NW: *There are clearly these parallels between Buddhism and Hume's philosophy, but there must be differences as well.*

AG: I think the biggest difference is that Buddhists see their philosophical project as being part of a broader therapeutic project. Although Tsongkhapa made pretty dry philosophy for most of his life, still it's all in aid of making people better, making people happier, and making people function better. So the Buddhists think if you have this combination of recognizing the scepticism and then recognizing that it doesn't really matter, you'll function better in the world—you won't suffer as much as you did before. And Hume doesn't really have that in his works. Hume is more detached. Hume doesn't think that doing this philosophy is really going to make you a better person or make you suffer less. It's something that he's more interested in in an abstract way.

NW: *When you were talking earlier about your psychological research into children, you suggested that children don't tend to have a sense of self, but they create it, which would seem to imply that you don't really subscribe to the Humean or Buddhist position on the self because adults (as opposed to children) have selves.*

245

AG: There's an interesting controversy both in Hume interpretation and in the Buddhist tradition about what exactly it means to say that the adult doesn't have a self. Tsongkhapa had what Buddhists call a 'middle way' view, which is that the self is an illusion, but it's a useful, important illusion—it's not an illusion you would want to get rid of. And I think you could argue that this is Hume's view as well. He thinks the self is an illusion, but he thinks it's an illusion that actually does some work. It is, as it were, a *real* illusion. That's exactly the way Tsongkhapa talks about it. And I think from a psychological perspective—from a developmental perspective—there's a good argument that, for instance, if we didn't think that our future selves were the same as our current selves, we wouldn't do things like save money for the future or do things like delay gratification. And actually one of the things we know developmentally is that the development of this autobiographical extended self is connected to abilities like delaying gratification, like not doing something now in order to get a benefit in the future. If you don't think that future self is you, then what's the point in doing things for that future being? Why should I be saving my money now for future Alison when she's eighty? Why not give that money to somebody else, some other eighty-year-old? My future self may well be as different from my current self as that other eighty-year-old. It's only when you have the illusion of the self that you can understand and act in a way that is helpful to you. And I think you could argue that both Hume and Tsongkhapa had that insight as well.

NW: *If the self is really just a folk psychological term—namely, if it's just a useful illusion—the question is, what use is it, because what is the future self that's going to benefit from having this illusion?*

AG: As a psychologist, and as a philosophical naturalist, I think that we can explain things about our intuitive psychology by thinking in evolutionary terms. And from an evolutionary perspective, especially when you've got creatures like human beings who have very complicated cognition, it is to our advantage, for example, to save up our grain from this year in order to feed ourselves next year. That actually makes us thrive and survive and reproduce in a way that we couldn't have done before. So, even if in some sense it's an illusion to think that there is a single person that's the same, it might very well be that doing the things that come from that illusion (like saving money or considering the future or making plans for the future) are things that really would help us to survive and thrive.

Further Resources

Owen Flanagan (2013) *The Boddhisatva's Brain*, MIT Press.

Alison Gopnik (2009) 'Could David Hume Have Known about Buddhism?', *Hume Studies*, 35:1/2, 5–28.

Alison Gopnik (2015) 'How an 18th-Century Philosopher Helped Solve My Midlife Crisis: David Hume, the Buddha, and a Search for the Eastern Roots of the Western Enlightenment', *The Atlantic*: http://www.theatlantic.com/magazine/archive/2015/10/how-david-hume-helped-me-solve-my-midlife-crisis/403195.

David Hume (2000) *A Treatise of Human Nature*, ed. David Fate Norton and Mary J. Norton, Oxford University Press.

Dario Perinetti (2018) 'Hume at La Flèche: Skepticism and the French Connection', *Journal of the History of Philosophy*, 56:1, 45–74.

Je Tsongkhapa (n.d.) 'In Praise of Dependent Origination', translated by Thupten Jinpa: http://www.tibetanclassics.org/html-assets/In%20Praise%20of%20Dependent%20Origination.pdf.

24

KATRIN FLIKSCHUH
Philosophy in Africa

David Edmonds: *When I studied philosophy, I don't remember there being a single African philosopher on the syllabus. Katrin Flikschuh thinks the curriculum needs updating. She believes that there are developments in African philosophy which are intrinsically interesting and which cast new light on old philosophical problems.*

Nigel Warburton: *The topic we're going to focus on is philosophy in Africa. Now, Africa is a big place, so you'd expect that there would be quite a lot of philosophy going on there. Is there something distinctive about African philosophy?*

Katrin Flikschuh: That's a good question and one that's actually debated hotly in African philosophy itself, with different African philosophers taking quite different perspectives on it. Some of them say that there's nothing distinctive other than that it is philosophy that happens to come out of this particular geographical location, and others take the extreme opposite view—that African thinking is very different from any other form of human thinking.

NW: *Presumably the post-colonial African movement has been an important influence on this.*

KF: That's been the case in more senses than one, I think. One very important aspect of this is that of course a lot of the first-generation post-independent African leaders, such as Nkrumah, Nyerere, and Leopold Senghor, were also all philosophers in some sense or another—they were either trained philosophers or thought of themselves in that way. That means that philosophy in Africa has always (in post-independence time) had a certain public function. I think that professional academic African philosophers are acutely aware of the public function that their thinking has, and that they have done so even though they work in a context in which the population is often still largely illiterate. Philosophy in Africa has a political purpose and that has a lot to do with the struggle for post-independence and the Pan-Africanism that came with it. This is not to say, of course, that every African thinker is a Pan-Africanist, but that the political thought is very much in the background of African thinking.

NW: *So presumably there is another aspect of African philosophy—there are lots of countries in Africa and you'd expect there to be many distinctively different African philosophies.*

KF: Yes. And again, you can see the colonial influences. If you look at thinkers such as Kwame Gyekye or Kwasi Wiredu, both from Ghana, as it happens, they come out of the Anglophone philosophical tradition—both were trained in Western countries. And then you can compare this with someone like Paulin Hountondji who is a Beninese philosopher, and comes out of the Francophone tradition. There are some very interesting methodological differences between those schools of thought, and it's interesting to see, despite their Western training, how their particular African context matters.

NW: *It would be easy to imagine that what's going on mostly in Africa is that there are Africans discussing philosophy that, as it were, was imported from other countries—so European philosophy or American philosophy or Australian philosophy—which just happens to be discussed in an African context.*

KF: I think that this is both the case and not the case. I spend quite a lot of time in the philosophy department at the University of Ghana. One of my colleagues there says that whilst the curriculum is often very much dictated by the Western curriculum, the real interest that students and philosophers alike have has more to do with particular problems and philosophical questions that emerge out of the African context. So you do get this rather strange bifurcation sometimes of a curriculum that is still an inheritance from colonial times (and there is a sense in which you can't do philosophy unless you know the Western tradition—although this too is hotly contested) but nonetheless it is all in the end meant to lead to the ability to engage with problems that really are preoccupying African social contexts.

NW: *I sense you think that this is a really interesting phenomenon—that there are specific ways of doing philosophy in Africa which we should know more about.*

KF: Yes, that's right. And I think that this is the conclusion that I've come to, rather than my starting point. My own starting point for engaging more with African thinking had more to do with a sense that our own thinking is really rather more parochial than we would like to think, and this comes out especially in the topics that I work a lot on—global justice—where there is often a claim to universal validity of certain principles or ideas or conceptions of personhood, where that claim to universal validity is just simply taken for granted and not really interrogated. And so I came into African philosophy in part because of a certain unease with that, and a feeling that we should engage more with perspectives that are not our own. But one of the unanticipated benefits of doing this was really that it led me to reassess a lot of our own thinking in light of engaging with African philosophical thinking. So it wasn't so much that I just wanted to hear what the African philosophers had to say, yet was still going to think in much the same way that I did before, but rather it showed me that we could look at the world from distinctly African perspectives as well.

NW: *Could you give a specific example of that?*

KF: Well, one of the African writers whom I really admire is Kwasi Wiredu, and I think it is very difficult not to admire him because he is such a clear and elegant writer. He is, of course, from our perspective, also a very traditional writer, in that he was trained in Oxford under Peter Strawson. So he is a very classic analytic thinker. He writes a lot on the philosophy of language, but he uses the tools of analytic philosophy in order to analyse concepts from his native language Akan, and then to question certain Western received theories. He's written an article in which he says that the theory of truth that is more or less taken as a given in much Western thinking—the correspondence theory of truth—would be virtually incoherent when applied to the Akan conceptual scheme, because the Akan language, Twi, does not have a terminological distinction between matters of fact and truth. The correspondence theory therefore can't really be articulated—you can't articulate the thought that truth is correspondence with fact because the words, as it were, are not available for that. So that would be one example where you suddenly realize that the world can look very different depending on what language scheme you work with.

NW: *But you could recognize that different people have different ways of looking at the world without giving them much heed. I mean, we know that there are lots of different religious beliefs, not all of which could possibly be true, and some of which are completely batty, but we don't have to explore the crazier outreaches of religion.*

KF: I'm not sure about that. I think that sometimes when one explores what prima facie strikes one as the crazier outreaches of a particular religion or worldview, the less crazy they begin to look. For example, I'm working at the moment on different conceptions of personhood, and I am very interested in the conception of personhood offered by Ifeanyi Menkiti, who is a Nigerian philosopher. He has a theory according to which many African traditions recognize what they call 'ancestors' as persons who are biologically dead (so physically not in existence) but spatio-temporally still in existence, so they are in a certain sense non-physical but spatio-temporal beings who are still with us and who ought to still be treated as persons. I think prima facie one might think this is a crazy view, in that it is obviously based on a pre-scientific conception of nature and as such is utterly crazy. So I'm comparing that with our own difficulty in dissociating ourselves entirely philosophically from our commitment to this idea of an immortal soul. Once one really looks into this and delves a little bit deeper, one will find that the Menkiti view is not that crazy or different from our Cartesian view of souls if you adjust your conceptual frame in certain ways. By the same token, though, it might begin to look to you that the immortality of the Cartesian soul is completely crazy—much crazier than you initially thought, in fact. So that's what I find most interesting—how looking at others' views impacts on how you then re-evaluate your own view.

NW: *That's one way of looking at African philosophy—that it's a way of giving you a different perspective on your own views. But there is another way, of course, where you could say that actually what's being said is very plausible, and true, possibly, and that it's a respectable philosophical theory. And presumably in the area of political philosophy, there must be African philosophers making significant contributions on the topic of democracy, say, as it emerges in Africa in different countries.*

KF: Interestingly, that debate is in a state of great flux, and in many respects, to my mind, remains quite underdeveloped. A lot of African thinkers who work on political philosophy face, of course, certain constraints that are quite different from the constraints that Western political thinkers face. This is because, I think, Western political thinkers are able to take for granted a certain history of more or less organic, open-ended, state formation. It just so happened that we ended up with states. And we have a 500-year-long history of political thinkers that take us down that route. And so then we can, with that history and with that tradition of political thought, tinker in our frame. From the African political perspective, the problem is quite different, because I think that the problem there is that there are these states and they can no longer be wished away, but they certainly didn't develop in a very organic or natural or open-ended manner, historically. So the problem becomes, very often, of trying to both differentiate the African political context from the Western context in order to avoid what Africans often think of as a sort of neo-imperialism, where the concepts are simply taken over. But on the other hand, it's difficult to work up pre-colonial or traditional political concepts that were more adequate to a non-state political form. So in Africa at the moment there's a lot of discussion, for example, about democratic theory. And this is in part because African thinkers want to avoid what they consider to be the trap of possible neo-colonialism or neo-imperialism whereby African states are constrained by taking on the whole liberal democratic value package. African philosophers want to come out with a distinctly African conception of democracy. The problem they have is that the pre-colonial, more traditional, concepts of political organization and rights do not, of course, fit very easily into the state forms that they have inherited from the colonial context. There is a tendency very often to contrast the liberal conception with what is perceived as the traditional consensus-based conception of democracy (i.e. not so antagonistic, not so individualistic, not multiparty based, but more consensus oriented)—to contrast those two without really thinking sufficiently hard about quite how that traditional conception would fit into the structure of an inherited post-colonial constitutional state.

NW: *I know that one area you're particularly interested in is the area of human rights. How does that go down in African philosophy? Is that seen as something that's been imported from the West?*

KF: The human rights issue is another very big can of worms. It's become hugely popular in Western thinking. It's actually described as a new lingua franca. And my own view towards it is a good deal more sceptical than that of most of my Western colleagues. I think in the African context too it's a very contested issue. The views range from those who think that this is actually an anti-communalistic doctrine, and therefore inconsistent with traditional African society (which is much more communalistic). I think there's much agreement amongst African thinkers that African society is communalistic in orientation. So one view on human rights would say, 'this is antithetical to everything we've always believed'. At the other extreme, you have people like Ajume Wingo who has written a paper saying that Africans thought of human rights long before Europeans thought of them. I think the dominant view is probably what Gyekye describes as a moderate communitarianism—i.e. a conception towards human rights that is not antithetical towards them, but that would want to say that individuals have duties towards their communities just as much as the communities owe rights to them. So for most African thinkers, there is unease about what they often perceive as the excessive moral individualism of human rights.

NW: *That's really interesting. So there's a sense in which human rights are perceived as protecting the individual, rather than contributing to a wider communal state.*

KF: Yes. And I think that that goes very much against the much more prevalent view in Africa of the person owing their identity to their community. You become a person through taking on obligations and entitlements, playing a role in your community, and that's what makes you a moral person. And I think the anxiety about human rights is that they often seem

to pitch the individual against the community, and that can of
course turn out to be socially very disruptive.

NW: *I think the only African philosopher that I knowingly studied as
an undergraduate was St Augustine. It's quite rare to study African
philosophy. If you were going to rewrite the curriculum for these
university philosophy courses, which philosophers would you think should
be on there, and how would you approach it?*

KF: That's a very good, very big, and very challenging
question. It is true that we engage very little with African
thinking. In the American context, things are slightly different
because of the large number of African-Americans, and so
there African-American philosophy has emerged. That,
interestingly, is often very much focused on questions of
race. And one of the interesting differences between
African-American philosophy and African philosophy is that
African philosophy is far less preoccupied with questions of
race. They are much more preoccupied with retrieving lost
concepts and lost metaphysical frameworks. So why do we
ignore it, I think, is perhaps the first question one would have
to consider. Chinua Achebe (an African writer who was not
awarded the Nobel prize for literature but should have been)
in his essay called 'An Image of Africa' criticized the European
perspective of Africa as a backwater, as hopelessly
underdeveloped, as having nothing to offer. And it is my sense
that that image is still very strong amongst Europeans, and I
think that that contributes to our oversight of this tradition.
Now, I personally have great admiration for Kwasi Wiredu—I
would definitely put him on any curriculum. I would also put
Kwame Gyekye on it, who is also a Ghanaian thinker. I would
definitely put Paulin Hountondji on it, who comes out of a

Marxist perspective—well, Marxist with Husserl—which is very interesting, and engages very much in this question of 'is African philosophy just a geographical denomination or is it something different?'. Gosh, there are certainly very many that one could plug into different curricula in order to afford us a new perspective on old philosophical problems.

Further Resources

Ada Agada (2018) 'A Truly African Philosophy', *Aeon*: http://aeon.co/essays/consolation-philosophy-and-the-struggle-of-reason-in-africa.

Emmanuel Chukwudi Eze (2008) *On Reason: Rationality in a World of Cultural Conflict and Racism*, Duke University Press.

Kwame Gyekye (1987) *An Essay on African Philosophy: The Akan Conceptual Scheme*, Temple University Press.

Paulin J. Hountondji (1996) *African Philosophy: Myth and Reality*, 2nd edition, Indiana University Press.

Lucius T. Outlaw Jr (2017) 'Africana Philosophy', *The Stanford Encyclopedia of Philosophy*, ed. Edward N. Zalta: http://plato.stanford.edu/archives/sum2017/entries/africana.

Kwasi Wiredu (1980) *Philosophy and an African Culture*, Cambridge University Press.

25

ANGIE HOBBS
Plato on War

David Edmonds: *Hobbes believed that without a state, conflict was inevitable—there would be war of all against all, and life would be solitary, poor, nasty, brutish, and short. Rousseau held that, on the contrary, man was born good and it was civilization that had caused our downfall. Two millennia earlier, Plato had himself addressed some fundamental questions about human nature and warfare. War, he proclaimed, was always an evil, though it was a good training-ground and a test of virtues such as courage. But are human communities bound to descend into warfare? Angie Hobbs is a philosopher who specializes in ancient philosophy at the University of Sheffield.*

Nigel Warburton: *The topic we're focusing on is Plato and war. What does Plato think about war—is it inevitable?*

Angie Hobbs: I think there are two questions we want to sort out here. Firstly, Plato asks if war is an evitable or inevitable feature of human civilization. Can there be a human community that could exist without war? The second question asks whether a community without war would be worth the price. Would we have to give up too much?

NW: *So we're talking about Plato in the* Republic, *here, are we?*

AH: Yes, he writes about war in a number of dialogues but it's particularly in the *Republic* that he tries to create a society from scratch to see if war inevitably grows in it.

NW: *Let's take the first question: can war be avoided?*

AH: Plato creates an initial classless, apolitical, pastoral society in the second book of the *Republic* (in 372), and in this pastoral version there is no war. The character of Socrates says that if we have no political classes, then we can have a community of economic producers and consumers who live this life of rustic serenity: they sit around, they chew roasted acorns, they sing hymns to the gods and enjoy each other's company. It all sounds pretty limited. They have no arts, no sciences, no philosophy as far as we can tell (an intriguing omission!), and there is no war and no poverty. Now, there's a key question about whether Socrates actually thinks this is a real, historical, empirical possibility, and my own personal view is that he doesn't. However, at least hypothetically, we are given the idea that there is this society which doesn't have war. But we might hesitate before calling it a 'civilization'. One of Socrates' interlocutors famously says that this way of life sounds awful, that this is a society fit only for pigs—perhaps a sly reference to the roasted acorns—what is needed are more luxurious material goods and more sophisticated entertainment. Socrates responds by bringing in all sorts of material goodies, such as gastronomic delicacies, perfume, cosmetics, fine clothing, couches, tables, gold, and a wide variety of arts. But he also says that as soon as you allow humans to indulge in what he calls 'unnecessary desires' (as opposed to the purely necessary desires required for survival that existed in the pastoral war-free society), then a problem arises due to the fact that such unnecessary desires are themselves unlimited, yet the resources to satisfy them are limited. The people are going to want more and more and they're going to appropriate more and more land. Neighbours are going to start to get jealous. You're going to get all sorts of land disputes and conflicts, and war is going to result; furthermore, says Socrates, you will need a separate, trained warrior class to fight the wars, so a political structure will start to emerge. And the traditional view of what Socrates is saying here is that, if you want civilization, if you want the arts, if you want life to be interesting and challenging and stimulating and at least fairly comfortable and luxurious, then you've got to accept war.

NW: *In this pastoral world, it looks as if there's no conflict at all. That's the opposite of Thomas Hobbes's state of nature where everybody fights each other for the limited resources.*

AH: Absolutely. And it looks at first sight as if Plato in the *Republic* is giving a diametrically opposed view to what Thomas Hobbes does in such works as *Leviathan*, *De Cive*, and the *Elements of Law*. Hobbes, of course, says that in a state of nature (by which he means in a state without a political structure) man is innately at war with man, and that we need a certain type of firm rule to fix this. Many people have interpreted Plato as saying that in the state of nature we are at peace and that it is the development of civilization and political structures in general that cause the problem. But I think that's too simple.

NW: *So you don't accept the traditional view?*

AH: I don't. I think people have been too quick to think that the introduction of war into the *Republic* and what Socrates calls the fevered war-prone society is fuelled simply by our unnecessary desires for expansion and aggrandizement, and that there is no way of developing a political structure and civilization that is also free from war. People think that's the end of the story and that's where we have to stay. But I don't think they're reading the *Republic* carefully enough. If you read on (to be precise, if you look at 399 in the *Republic*), you'll see that Socrates asks if there is a chance of purifying our inflamed war-prone state, and the answer given is yes. The problem is *not* that aggressiveness is itself innate in the human psyche, ready to erupt as soon as we permit any desires and activities not strictly necessary for biological survival. If you look very carefully, says Socrates, at what *causes* aggression between humans, you will see that its origin lies in certain other desires which *are* innate—desires for material goods, desires for physical pleasures, desires for honour. Now, in the wrong kind of society, with the wrong kinds of objects of desire on offer and revered, our innate desires (whether for material goods and physical satisfactions or for honour) will become perverted and corrupted: we will end up desiring things which are in scant supply and for which we need to fight with other people. The worst problems arise when honour and status become conflated with the acquisition and display of material goods. However, if we were to grow up in a very different society—say, one run by beneficent Philosopher-Rulers—then in fact our innate desires for material comfort, for physical satisfaction, for honour, and for a certain amount of status and self-respect could be satisfied in such a way that we did not end up in conflict with our neighbours over scant resources. So although it looks as if Plato and Hobbes are saying diametrically opposed things about the solution to war, I think it is more complicated than that. They may differ about the original state of nature, but they are not as far apart as has sometimes been supposed about the relations between a political state, aggression, and war.

NW: *So you're saying that by the introduction of classes, with Philosopher-Kings at the top, and also by educating the citizens or the people, Plato thinks you can actually eliminate war both within the society and eliminate the aggression that might be felt towards other states?*

AH: Yes. He does at least think that it's a possible option that you can avoid aggressive war if you've got the Philosopher-Rulers (and there are going to be Philosopher-Queens too, I'm delighted to say) running the show. Now, there will still be a high price to pay, we might think, because the philosophers are going to run the show in such a way that the arts are going to be heavily censored, and education is going to be very strictly controlled. The individual is seen as part of a greater whole; we're going to have—let's make no bones about it—a totalitarian state. And very few of us would be prepared to accept that price. However, I think the positive message here is that we don't have to go down the totalitarian route to learn something from what the character of Socrates is saying in the *Republic*. He is saying that we've been too lazy in our thinking about what causes war and aggression in human society. We've just assumed that war and aggression are inevitable because we see them all around us and they have always been around us. We're not really thinking clearly and hard enough about this. And he says that if you do think hard, to start with you're going to see that war itself is a cultural phenomenon and the desire for it has to be learned. So nobody is ever born with an innate desire precisely to make war—that has to be learned later. Secondly, and more controversially, I believe that Socrates is saying that not even aggressiveness in itself is innate. The *potential* for aggressiveness is innate, because what *is* innate are these desires for physical satisfaction and the desire for honour. Things would look different if you grew up in a society which felt that you don't need elaborate confectionery and ornaments to satisfy your physical desires, that lentil soup and a few green beans are absolutely sufficient and will make you happier in the long run; and that you don't need to go out and kill a lot of people to get honour and status. You can also receive honour and status— indeed more so—by being a philosopher. You don't have to be Achilles to be treated as a hero; you can also be a heroic Socrates. So what Plato is doing here is reworking and expanding the whole notion of what it is to be a fine human being.

NW: *Is there something we can learn today from Plato on war?*

AH: I absolutely think there is. Though I certainly wouldn't want to endorse Plato's totalitarian regime, I think we can still learn a lot. The character of Socrates is asking us to think about where aggression comes from: what causes human aggression? And not enough people have asked that question—they've assumed too readily that aggression is the starting point. Plato doesn't assume that. He asks what causes human aggression and he comes up with these innate desires which are *already* perverted and corrupted by the time we get to aggression. He says that there are other ways of channelling those desires and educating them. So even if we can't avoid war altogether (and Plato is fairly pessimistic about that, as he thinks it's very unlikely that there'll ever be *one* Philosopher Ruler, let alone *a whole world* run by Philosopher-Rulers), even if we can't get to that ideal, we can use the ideal as a blueprint to strive towards and we can at least reduce human aggression by redirecting our innate desires onto different objects. And the message about redirecting these innate desires onto different goals is important even if, like me, you don't want to treat the state run by Philosopher-Rulers as a blueprint! But whatever ideal of community you have in mind, the redirection of innate desires will be a major task, as it will require substantial social reform: we are trying to create a society that honours different people and things and behaviours. But if there is any chance at all of reducing aggressiveness and reducing the risk of war, we would do well to take the trouble to learn from Plato.

Further Resources

Thomas Hobbes (1991) *Leviathan*, ed. R. Tuck, Cambridge University Press.

Angie Hobbs (2000) *Plato and the Hero*, Cambridge University Press.

Angie Hobbs (2002) 'Plato on War', in D. Scott (ed.) *Maieusis: A Festschrift in Honour of Myles Burnyeat*, Oxford University Press, 176–194.

Plato (2007) *The Republic*, translated by D. Lee with an introduction by M. Lane, Penguin Classics.

Nigel Warburton and Andrew Park (2016) 'Plato's Philosopher Kings', BBC Radio 4 and *Aeon*: http://aeon.co/videos/why-plato-believed-that-philosopher-kings-not-democracy-should-run-the-state.

26

HELEN BEEBEE
Possible Worlds

David Edmonds: *I'm pretty sure that you're reading this right now. But presumably you could have chosen to do something else—you could have decided to go shopping instead. What other worlds are possible? Is it possible to imagine that rather than reading Philosophy Bites, you chose instead to buy a one-way ticket to North Korea? Helen Beebee is fascinated by possible worlds.*

Nigel Warburton: *The topic we're going to focus on is possible worlds. That sounds like something out of science fiction. What is a possible world and why would it matter to a philosopher?*

Helen Beebee: Perhaps the best way to start thinking about it is to think about the way in which possible worlds were introduced into philosophy, which happened a really long time ago. Gottfried Leibniz, in the late seventeenth to early eighteenth century, very famously said that we live in the best of all possible worlds. And he said that in the context of worrying about the problem of evil—the problem of how it can be that there's an omniscient, benevolent God who creates a world where there's all this pain and suffering. And Leibniz's thought was that God had a choice when he created the universe—he could have set up the initial conditions differently, and he could have set up the laws of nature differently. But because he's benevolent, and clearly does things for a reason, this must be the best of all possible worlds (otherwise he would have selected one of those other possible worlds and we'd be living in that one and not this one). So Leibniz believed in possible worlds—he thought of them as ways the world could be, where God sets up the initial conditions and the laws, and has lots of choice about how he might do that. Then, once you've set up the initial conditions and the laws, you can just let everything run its course. But of course if you set the initial conditions and the laws up differently, you're going to get a whole different kettle of fish—things will pan out in different ways as a result. And it's not just Earth that would be different—it's whole alternative universes. Now, as for the *actual* world, the one we are in right now: we've got the universe; we've got galaxies; we've got stars; we've got the Earth; we've got human beings; and so on. But presumably there are going to be alternative universes where nothing very much happens at all: you're going to get ones where the Earth never comes into existence; you're going to get ones where human beings never evolve; and so on. So that's the basic idea of possible worlds. Another way you might think of it is when you read a work of fiction (especially science fiction because their scope tends to be so broad) you can think of what the author is doing as, in a way, telling you about a small corner of a possible world. For example, take the Sherlock Holmes stories—you might think of that as saying a little bit about some very constrained spatio-temporal region of some possible world where there are all these people (Sherlock

Holmes, Moriarty, and so on). And if you start with that, then you can think about what it would take to tell a story about the *whole* of that possible world. You could take the Sherlock Holmes stories and expand them back in time and forward in time and across all of space—fill out all of the details, as it were—and then you've got a possible world.

NW: *Going back to the example from Leibniz—Voltaire famously mocked that in* Candide *because it was fairly obvious to him that there must be some possible world in which people are much nicer to each other than they are in the real one.*

HB: Yes, that is a worry for that particular response to the problem of evil. Once you take the idea of possible worlds seriously, it's very hard to agree with Leibniz that there really couldn't be a better possible world than this one. Take any bit of suffering—surely there's a possible world where that didn't happen, and surely that's a bit better than the actual world! So, yeah, I don't think that's a very convincing response to the problem of evil.

NW: *Let's now talk about the word 'possible'. Just because we can imagine something doesn't mean it could actually happen, does it?*

HB: That's a worry for talk about possible worlds. The reason why philosophers nowadays are really interested in possible worlds is because they're really interested in making sense of what's known as 'modality'—claims about what's necessary, what's possible, what might have been, and how things might have gone differently. Philosophers obviously find *everything* puzzling, but they find modality *particularly* puzzling. We (that is, not just philosophers, but everyone) make distinctions between things that could've been different (e.g. I woke up on

time, but I might have overslept this morning, or I didn't miss
the bus, but I might have done if I'd slept for longer), and
things we think couldn't have been different (e.g. two plus two
is four—it's very hard to see how that could have been
different, so that seems like it's not just a contingent truth, but
rather a necessary truth). Philosophers want to make sense of
this difference. And they also want to make sense of what's
known as counterfactual talk. For example, I say things like, 'if
I'd have overslept by five minutes this morning, I still would
have made it in time, but if I'd overslept by an hour, I would
have been late'. We're very good at making those kinds of
counterfactual claims in general everyday life. We might argue
about some of them but we have quite a good grip on which
ones are true and which ones aren't. And again, that's very
puzzling. What makes these claims true or false? What possible
worlds give you is a way of understanding such talk. So when I
say that it's just contingently true that I'm sitting here today (in
that it could have been otherwise, I might have been somewhere else), you can understand that in possible worlds talk by
saying that it is true in the actual world that I am sitting here
today, but there are possible worlds where it's not true, as there
are possible worlds where I'm not sitting here and I'm doing
something completely different right now. And similarly, when
you say that something couldn't have been different (for
example, when I say that two plus two is four and is a necessary truth), we take that to mean that 'two plus two is four' is
true in *all* possible worlds. So possible worlds give us a way of
understanding or reducing that really puzzling modal
talk—talk about what might or might not have happened—into
some talk about possible worlds. It's a really useful thing for
philosophers.

NW: *But why is it useful to be able to describe it in those terms? Why is it useful to be able to interpret 'if I had overslept, I wouldn't be here' as 'there is a possible world in which I overslept and didn't get here'—what's the use of that different way of talking?*

HB: It's partly just a bit of technical machinery. We have these unanalysed notions of necessity and possibility and contingency. The idea is that we get to analyse all of those in the same way just by using this very straightforward device. But there is a deeper metaphysical reason why you might want to do that as well. So the American philosopher David Lewis was partly interested in possible worlds because he was really puzzled by the nature of necessity, specifically. David Hume, a couple of centuries ago, was also really worried about the nature of necessity. Hume was worried about causation and he didn't really see how it could make sense to say that one thing guaranteed that something else would happen (in other words, how it would necessitate it). He found this to be a really puzzling notion. And I think Lewis shared some of that puzzlement about the nature of necessity. What you get to do when you move from talking about necessity to talking about possible worlds is, as it were, suck all of the necessity out of the world—you don't need to think that there's any necessity in the world because all of our necessity talk just gets cashed out in terms of all these other possible worlds. So you don't need to think of necessity as being a part of any world, as you get necessity talk coming out of talking about the space of possible worlds. That's a metaphysical reason for wanting to take possible worlds seriously, in order to dispense with necessity *in* the actual world.

NW: *Whilst we're on the topic of metaphysics and what exists, I think I'm right in saying that some philosophers don't just use this as a tool, but rather they really believe that these other possible worlds actually exist in the same sense as the one we're now in.*

HB: Yes: David Lewis very famously did believe that, and he did say that typically the response he got to expressing that belief was what he called the 'incredulous stare'. He questioned whether the incredulous stare counted as an argument and could carry any weight in philosophical debate. Lewis's view was that possible worlds are an incredibly useful device, not just for understanding modality, but for a whole range of other things too. And his line of argument was that when something's *that* useful, you should just believe in it. He made the analogy with sets in mathematics: sets are a really strange thing, for example there is Nigel and then there's this other thing—the set that has Nigel as its member—which is really puzzling. Lewis's philosophical position conceded that they're a bit strange, but you can't do maths without sets, and so you should believe in them. Similarly for possible worlds. Lewis thought that what possible worlds are are real, concrete entities. There's a real alternative universe where there are people going around doing the things that happen in the Sherlock Holmes stories: they're real flesh-and-blood people—the Sherlock Holmes there is smoking a real pipe and eating real food and sitting at a real table, just as much as we are. They're not strange abstract entities, they're real concrete things.

NW: *Just to get that clear—David Lewis believed that there is a possible world in which England won every single World Cup ever.*

HB: That's exactly right. You are giving me the incredulous stare now, and I'm very sympathetic to the incredulous stare, but I'm not really sure what to think. I'd like there to be another story about what possible worlds are that is less weird than this realist story. And there are other stories out there. For example, there's a position that's known as 'ersatzism', which says we should think of this as a kind of story. So, instead of thinking of the possible worlds as existing, the ersatzist thinks of them as just stories. When we say that something's true in a possible world, all we mean is there's a consistent story in which that happens. For example, there's a possible world where there are talking donkeys. Lewis (who's a realist about possible worlds) and the ersatzist agree that that claim is true, and that's why it's true that there could have been talking donkeys. But what the ersatzist says is that we don't need to believe in real talking donkeys; we can just say that there's a perfectly sensible story you can tell about an alternative universe in which talking donkeys feature. So the story is kind of like this abstract entity and that's what other possible worlds are.

NW: *That seems more attractive to me because the notion of a possible world is surely one that isn't actual. I mean, we call it 'possible' because it's not actual!*

HB: There are two things to say about that. One is that Lewis thinks that all that the word 'actual' is doing is locating us in one of those many possible worlds. So it's not as though the other possible worlds have some sort of shadowy existence—they really exist. All we're doing when we say this thing actually happened is saying that it happened in this world rather than some other world. It's a bit like when I say, 'this is happening *here*', I'm locating where it's happening—it's not that wherever here is has some special metaphysical status relative to other places. And the second thing to say is a worry that Lewis had about that ersatzist position where you just have these abstract stories: namely, we need to have some constraints on what counts as a legitimate story, but what's the constraint? Well, the story has to be internally consistent. If you take all the Sherlock Holmes stories and discover that they differ on a certain point—say, the year that Sherlock was born—and then you put them together to think of it as one big story, the result is that you have an internally inconsistent story. And there can't be a possible world where that story is true because it would be a story that has a contradiction in it. So consistency is a constraint on what can count as a legitimate story that is a possible world. But the problem arises when we notice that consistency is a modal notion—to say that some sentences collectively are consistent with each other is just to say that they can all be true together. And the idea of 'they can all be true together' or 'it's possible for them all to be true together' is just another modal notion. So Lewis's worry was we haven't really filtered out all the modality. If we do the ersatzist story, we're still left with this primitive notion of what's possible and what's necessary, and that was exactly the notion that we were supposed to be using possible worlds to do away with.

NW: *You've talked about questions about necessity. Are there other areas of philosophy that are enlightened by introducing this way of speaking?*

HB: Yes: one is the notion of a counterfactual conditional. Again, take the example of me saying, 'if I got up five minutes later, I still would have arrived on time, but if I got up an hour later, I would have arrived late'. Lewis thinks (and this is a standard view) that you can give a possible world story about that counterfactual conditional claim, and it basically amounts to imagining a possible world that's very similar to the actual world in almost all respects but it has a few minor differences that make it the case that I get up an hour later, and now we run the laws and see what happens in that world. As it turns out, in that world—the closest, most similar world—what happens is that I arrive late. That's why it's true that had I woken up an hour later, I would have been late. Now Lewis uses that to analyse the notion of causation, which is a really important notion in metaphysics. He thinks that one thing causing another really just is a matter of it being the case that if the first thing hadn't happened, then the second thing wouldn't have happened. He also thinks that you can use possible worlds for a whole bunch of other things too. For example, there's the notion of a property—you have two red things, there's this property 'redness' that they share. Again, this is a big issue in metaphysics: what does it mean to talk about properties? Lewis thinks that we should just think of properties as sets of possible individuals. So think of the set across all the possible worlds, all the individuals in those possible worlds that are red—that just is what redness is. Similarly, there's the notion of a proposition—when I say 'snow is white' and you 'Schnee ist weiss', we're uttering different sentences but they mean the same thing. A standard line to take in philosophy is that they're expressing the same proposition, just doing so in different languages. But now there's the question of what a proposition is, as that seems like a really peculiar entity.

Lewis's view is that a proposition is just a set of possible worlds again. So the proposition that snow is white is just the set of all possible worlds where it's true that snow is white. (That sounds a bit circular, but you could do it in a way that sounds a bit less circular.)

NW: *In the philosophy that you do yourself, have you found this notion of possible worlds has helped you?*

HB: Oh, yes. For most people who work in metaphysics, philosophy of language, and all kinds of areas of philosophy, possible world talk is just part of the currency: everybody talks about possible worlds and just uses that machinery all the time. As for me, I worry about causation quite a lot and possible world talk comes up there a lot. But in using that machinery, we run up against that question constantly—what are these things, these possible worlds? I'm not sure I want to sign up to the Lewisian view that these are real, concrete entities. That's a worry for me, and it's a worry for a lot of philosophers that we're not really sure what to do about that. I think what we tend to do in practice is just think that there's a kind of division-of-labour thing going on here, and that there are other people that worry about what metaphysical story we should tell about possible worlds—we're going to leave it to them to sort out and we're just going to happily carry on talking the talk.

Further Resources

Helen Beebee and Julian Dodd, eds. (2006) *Reading Metaphysics: Selected Texts with Interactive Commentary*, Blackwell, chapter 5.

Nikk Effingham (2013) *An Introduction to Ontology*, Polity, chapter 5.

David Lewis (1983) *On the Plurality of Worlds*, Blackwell.

Christopher Menzel (2017) 'Possible Worlds', *The Stanford Encyclopedia of Philosophy*, ed. Edward N. Zalta: http://plato.stanford. edu/archives/win2017/entries/possible-worlds.

27

TAMAR SZABÓ GENDLER
Why Philosophers Use Examples

David Edmonds: *If a murderer is at your door and asks for the whereabouts of a potential victim whom you're sheltering, are you permitted to lie to him? You might recognize the example from Immanuel Kant. But why does Kant use the example in the first place? Why do any philosophers use examples, rather than just deploy pure abstract reasoning? Here's Tamar Szabó Gendler.*

Nigel Warburton: *The topic we're going to focus on is why philosophers use examples. That's a really interesting question. So why do philosophers use examples?*

Tamar Szabó Gendler: One of the most striking things when you pick up one of the works in the Ancient Greek philosophical tradition—take something like Plato's *Republic*—is that, on the one hand, it's full of all sorts of abstract argument, and on the other hand, it's full of all sorts of vivid cases. And I think Plato gives a clue as to why it is that the works—the dialogues—include these two sorts of things, when he talks about the human as having a multipart soul. Plato says famously in the *Republic* and in several of the other dialogues that human beings are composed in part of what he calls reason or rationality, and in another part what he calls spirit and appetite. And this recognition that human beings, on the one hand, have a capacity that gauges and understands the world in terms of reason and argumentation, and on the other hand have aspects of themselves that understand the world in other ways, is actually a central theme both in the Western and the Eastern philosophical traditions, and the role of examples is to talk to the other parts of the soul.

NW: *So when Plato uses the famous example of the cave—these prisoners chained facing a wall and just seeing the flickering shadows of reflections cast by people carrying shapes in front of a fire—that elaborate metaphor isn't there to appeal to the rational part?*

TSG: Well, it's doing two things. One of the really interesting things about the allegory is that there's a way of understanding it analytically—you can see what its structure is—but it also does what all metaphors do, which is it makes you attentive to patterns in the world. One of the things that metaphors do is they help direct your attention towards relations that hold between things that you might not otherwise recognize. So the allegory of the cave is, in an incredibly self-referential way, appealing to the rational part of the soul (by pointing out to you what these various levels and their relations are), but it's also appealing to the other parts of the soul (by giving you vivid imagery that you can hold on to at the moments when you're trying to understand the nature of the world).

NW: *If somebody describes architecture as frozen music, then you get a new way of framing the world—is that the idea?*

TSG: That's right. And in fact, there are cases where we're resistant to certain sorts of metaphorical aberrations because we don't want those ways of looking at the world to be available to us. So, some of the amazing literature on dehumanization suggests that one of the main things that was done by various fascist governments in the middle of the last century was to use metaphors that equated certain groups of humans with nonhumans. And those sorts of patterns of making sense of the world end up affecting our apprehension of things in pretty profound ways.

NW: *Now those are metaphors—are they really examples?*

TSG: It's an interesting question. One of the things that is hard to distinguish when you start pressing almost any dichotomy is where things that seem to lie along a spectrum belong on it. So I think we're pretty clear that there's a notion of abstract logical relation, that in its purest form is manifest in things like mathematics and logic—that's part of why Plato was so obsessed with those as being the aspects that are unadulterated by the other parts of the soul. And then we can continue down from there to things that appear to affect only the non-rational parts of the soul. For example, Plato is very interested, in the middle of the *Republic*, in the ways in which rhythm in music, marching together, dance movements, and so on interact with the parts of the soul that he thinks of as non-rational. Examples, metaphors, and so on fall somewhere in the middle of that spectrum.

NW: *I'd have thought that the Republic was directed at Philosopher-Kings or potential Philosopher-Kings, and shouldn't they just be swayed by reason, not by passion?*

TSG: I think all human beings (and this is something that Plato recognizes, it's something that Aristotle recognizes, it's something that the early moderns recognize) are evolved creatures. One of the things that is so striking about the *Nicomachean Ethics* and also the *Republic* is the emphasis they place on early childhood. The reason they place this emphasis on early childhood is they're interested in the cultivation of the right sorts of instincts and habits in the non-rational parts of the soul. Aristotle is constantly worried about what the 'non-well-raised one' will be able to do. And so although one might think there's a kind of idealized picture where the reason and the spirit and appetite are in harmony as the result of the proper cultivation (Plato describes these in the middle books), as a matter of fact no one reading the book has been raised in the way that Plato describes—nobody reading Aristotle's *Ethics* is truly a 'well-raised one'—and as a consequence, the argumentation needs to include things that appeal not just to the rational part of the soul.

NW: *That explains why Plato was using this—because of his particular theory about the soul. But are we all footnotes to Plato, to that extent? Is the subsequent history of philosophy and history of people just playing out what was implicit in Plato?*

TSG: Well, one of the things that's interesting is that it's not just in Plato that you see this. In the non-Western philosophical tradition, you have a similar metaphor—the Buddhist tradition speaks of a person riding on an elephant. So instead of the metaphor that Plato uses (the charioteer and the horses), the Buddhism has the rider and the elephant. And there are similar metaphors in most world wisdom traditions of a human being (it's interesting that we are identified humanly with the rational part) and then of some sort of nonhuman animal who's also co-present. As such, the extent to which we're footnotes to Plato in using examples is just the extent to which Plato is, metaphorically speaking, a footnote to Darwin—that is, as a matter of fact, we're all evolved creatures, and as a consequence we have parts of the brain which respond as the result of certain sorts of evolved patterns.

NW: *I really like this idea, but I'm sure that many of the times I've used examples in philosophy, what I'm doing is illustrating something which I've made a generalization about and I'm clarifying what that generalization really means by giving one or two cases, so that the listener or reader can follow exactly what I meant.*

TSG: Good. And it's certainly the case that if something is universally true then it's true in each instance, and if something is true in a series of instances then we can make a generalization about it. But one of the interesting things is that the way that we process information about generalizations and the way that we process information about particulars tend to be quite different. Whereas the processing of information about generalizations, roughly speaking, uses what Plato would call reason, the processing of information about particulars brings with it all sorts of additional features. So, some of the literature that we confront when we try to think about the relation between the statement of abstract moral principles, on the one hand, and instances where those principles are applied—the debate about particularism in ethics—is in fact the debate about exactly what you just raised. The particularists say that there's no way that we can actually come up with a generalization, we just need to look at the particular cases. And those who say any particular instance will in some sense distort what the universal claim was are concerned with the tension between these two modes of processing information.

NW: *And often the selection of a particular example is rhetorical because you're pushing a card to somebody—you really want them to believe your generalization so you choose the best example to persuade them.*

TSG: That's right. And, in fact, one of the implicit background topics at play here is the debate between the philosopher and the rhetoricians. So in the Ancient Greek world, but also throughout other wisdom traditions, there's a distinction between coming to understanding through reason and coming to understanding through some alternative mode of bringing about a change of heart. And two of the most famous of those modes are 'revelation', on the one hand (which involves a change of heart that comes not through reason but through the sudden production of insight), and 'rhetoric', on the other (which in its best versions involves a similar bringing to insight but in some cases involves the bringing about of a change of attitude that ultimately isn't grounded in what the person would reflectively endorse).

NW: *That's really interesting because philosophy is often portrayed as the subject which focuses on reason and tries to play down, not just rhetoric, but also appeals to the passions generally.*

TSG: Yes. I don't think that if you look at philosophy as a practice that in fact accords with what it is that philosophers (for the most part) are doing. Take one of the purest instances—the kind of argument that Kant gives about morality, where the claim that Kant's making is the incredibly deep and profound claim that freedom comes only with being a self-lawgiver, and that giving of the law to one's self takes the form of the Categorical Imperative. Even in that work, Kant feels compelled both to give you multiple formulations of the Categorical Imperative so that it can become intuitively appealing in the right sorts of ways, and to give a number of instances—they're to help make vivid what it is that this very abstract formulation is saying. So, although it is an ideal of some but not all strands in the Western philosophical tradition that reason has primacy, it's also the case that in their practice nearly all philosophers recognize (whether implicitly or explicitly) that some of their argumentation needs to be involved in bringing onboard the non-rational parts of the soul.

NW: *And actually, in Philosophy Bites interviews we often ask people to give an example to clarify exactly what they mean, but presumably also to make the view more plausible to people who haven't quite got what the generalization was.*

TSG: That's exactly right. And often we ourselves don't quite have a sense of what it is that we're looking for at the most abstract level, but we have several concrete cases on which we're triangulating. And sometimes presenting those helps us see what the pattern was that we were trying to pick up on.

NW: *So are you suggesting there's a kind of reflective equilibrium moving between the universal and the particular?*

TSG: I don't know that we ever reach the sort of status that an equilibrium would suggest. The notion of reflective equilibrium is one that's meant to articulate what it is that happens when you work with a principle and then you work with cases and then you work back to the principle correcting for cases and so on. Equilibrium suggests that there's a point at which you come to a stable relation between them. But if the rational articulation of the general principle is appealing to one part of the soul and the particular cases are appealing to another, it becomes a question whether that sort of equilibrium will in fact ever be reachable or whether in fact there might be inevitable tension between them.

NW: *Do you think this pattern of philosophical communication maps discoveries in neuroscience about the way that the brain works?*

TSG: One of the things that's really clear about the way that the brain works is that a very, very small part at the front of it—the prefrontal cortex—does the work that Plato thought the charioteer did, and that pretty much everything that happens in real time all day long actually happens through various kinds of routines and habits and overlearned evolved processes in the back of the brain. So if you wanted to make a prediction, what would neuroscience tell us? What neuroscience would tell us is that if anything, the metaphor of the parts of the soul understates the degree to which we should expect there to be tensions. It's only because what we perceive in manifest behaviour comes out through limited sensory organs—that is, we speak, we do things with our arms and legs, we do things with our eyes—that there was ever any illusion that we spoke with one voice. And, in fact, the literature on the discrepancies between verbal and nonverbal communication—the literature that looks at eye gaze as a predictor of what responses will be—suggests over and over again that with regard to almost all of our responses to the world, there are multiple factors coming into play and one becomes dominant, but the others were pre-potently present all the way through.

NW: *Am I right in suggesting that your view is that it's a good thing that we as philosophers use examples and appeal to the passions, not just hover in that world of abstraction and universals?*

TSG: Well, you might think that's how we do philosophy for people with brains, where what I mean by having brains is people who are evolved members of an animal kingdom (of which humans are one sort). So, to do philosophy for angels might look like a different endeavour, but to do philosophy for human beings needs to look like this.

Further Resources

Tamar Szabó Gendler (2010) *Intuition, Imagination and Philosophical Methodology*, Oxford University Press.

Alan Hájek (2017) 'Philosophy Toolkit', *Aeon*: http://aeon.co/essays/with-the-use-of-heuristics-anybody-can-think-like-a-philosopher.

Plato, *The Republic*, Translated by GMA Grube revised by CDC Reeve, Hackett Publishers.

Timothy Williamson (2007) *The Philosophy of Philosophy*, Blackwell.

28

REBECCA NEWBERGER GOLDSTEIN
Progress in Philosophy

David Edmonds: *'All philosophy is just footnotes to Plato'. That's a famous quote, but also a rather depressing one, because it suggests that philosophy hasn't made much progress since the fourth century* BCE. *Here's Rebecca Newberger Goldstein to cheer philosophers up.*

Nigel Warburton: *The topic we're going to focus on is progress in philosophy. It seems to many people that there isn't any progress in philosophy because we're still discussing the same sort of problems that Plato was discussing.*

Rebecca Newberger Goldstein: Well, in a sense we are—but many of the questions that he was discussing have developed since he first posed them. Part of the progress is refining the problems. Plato is terrifically significant because he raises almost all of the paradigmatic philosophical questions, and raises up, in the process, all the different subgenres of philosophy: philosophy of language; philosophy of mathematics; philosophy of science; philosophy of religion; epistemology; metaphysics; political theory;

ethics ... I think that in that sense there's some justification for Alfred North Whitehead's statement that all that philosophy consists of is a series of footnotes to Plato. But Whitehead's statement isn't justified if we interpret it to mean that Plato gave us the right answers to the questions he posed. And Whitehead's statement isn't even justified if we interpret it to mean that, in posing his problems, he asked all of the right questions. So, for example, he posed that very fundamental moral question concerning the nature of justice. And yet, when considering the question of justice, he didn't think to pose the question of whether slavery can ever be just. It would take quite a few centuries for people to see that the answers they had already accepted regarding the nature of justice meant that they had to confront the unjust nature of the institution of chattel slavery. The U.S. eventually fought a civil war over this issue—not that all forms of slavery have been wiped off the face of the planet even today. Good on Plato for putting the question of justice on the table. But that question, thankfully, has itself developed beyond the way Plato understood it.

NW: *We've made social progress, that's for sure; we got rid of slaves to some degree. But questions about metaphysics and questions about the nature of the mind, they're still mysterious. And some people think we'd better give up on philosophy because we've had literally thousands of years discussing these issues and not got very far. We are still going back to Aristotle for ethics—why are we doing that? If that's all we've got, surely what we should be doing is going to science.*

RNG: For us to make sense out of our lives, there are two sorts of fundamental questions: (1) what is; and (2) what matters. I would argue (and I would need a philosophical argument to argue this) that science gives us the best answers to questions concerning *what is* the case. Our ontology is really best revealed through science. We live in a world of energy, matter, space, and time, where, it turns out, matter and energy and space and time are not as they seem to us in sense perception. Theoretical physics has corrected our conceptions of them. The same goes for the nature of the mind, as I think we have to get rid of the whole idea of disembodied minds that has been taken so seriously in the history of philosophy—get rid of this idea because of what we've learned from both evolutionary biology and neuroscience, no matter our intuitive predispositions to believing in disembodied minds. But this very claim that I've made, that science is superior a description of reality than our pre-scientific intuitions (which is an assertion of what we call 'scientific realism'), itself depends on a philosophical argument. Scientific realism is a philosophical view, requiring philosophical arguments. In that sense, philosophy is very necessary, even for science to make its ontological claims, much less assert that its ontological claims trump pre-scientific claims.

NW: *Could you give an example of what you mean there?*

RNG: In the philosophy of science there are two very different views of what it is that we're doing when we're doing science. Does science extend our ontology—our knowledge of *what is*—beyond sense perceptions, or is science simply an instrument for making further predictions of what our senses will perceive? There are many scientists who have argued for the latter. In fact, the view—instrumentalism—used to be the more popular view in physics because of some of the problems of interpreting quantum mechanics, which is a pretty weird and counter-intuitive theory. What was called the Copenhagen Interpretation, in honour of Niels Bohr, was an anti-realist interpretation of quantum mechanics and thus of science in general. Nowadays physicists who care about these foundational questions have mostly dropped the Copenhagen Interpretation and instead advocate either for what is called Bohmian Mechanics, after the physicist David Bohm, or the Many-Worlds Interpretation. Now both of these are, in contrast to the Copenhagen interpretation, realist interpretations of quantum mechanics, though they offer us startlingly different pictures of reality. So here we have one scientific theory—an extraordinarily useful scientific theory given its powerful predictions—but three very different interpretations as to what this theory is actually telling us about the world. The theory itself—its empirical predictions—can't decide this question for us. Advocates of the Copenhagen Interpretation, of Bohmian Mechanics, of the Many Worlds Interpretation all agree on the empirical content of quantum mechanics, but they radically disagree on what this theory means—on what, if anything, it is telling us about *what is*. The question of what science is telling us isn't itself empirically decidable. It isn't a scientific question. What we have to go on is philosophical arguments.

NW: *What you're saying relies on our notion of a philosophical argument. So at this point it might be quite useful to get your answer to the question: 'what is philosophy?'*

RNG: Here's my understanding of philosophy. It's influenced by the view of the twentieth-century philosopher Wilfrid Sellars. A little personal history: I came into philosophy from science—from physics, specifically—and it was actually my difficulties in understanding what quantum mechanics was telling us about the world that drove me to philosophy. But when I made the switch to philosophy, I was worried—isn't it ultimately a scientific matter how one interprets quantum mechanics? And then I read Wilfrid Sellars' 'Philosophy and the Scientific Image of Man'. (Unfortunately, he uses the word 'man', where we would now say 'of the human' or something of that sort.) Sellars' view of philosophy is that it tries to reconcile what science is telling us about ourselves and the world—ourselves *in* the world—with pre-scientific intuitions. There's science on the one hand, what Sellars calls the scientific image of us, and then there are extra-scientific intuitions on the other hand, what Sellars calls our manifest image. Some of the intuitions that go into our manifest image are utilized in the scientific image—such as the standards of evidence and justification, the belief in what Hume called the uniformity of nature. In this sense, not only are our manifest and scientific images consistent with one another, but the scientific image actually depends on elements of the manifest image. But sometimes we discover inconsistencies or tensions between the scientific and manifest images. And science can't itself solve these tensions. That's where, according to Sellars, philosophy comes in. So, take the idea of souls, for example, which seems to come pretty naturally to us, the idea that our consciousness and our very identity is located in an immaterial substance that can survive the death of the body. We have to let that go. It is inconsistent with what we know of evolutionary biology and neuroscience. But the notion of the self—the self that matters so that I care about that self and I try to carve out a meaningful life for it: Does that notion, too, have to go because of what science is telling us? Can it be reconciled with neuroscience or not? Philosophy is a bit like a marriage counsellor in its efforts to reconcile claims coming from two sides. Philosophy is trying to expand our coherence, taking our scientific knowledge of the world and seeing which aspects of the manifest image can be justified by it, which can be reconciled with it, and which have to be abandoned.

NW: *Isn't that definition of philosophy begging the question? There are some psychologists or neuroscientists who say that they have done the research, and the conclusion is that there is no self, so we need to get over it. And your definition of philosophy seems to smuggle in that the notion of self (the folk psychology notion, as philosophers might call it) matters.*

RNG: If psychologists and neuroscientists ever did get to that state of knowledge where it is clear that the notion of the self is just not reconcilable with scientific findings, that would be something to be worked at within philosophy. We would have to work out a transformed notion of pursuing a life in the face of the non-existence of the self. But science hasn't legitimately reached that point yet (a philosophical judgement on my part). Here's where they've gotten to: on the neuro-level, we can't find the kind of unity-of-self that is reflected in our intuitive notion of the self. But to conclude from that absence that the notion of a self must be abandoned, in the same way as the notion of the immaterial soul, is unsound. Indeed, it is *they* who are begging the question, by saying that if you can't find it on the current neurological description, then it simply doesn't exist. But after all, we can't find consciousness in the current neurological description of the brain. That's the famous hard problem of consciousness. Clearly, the neurological descriptions that we have to date are incomplete. You can argue for the non-existence of the self on philosophical grounds, as Parfit does, but it's premature to do so on the basis of neuroscience.

NW: *Philosophers have been trying to answer these intractable questions about the nature of free will and the nature of consciousness for millennia, and not really got that far. Isn't it more likely that scientists will make progress in this area than philosophers?*

RNG: Yes, it is. What philosophy can do, though, is to point out when science is still falling short of being able to draw an ontological conclusion. I agree that in terms of all these questions of 'what is', it is science that we have to rely on. But often what we need outside of science, and what we need philosophers for, is to make clear exactly how much is implied by the scientific findings and how much isn't. Scientists often overreach when making claims concerning the contents of their findings, sometimes because they're not sensitive to the philosophical issues involved. With the question of consciousness, for example, I am convinced that the hard problem of consciousness has not been solved yet. From the neuroscientific description of the brain, we cannot yet understand why it feels like something to *be* this brain. The subjective aspect of being a brain doesn't make itself manifest in the neuro-description. A neuroscientist might say that the fact that consciousness is not there in the current neuro-description entails that there is no such thing as consciousness. If we can't get it out of the scientific description, then there's just not such a thing. But to argue in this way is to wander into some deep philosophical waters, perhaps over one's head. Does it make sense to say that there is no consciousness, that there only *seems* to us to be consciousness? Do away with consciousness and one does away with all facts about how things seem to us. Philosophy has this role of looking at what the science is and what it does and does not entail. This requires keeping abreast of science, if a large part of being a philosopher is the art of reconciling science with other intuitions, as Sellars maintained. The late Stephen Hawking attacked philosophers for being ignorant of science—from which I conclude that he was talking to the wrong philosophers. Philosophers always have to know what's going on scientifically—what's the content of our best science at the moment, and then consider: what does it entail and what doesn't it entail, and which intuitions can we hold on to, and which must we abandon? That's mediating between sides, and that's what they're trained to do. There's a division of talents—a division of labour. Philosophy is joined at the hip to science but it's doing something different from science. Philosophy is not just bad science, although sometimes it is.

NW: *You said there are two important questions: 'what is' (which we've been discussing through science); and also 'what matters'. Now, presumably the area of philosophy that deals with what matters is moral and political philosophy.*

RNG: Yes, but I'd also include epistemology to a certain degree as well, because we're committed to the fact that truth matters. And because truth matters, justification matters and figuring out what counts as justification matters. As such, I would say that these normative questions include ethics, aesthetics, political philosophy, but epistemology as well. And since science presumes certain epistemological answers, here, too, we can see that science presumes philosophy.

NW: *Now, here it's perhaps even more controversial to talk about progress because many people are moral relativists (or profess to be) and that's a position that was held in ancient times as well. We don't seem to have got far beyond that. And if people think, 'well, that's just your morality and this is my morality and there's no place to judge them', it seems that there's no progress being made at all.*

RNG: I don't believe that people really hold that relativist view. I think it's an intellectual pose. Anybody who ever feels righteous indignation, even on their own behalf, feels that their rights are being violated, and that entails a recognition of rights. If you show me a person who's never felt that—who's never felt indignation or moral outrage because their own rights are being violated—then I would say that such a person can consistently be a moral relativist. Suppose you're lying on the beach and some big fat guy wants to get from point A to point B and you're lying there prone in between. So say he takes the shortest distance between two points and steps on your stomach, and you quite naturally protest, saying something along the lines of, 'how could you possibly have done that? Don't you know the pain you've caused me? What reason could you possibly have had to cause so much pain to me when avoiding it would have cost you nothing?' You are already on moral grounds when you make such a claim. You're already violating the terms of your relativism in just having normal emotional reactions of righteous indignation on your own behalf.

NW: *So there seems to be some progress in morality—you mentioned earlier the idea that we have got rid of slaves. It is not that we've got rid of all slaves, but surely many people feel it's wrong to enslave someone, and that wasn't true in Plato's Athens. As such, this* *is progress. But should philosophers take any credit for the progress that's occurred?*

RNG: Philosophers can't take total credit. Social activism, including on the part of slaves, was certainly necessary. But let me broaden the question. I would say to be a moral person is to hold yourself, your behaviour, accountable. But the question is: to whom? To whom am I beholden to account for my actions? Before it was assumed that the relevant class was white propertied males. One way that we can count moral progress is the widening of this class of those to whom we're beholden in accounting for what we do. Do we all have to be accountable to the poor, to the colonialized and disenfranchised and enslaved, to women, to children, to gay people, to animals? What have philosophers contributed to the progress we've made with the question of those to whom we're accountable? I'm really interested in this question because I don't think philosophers can do it all on their own. I think they are necessary and that if you go through the history of moral progress or social progress, you will find it always beginning with a philosophical argument. This is in just the same way that we've seen Peter Singer in our own day begin with a very philosophical argument (which many thought some decades ago was rather batty) regarding what we owe animals. It is in an argument for including animals in the class of those to whom we must hold ourselves accountable. But then you start taking the argument seriously, on its own terms, and it becomes a social movement—a step that's absolutely necessary—in fully coming to terms with the argument that animal suffering matters. To claim that it matters is to claim that, in principle, we have to make ourselves accountable to animals, and that involves some substantial revisions. We're reluctant to make these revisions, both out of intellectual laziness and, even more, because we then will see we're not permitted to act in ways we'd like to act. But one of our saving graces is not just empathy, some limited amount that we seem to have, but also that we don't like inconsistency, including moral inconsistency. And it's the job of a philosopher to point out inconsistency and to keep rubbing our noses in it, until we feel intolerably uncomfortable. I know this is what happened to me with this argument of Singer's, and as a result I eventually had to change my life.

NW: *One sense in which philosophies progressed is there are more philosophers around now—more trained philosophers—than ever before in the history of humanity. The university system is churning out philosophers every minute. We haven't got 'Philosopher-Kings', but we've got many people with philosophical training. Does that mean we now have philosophical experts?*

RNG: I think it is really interesting that Plato put his finger on so many things, including this—the problematic role of the philosophical expert in society. He has this incredible passage in the *Protagoras*. Plato is in the midst of creating the field of philosophy, and yet he's always aware of the fact that people will inevitably resent philosophers, that it's in the nature of philosophy to incite resentment. There he is, at the dawn of philosophy, and Plato asks why this is the case. In answer, he asks us to imagine that there's a would-be flute player who really plays badly, who has absolutely no talent, and he wants to get up and perform for an audience. His family is going to try to dissuade him, telling him the hard truth so that he does not embarrass himself or the family at large. The would-be flute player is going to be rather disappointed to learn he has no future as a flute player, but he'll be able to adjust—to give up his pretensions of musical ability and find something else to occupy him. Now, in contrast, imagine somebody who says, 'I know the difference between what's true and what's false. I believe what's true and I have good reasons for it. I certainly know the difference between what's right and what's wrong. And I'm living a life that matters—I'm living a life worth living.' And then here come these professional philosophers who say that he doesn't have any right to these opinions, because that's their field; they are the experts, and he's just embarrassing himself with his amateur opinions on epistemology and ethics. He doesn't even know how to begin to think about these subtleties and should just forget about it. But he can't just forget about these questions since that's to forget about what it means for him to be human. The philosophers are demeaning his very humanity in some sense, because to be human is to have a stake in these questions—believing the true, doing the right thing, living a life that matters. So it's not like flute-playing, and it's not like a theoretical physicist saying, 'I know more about string theory, sit down and be quiet and let the experts take over'. We all recognize that he has the authority to lecture us on string theory, and we all recognize that there are some flute players who merit an audience, but for a philosopher to lay claim to expertise on these core humanity issues is tricky (and it's somewhat insulting). To be human is to lay claim to being an expert on the right grounds for believing and the right grounds for acting and pursuing a life worth pursuing. Some know-it-all emerges from the academy and says, no, I'm the expert on these core activities of being human: this seems to diminish others' humanity. There's a real issue here, implicit in the very field that Plato was in the process of creating, and he recognized it. We may not like the way he opted to resolve the issue, which was to propose arranging society so that non-philosophers pliantly behave the way the untalented flute player behaves, but at least we have to give him credit for spotting the issue. And again, that's the crux of the truth in Whitehead's claim.

Further Resources

Nancy Cartwright (1983) *How the Laws of Physics Lie*, Oxford University Press.

Rebecca Newberger Goldstein (2016) *Plato at the Googleplex: Why Philosophy Won't Go Away*, Pantheon.

J. L. Schellenberg (2018) 'Philosophy's First Steps', *Aeon*: http://aeon.co/essays/why-philosophy-is-taking-its-time-to-answer-the-big-questions.

Wilfred Sellars (1962) 'Philosophy and the Scientific Image of Man', in R. Colodny (ed.) *Frontiers of Science and Philosophy*, University of Pittsburgh Press, 35–78.

Andrew Whitaker (1996) *Einstein, Bohr and the Quantum Dilemma*, Cambridge University Press.

29

MARY WARNOCK
Philosophy and Public Life

David Edmonds: *Can and should philosophers contribute to public life? Well, one philosopher, Mary Warnock, has certainly done her bit. She sits in the House of Lords, and has been selected by the British government to head up two major inquiries—both of which have had an enduring influence. The first inquiry was into how the education system should accommodate children with emotional and physical difficulties (in the jargon: 'special needs'). The second inquiry looked at how the government should regulate fertility treatment and embryo research, which covered numerous issues from surrogacy to IVF. Among the recommendations was that scientific research be limited to embryos less than fourteen days old.*

Nigel Warburton: *I'm really interested to talk about your role in public life. It's comparatively rare for philosophers to have an active role in public life, but you've chaired commissions, and you've been an active member in the House of Lords for quite some time now. I wondered how philosophy prepared you for these things.*

Mary Warnock: I think that being a professional philosopher makes you tremendously anxious to distinguish things that differ that tend to be lumped together all in one concept.

It makes you quite alert to the need to pick conceptual muddles to pieces, and recognize that the way you say things is actually terribly important. I always find myself when chairing some committee being very bossy about pointing out that there are two different things at play here: one is your gut reaction or squeamishness about something; and the other is whether the thing is really harmful or not. Take a current example—there was a case of a woman who was paralysed and was asking that her tubes and breathing apparatus should be switched off at the moment when she said she wanted to switch it all off (it wasn't nigh, but she knew it would be in a month or two). There were a lot of doctors who said that she was asking them to kill her, and that they wouldn't like to do that. But hang on—other people are entitled to say that they don't want any more treatment, yet she was being denied. She was completely paralysed and couldn't switch off the equipment for herself. Were the doctors really entitled to say she might not have that freedom to choose when the treatment was enough? Were they entitled to say she might not have that freedom just because she couldn't do it herself? That is the kind of distinction that I think philosophers are quite alert to making and that is a very useful talent if we're going to have to chair committees and deal with people who say, 'I'm not happy about that'. I want to have members that say, 'I'm not asking you to be happy, we're not brought into this life to be happy'. And with regard to research using human embryos, there was this woman who kept saying that she wasn't happy, where I was bound to respond with, 'who cares whether you are happy? Is it right?'

NW: *You've been involved directly in legislation and informing legislation. I wonder if you could say a little bit about the main areas that you've worked in.*

MW: Well, the first government committee of inquiry I chaired was on special educational needs. That was extremely interesting, because in order to justify spending money on special educational needs one had to have a concept of education that included *everybody*. That meant it was worth spending government money on people who would actually never contribute to the economy or do anything except improve their own experiences. The second inquiry that I worked on was totally different. It was an inquiry into human fertilization and embryology, and there I was even more ignorant when I started. It was great fun in a way, but far more fraught than the first inquiry. That was because in the first case we all knew what we wanted, which was to improve the lot of disabled children. But in this second case we didn't all know what we wanted. We didn't know at all what the consequences of the new technologies would be and we had to try to work that out. So it was much more difficult.

NW: *On ethics committees generally, there's a sense in which people with a religious position are often co-opted. I wonder how you deal with somebody who's coming from a particular, perhaps quite dogmatic, standpoint? Philosophy, if anything, is anti-dogmatism, in that we have to defend our conclusions with reasons and evidence.*

MW: That is the most important thing that philosophy is—that philosophy prepares you to be non-dogmatic. And it is terribly important, I think, in any issue which is going to result in legislation. As such, I believe that actually philosophers are very good people to produce a cultural critique of legislation. If the House of Lords consisted entirely of philosophers, I wouldn't complain, because the role of the House of Lords is to criticize and scrutinize legislation. But what philosophers don't have, of course, is a lot of specialized knowledge. You could say that they are parasitic on other people's specializations. Nevertheless, to have some philosophers around while doctors or lawyers or engineers or people who know about the environment are making legislation is a very useful thing.

NW: *I'd like to come back to the question, though, about dealing with religion, specifically, because that to me is, in some areas, treated as synonymous with having authority and ethics.*

MW: The role of religion just seemed to me extremely difficult. I certainly wouldn't want to deny that religion has a place. And although I could be described as an atheist, I don't think that is an accurate description. I really do like the ritual and ceremonial aspects of religion, and having a space where you are prepared to say, 'I don't know' but which gives you a chance to express gratitude or humility or regret. But the trouble is that some people don't like them and don't feel any need for them, and therefore it seems absolutely wrong that legislation, and the rule of law, which have to bind *everybody*, are far more important than any particular dogma, it seems to me. I talk with passion about this because I'm involved very much in changing the law about euthanasia, assisted suicide, and assisted death. And anybody who produces the argument against such legislation (which I admit is terribly difficult to formulate) that human life is a gift from God is just simply talking irrelevantly because not everybody believes that. How can their particular religious belief possibly be brought in to justify blocking any attempt at legalizing assisted suicide? I mean, obviously people who are religious very often have extremely good and acceptable moral views, but they have no special access to what would be a good and solid basis of legislation in a matter like that (which is a moral, and not religious, matter).

NW: *I'm intrigued to know whether you think that philosophers have any expertise beyond the skills of rational analysis of argument that they can bring. For example, is there such a thing as a moral expert?*

MW: I don't believe there's any such thing as a moral expert. I think there are people who are more accustomed than others to dealing with moral problems, but that has nothing to do with philosophy. Instead, you might say that a doctor, or a psychiatrist, or a social worker was more of a moral expert in that sense. I still think that philosophers are useful in the discussion of moral issues because of their clarity in distinguishing one kind of question from another. One very important question when it's a matter of public policy and not on a private moral decision is trying to separate out what the consequences of passing a particular measure would be from any gut reaction you may have. I'm separating squeamishness from genuine conscience. Those sorts of distinctions I think are very important.

NW: *There's a caricature of a philosopher as an ivory tower don who cannot really boil an egg or deal with anything practical—isn't it a bit dangerous putting these sorts of people into the public realm where life and death decisions are actually made and not just theorized about?*

MW: I think philosophy has changed enormously, certainly since the immediate post-war time when I read philosophy and then went on to teach it, where the ivory tower, head-in-the-clouds philosopher was not in fact a caricature. That's what we were all like. We did actually think it wasn't part of our duties to think about real issues. But all that has radically changed, and it changed a long time ago. I think it changed in the Vietnam War when there was a huge student revolt against being called up, and draft-dodging was what students did and they wanted their philosophy tutors and other tutors to help them justify draft-dodging. And I think that was an enormously important point in history. And after that it became inevitable that philosophers (and everybody else, but philosophers in particular) should begin to have views on political issues. I do think that has made a huge difference.

NW: *Within British universities, though, there's been a strange kind of professionalization of philosophy. So there's an incredible demand to churn out peer-reviewed articles in often quite narrow journals. And that seems to me a force that's driving people employed within universities away from engagement with public issues. I wonder if that is your feeling too?*

MW: I'm afraid it is, and I think it's a very sad thing. I think it's an Americanization of philosophy, and also it's part of the ghastly way in which academics are now judged by government departments and by government bodies that dish out funds. You've got to publish now—teaching is not enough. And if you publish, then you've got to publish according to the American style with the whole apparatus—the critics and the references to your colleagues and the endless tedious reference to other people who've been working in the same field—because if you don't, you won't get published in the professional journals. And to me, it does make the whole task of philosophy really quite pointless. So if you refer to me as a philosopher, you probably have to put in a little caveat that I'm not an academic philosopher any longer. I adored teaching philosophy, it was the most wonderful thing to do, but nobody pays any attention to teaching now. I could never write an accurate peer-reviewed article without employing about six research assistants to look up the references, and I wouldn't even want to. But one interesting thing about that is that it might mean that philosophy is going to be better pursued in schools now, rather than in universities, because they'd have teachers who are people like me who actually love the subject, and not people who always had to have (for their own professional career necessity) their eye on publication.

Further Resources

Jane O'Grady (2019) 'Lady Warnock Obituary', *The Guardian*: http://www.theguardian.com/books/2019/mar/21/lady-warnock-obituary.

Mary Warnock (1978) 'Warnock Report', in *A Dictionary of Education*, 1st edition 2009, Susan Wallace (ed.), Oxford University Press: http://www.oxfordreference.com/view/10.1093/oi/authority.20110803121057612.

Mary Warnock (2000) *A Memoir: People and Places*, Duckworth.

Rachael Wiseman (2015) 'Meeting Mary Warnock in the House of Lords', *Women in Parenthesis*: http://www.womeninparenthesis.co.uk/tag/mary-warnock.

ABOUT THE INTERVIEWEES

Helen Beebee is Samuel Hall Professor of Philosophy at the University of Manchester. She works mostly on contemporary metaphysics, especially causality and free will. Her books include *Hume on Causation* and (with Michael Rush) *Philosophy: Why It Matters*.

Teresa M. Bejan is Associate Professor of Political Theory at the University of Oxford. Her research brings historical perspectives to bear on contemporary political questions. She is the author of *Mere Civility: Disagreement and the Limits of Toleration* and is currently at work on a new book about equality before modern egalitarianism. She also writes regularly for popular venues, including *The New York Times*, *The Atlantic*, and *The Washington Post*.

Emma Borg is Professor of Philosophy at the University of Reading and Director of the Reading Centre for Cognition Research. In the past, her research has focused on the philosophy of language (as in her two books *Minimal Semantics* and *Pursuing Meaning*), but she has become increasingly interested in issues at the interface with psychology (working on projects on understanding pain, and on agency).

Kimberley Brownlee is Professor of Philosophy at the University of British Columbia. Her areas of expertise lie in moral, political, social, and legal philosophy. Her current research focuses on loneliness, belonging, and social human rights. She is the author of *Being Sure of Each Other* and *Conscience and Conviction: The Case for Civil Disobedience*. She is also the co-editor of *The Blackwell Companion to Applied Philosophy*, and of *Disability and Disadvantage*.

Patricia Smith Churchland is a Professor Emerita of Philosophy at the University of California, San Diego, and an adjunct Professor at the Salk Institute. Her research focuses on the interface between neuroscience and philosophy. She is the author of the pioneering book *Neurophilosophy*, and co-author with T. J. Sejnowski of *The Computational Brain*.

Katalin Farkas is Professor of Philosophy in the Central European University. Her main philosophical interests include epistemology, philosophy of mind, and the philosophy of law. In her book *The Subject's Point of View*, she defended an uncompromisingly internalist view of the mind. She is currently writing a book on *The Unity of Knowledge*.

Sarah Fine is a Senior Lecturer in Philosophy at King's College London. She specializes in issues relating to migration and citizenship. She is also interested in work at the intersection of philosophy and the arts. She is co-editor (with Lea Ypi) of *Migration in Political Theory: The Ethics of Movement and Membership*. Recent papers include 'Refugees, Safety, and a Decent Human Life', *Proceedings of the Aristotelian Society*, 119:1 (2019), 25–52.

Katrin Flikschuh is Professor of Modern Political Theory at the London School of Economics. She has a BA in Politics, an MA in African Studies, and a PhD in Philosophy. She has published widely on the political philosophy of Immanuel Kant and works more recently on modern African philosophy. From 2014 to 2017 she led an international networks project funded by the Leverhulme Trust that sought to bring together African and Western philosophers and political theorists on aspects of the global justice debate. Aside from numerous journal articles on Kant and African philosophy, she is the author of *Kant and Modern Political Philosophy*, *Freedom: Contemporary Liberal Perspectives*, and *What Is Orientation in Global Thinking? A Kantian Inquiry*.

Miranda Fricker is Presidential Professor of Philosophy at the Graduate Center, City University of New York, and Honorary Professor in the Department of Philosophy, University of Sheffield. She is the author of *Epistemic Injustice: Power and the Ethics of Knowing*; co-author of *Reading Ethics: Selected Texts with Interactive Commentary*;

and co-editor of a number of edited collections. She is an Associate Editor of the *Journal of the American Philosophical Association*, a Fellow of the British Academy, and a Fellow of the American Academy of Arts and Sciences.

Tamar Szabó Gendler is Dean of the Faculty of Arts and Sciences and Vincent J. Scully Professor of Philosophy and Professor of Psychology and Cognitive Science at Yale University. Her books include *Thought Experiments: On the Powers and Limits of Imaginary Cases* and *Intuition, Imagination and Philosophical Methodology*.

Alison Gopnik is Professor of Psychology and Affiliate Professor of Philosophy at the University of California, Berkeley. She mainly writes about children but also artificial intelligence, Hume, and causal inference. Her books include *Words, Thoughts and Theories*, *The Scientist in the Crib*, *The Philosophical Baby*, and *The Gardener and the Carpenter*, and she also writes for *The Wall Street Journal*, *The Atlantic*, and *The New York Times*, among others.

Katherine Hawley is a Professor of Philosophy at the University of St Andrews. She is the author of *How Things Persist, Trust: A Very Short Introduction*, and *How to Be Trustworthy*, all published by Oxford University Press. She is currently thinking critically about what impostor syndrome is supposed to be.

Angie Hobbs is Professor of the Public Understanding of Philosophy at the University of Sheffield. Her main interests are in ancient philosophy, and ethics and political theory from Ancient Greece to the present; her publications include *Plato and the Hero* and *Plato's Republic: A Ladybird Expert Book*. She contributes regularly to radio and TV programmes and other media.

Susan James is a Professor of Philosophy at Birkbeck College, London. She writes mainly on early modern philosophy and political philosophy. Her most recent books are *Spinoza on Learning to Live Together* and *Spinoza on Philosophy, Theology and Politics: The Theologico-Political Treatise*.

Kate Kirkpatrick is Fellow in Philosophy and Christian Ethics at Regent's Park College, Oxford. She writes mostly on Beauvoir, Sartre, ethics, and philosophy of religion. Her books include *Sartre on Sin*, *Sartre and Theology*, and *Becoming Beauvoir: A Life*.

Christine M. Korsgaard is Arthur Kingsley Porter Professor of Philosophy at Harvard. She works on moral philosophy and its history. She is the author of *The Sources of Normativity*, *Creating the Kingdom of Ends*, *The Constitution of Agency*, *Self-Constitution: Agency, Identity, and Integrity*, and *Fellow Creatures: Our Obligations to the Other Animals*. She is currently working on a book to be called *The Natural History of the Good*.

Katherine J. Morris is a Fellow in Philosophy at Mansfield College, Oxford University. Her books include *Descartes' Dualism* (with Gordon Baker), *Sartre*, and *Starting with Merleau-Ponty*. She has published widely on these authors and on Wittgenstein, and teaches an option on Feminist Perspectives on the Body for the Oxford Women's, Gender and Sexuality Studies Master's course.

Jennifer Nagel is Professor of Philosophy at the University of Toronto. Her recent work focuses on intuitive impressions of knowledge and belief, on the guidance that these impressions provide in the ordinary course of conversation and social interaction, and on what these impressions can tell us about knowledge itself. She is the author of *Knowledge: A Very Short Introduction*.

Rebecca Newberger Goldstein is the author of ten books, including *Incompleteness: The Proof and Paradox of Kurt Gödel*, *Betraying Spinoza: The Renegade Jew Who Gave Us Modernity*, and *36 Arguments for the Existence of God: A Work of Fiction*. In 2015 she received the National Humanities Medal from President Obama.

Martha C. Nussbaum is the Ernst Freund Distinguished Service Professor of Law and Ethics at the University of Chicago, appointed in the Law School and Philosophy Department. She is an Associate in the Classics Department, the Divinity School, and the Political

Science Department, a Member of the Committee on Southern Asian Studies, and a Board Member of the Human Rights Program. Her most recent books include *The Monarchy of Fear: A Philosopher Looks at Our Political Crisis* and *The Cosmopolitan Tradition: A Noble but Flawed Ideal*. She has also edited twenty-one books and published over 450 articles.

Onora O'Neill combines writing on political philosophy and ethics with public life. She has been a crossbench member of the House of Lords since 2000, and is an Emeritus Honorary Professor of Philosophy at Cambridge. Her recent publications include *Justice Across Boundaries: Whose Obligations?* and *From Principles to Practice*. She has been awarded the Kant Prize, the Holberg Prize, and the Berggruen Prize.

Anne Phillips is the Graham Wallas Professor of Political Science at the London School of Economics but, despite the title, is a political theorist, working largely in the field of feminist political theory. Her books include *The Politics of Presence, Multiculturalism without Culture, Our Bodies, Whose Property?* and *The Politics of the Human*. She is currently working on a manuscript titled *Unconditional Equals*.

Janet Radcliffe Richards is Professor Emerita of Practical Philosophy at the University of Oxford, and Distinguished Research Fellow at the Oxford Uehiro Centre for Practical Ethics. She has degrees in Philosophy from Keele (BA 1966), Calgary (MA 1968), and Oxford (BPhil 1972), and was formerly Lecturer in Philosophy at the Open University and Director of the Centre for Bioethics at University College London Hospital. She originally worked in metaphysics and philosophy of science, but since writing *The Sceptical Feminist* in 1980 has switched to problems concerning the use of philosophy in a range of controversial contexts.

Rebecca Roache is Senior Lecturer in Philosophy at Royal Holloway, University of London. She is putting the final touches to a monograph on swearing, and plans next to write about how we manage to communicate offensive things to people without explicitly saying anything offensive.

Jennifer Saul is Waterloo Chair in Social and Political Philosophy at the University of Waterloo and Professor of Philosophy at the University of Sheffield. In addition to implicit bias, she works in philosophy of language and in feminism. Her current research project is entitled 'Pragmatics in the Age of Trump and Brexit'.

Elisabeth Schellekens is Chair Professor of Aesthetics at the Department of Philosophy, Uppsala University. She has published widely on the relation between aesthetic, cognitive, and moral value, non-perceptual art, aesthetic normativity, and more. Her books include *Aesthetics and Morality* and, with Peter Goldie, *Who's Afraid of Conceptual Art?*. She is currently Principal Investigator for the research project 'Aesthetic Perception and Cognition' and Leader of the Research Network 'Ethics, Conflict and Cultural Heritage'.

Amia Srinivasan is Chichele Professor of Social and Political Theory at All Souls College, Oxford. She writes about epistemology, political philosophy, and the history and theory of feminism. Her book of feminist essays, *The Right to Sex*, is forthcoming with Bloomsbury.

Ashwini Vasanthakumar is Queen's National Scholar in Legal and Political Philosophy and Assistant Professor at Queen's Law School, Ontario. She works in political and legal philosophy, and writes mainly on political authority and obligation in the context of exile and oppression. Her book, *The Ethics of Exile: A Political Theory of Diaspora,* is forthcoming with Oxford University Press in 2021.

Mary Warnock (1924–2019) was best known, as a philosopher, for her writings on Sartre, on imagination, and for the controversial *An Intelligent Person's Guide to Ethics*. In public life she chaired a number of high-profile government committees of enquiry, and she was created a Life Peer in 1985.

ABOUT THE EDITOR

Suki Finn is a Lecturer in Philosophy at Royal Holloway, University of London. She researches in the areas of metametaphysics, the philosophy of logic, the metaphysics of pregnancy, the epistemology of love, and feminist and queer theory. Suki has published her work in various philosophy journals, edited collections, and in the online magazine *Aeon*. *Women of Ideas* is Suki's first book. Suki is on the Executive Committee for the Society for Women in Philosophy UK, and on the Council for the Royal Institute of Philosophy. In her other life, Suki is a musician.

ABOUT THE FOUNDERS OF PHILOSOPHY BITES

David Edmonds is the author or editor of a dozen philosophy books including *The Murder of Professor Schlick, Would You Kill the Fat Man?*, the children's novel (with Bertie Fraser) *Undercover Robot,* and (with John Eidinow) the international best-seller *Wittgenstein's Poker.* He is a Distinguished Research Fellow at the Oxford Uehiro Centre for Practical Ethics. He and Nigel Warburton founded Philosophy Bites in 2007. On Twitter he is @DavidEdmonds100.

Nigel Warburton is a freelance philosopher, and consultant editor for the online magazine *Aeon* and for the *Five Books* website. He was formerly a university philosophy lecturer for over twenty years. His books include *A Little History of Philosophy, Philosophy: The Basics, Philosophy: The Classics, Thinking from A to Z, The Art Question,* and *Free Speech: A Very Short Introduction.* With David Edmonds he makes the podcast Philosophy Bites and they have already jointly edited three books based on the series. On Twitter he is @philosophybites.